To Jerry
Happy Valentine
Love anne.
2012

Quebec

The Story of Three Sieges

Quebec

The Story of Three Sieges

STEPHEN MANNING

continuum

London • New York

Continuum
The Tower Building
11 York Road
London SE1 7NX
www.continuumbooks.com

80 Maiden Lane
Suite 704
New York, NY 10038

British Library Cataloguing-in-Publication Data
A catalogue record for this book is available from the British Library.

ISBN: 978 144111 359 7

Library of Congress Cataloguing-in-Publication Data
A catalog record for this book is available from the Library of Congress.

Typeset by BookEns Ltd, Royston, Herts.
Printed and bound in Great Britain by MPG Books Ltd., Bodmin, Cornwall

To Professor Jeremy Black, a true friend and a great inspiration

Contents

List of maps

Introduction

Although this is a story of the three sieges of Quebec, it must be acknowledged that there were in fact four attempted sieges of this great Canadian city during the eighteenth century. The first, in 1711, was part of the wider conflict known as the War of the Spanish Succession (1701–14) and was marked by both farce and tragedy. On 30 July, an invasion fleet, commanded by Admiral Sir Hovendon Walker, left Boston harbour bound for Quebec. The fleet consisted of some 70 sailing ships, including nine men-of-war, and carried approximately 12,000 troops, led by General John Hill. The attack was so secret that even Walker had not been briefed as to his destination, and was ordered to open his instructions only once at sea. He discovered, to his horror (for history has recorded that Walker was not a brave man), that he was ordered to proceed to Quebec. Walker convinced himself, and his captains, that the St Lawrence was still likely to be icebound and that his vessels would become embedded in the ice and all would starve. After three weeks of procrastination, the fleet met with gales and then fog above Anticosti. Walker lost his bearings and thought he was heading for the south shore, when in fact a southwesterly was driving him onto the rocks of the north shore. On the very dark night of the 23 August, lookouts spotted rocks with waves breaking violently over them. The alarm was raised and a number of the vessels managed either to anchor, or to beat back into deep water, but eight transports and two supply ships were driven onto the unforgiving coast. The survivors spent a chilling night listening to the cries of their drowning comrades. The morning light revealed a scene of carnage: although 500 exhausted men were rescued from the sea's clutches, nearly 1,000 British dead lay on the shore, including 35 women. Three days later, a panicky, and shocked, Walker decided to agree with the advice of his pilots that the St Lawrence was impossible to navigate and the battered fleet headed for England. It was an ignominious end.

Walker's half-hearted expedition was not the first time that Quebec had been a military target. In 1629, Quebec was little more than a French fur-trading settlement, with a shifting population of officials, merchants and priests. In that year it was captured for the British by Sir David Kirke, but British control lasted a mere three years as it was returned to the French by the treaty of Saint-Germain-en-Laye. In 1663, the colony of New France was created, with Quebec as its capital. In October 1690, the city again experienced conflict when Sir William Phips, governor of Massachusetts, attempted to capture Quebec, with an army of fishermen and farmers and a fleet fitted out in New England. However, he was defeated, at the gates of the city, by a combination of the stubbornness of the French governor, Frontenac, French cannons firing down onto his fleet from the city walls and the harshness of the approaching winter weather.

Despite such a violent past, Quebec is no historical exception, for history is littered with examples of battles fought over the same piece of ground, whether a city, a fortification, a natural feature or man-made phenomenon, such as a road junction, and it is common for such incidents to have occurred during a particular conflict. For example, St Albans witnessed two clashes during the War of the Roses (1455 and 1461) ; Newbury was fought over twice in the English Civil War (1643 and 1644) , the railway junction of Manassas hosted two significant battles during the American Civil War (1861 and 1863) and the Belgian town of Ypres was fought over on three separate occasions during the First World War, to name but four. Although Quebec can be said to have been the scene of three major tussles, it differs from the earlier quoted battles for it was crucial to events in two separate eighteenth-century conflicts; the Seven Years' War and, within that, the lesser French-Indian War, and the American War of Independence. Both wars shared the same outcome in that, at their conclusion, two European Empires in North America were defeated.

The importance of Quebec in these two separate eighteenth-century conflicts altered significantly between the two wars. In the Seven Years' War, although Quebec was central to French power in North America, the need for its capture was essentially tactical, for in a war in which the French had the significant advantage of controlling internal communica-

Introduction

tions, the use of rivers for the transfer of men and resources provided the only means by which such large movements could be made by British forces advancing from the north. The St Lawrence river, thought by the French to be impossible to navigate by a British fleet, was the means by which Wolfe was able to bring his army to the walls of Quebec in 1759, and allowed his successor, Brigadier-General James Murray, to journey on to the last remaining city under French control, Montreal, in the following year. In contrast, during the early months of the American War of Independence, Quebec was viewed by the Revolutionary Americans as the bastion of British rule in Canada and, as such, if it could be taken by force then the Americans would have gained a significant strategic victory, which would have severely dented British morale and might even have led to an early end to the conflict.

Consequently, Quebec maintained its importance in two major conflicts and held its ability to draw individuals to it across the years, for, despite the fact that the conclusion of the Seven Years' War and the beginning of the American War of Independence were separated by more than a decade, the names of a number of people appear in both histories of the two conflicts and the history of Quebec. For example, the British Governor of Quebec in 1775 was Sir Guy Carleton, who had served under General Wolfe during the attack on the city in 1759. Benedict Arnold, who led an American force on Quebec in 1775, had visited Quebec on several occasions in his role as a merchant and had supplied British troops there. George Washington, one of the leading advocates of the American attack on Quebec, had fought alongside the British during the Seven Years' War and the commander of American forces that attacked Quebec on the night of 31 December 1775, Richard Montgomery, had been a former British officer during the earlier conflict with the French in Canada.

Quebec is set in striking surroundings and the gifts bestowed upon it by nature has made the city a natural fortress. The French explorer, Jacques Cartier, first discovered a native Indian settlement there in 1535 and named the imposing cliffs, which rises up from the St Lawrence, Cap Diament (Cape Diamond). The area that was to become Quebec was atop the cliff, on the north shore of the St Lawrence, with a small tributary, the St Charles river, running by its western edge. Cartier constructed a small fort, the first in Canada, and a more significant settlement began in 1608. Although Quebec is nearly 700 miles from the open waters of the Atlantic Ocean, it was the first great centre to be encountered on a journey up the river. In the native language of the Algonquin people, Quebec literally means 'where the river narrows' and here the strong current of the St Lawrence, contracted to a breadth of about 1,000 yards, washes the base of the high cliffs on which the city stands and then broadens into a great basin four or five miles wide. At Monmagny, some 32 miles below the city, the width of the river is twelve miles. There is little doubt that Quebec grew because of the narrowing of the St Lawrence at this point, for the sheer nature of the rock made any attack difficult, both directly from the river and the east, whereas an attempt from the west would mean that any vessels would first have to brave the artillery fire from the city, at the narrowest point of the river, before landing troops. Furthermore, any attacking force would have to climb cliffs 150 to 250 feet high, which at first glance presented a formidable, if not impassable, barrier to landings from the river.

On the east side of the basin, the fertile island of Orleans divides the river into two channels, a narrow and intricate one to the north and broad one to the south. Quebec stands at the east end of a plateau, seven or eight miles long, and in places two or three miles wide. At the north of the plateau, the river St Charles flows into the St Lawrence near the base of the high ground and constitutes a natural barrier for any army to cross. In 1759, the French had a pontoon bridge in place across the St Charles, to allow for the rapid passage of troops from the east to the west of the city. Six miles to the north-east of the city, the apparently insignificant Montmorency river empties its waters into the St Lawrence over a spectacular waterfall, which is more than a hundred feet higher than Niagara. On the east and south side the plateau falls in steep cliffs to the strand of the St Lawrence. On the west side, the drop to the valley of the Cap Rouge river is no less sheer. On the southern shore of the St Lawrence, where the river is a mere 1,000 yards wide, rises Point aux Pères and the nearby Point Lévis, two positions which would feature significantly in Wolfe's attempts to take the city.

Quebec, surrounded as it is by natural beauty, drew to it merchants to trade and later soldiers and sailors to fight over the control of not just the city, but its hinterland and the very country of Canada itself. Furthermore, the eighteenth-century combatants who fought over the control of Quebec knew that their success or failure could well determine the fate of both nations and empires. Few cities in history had such power to determine the continuance of empires. The story of the three sieges is one of military brilliance, as well as incompetence, of cowardice and extraordinary bravery and fortitude, and it incorporates the lives of many of the best-known historical figures from Britain, America, France and Canada.

I have recently been described as a 'gentleman scholar', although I assert no claim to either the former or the latter, but I would wish to offer my upfront apologies to all the learned, and respected, academics, living and now no longer with us, who have worked so diligently to research and record the events surrounding the sieges of Quebec. This book owes so much to their previous work and writings and I offer my thanks to them all. In producing a one-volume work I decided that I would write a book which would be accessible to all and not littered, or perhaps even hindered by, footnotes. Thus I make no scholarly pretensions for either myself or this book, but simply state that the story of the 'three sieges' is a rich and absorbing one and, for the first time, it is told in a single concise volume. I hope you will agree that it is a fascinating tale.

Stephen Manning
Colaton Raleigh, Devon, England
January 2009

1

The Road to Montreal

In the early morning of 13 September 1759, a breathless James Wolfe reached the top of the demanding slope of the Anse au Foulon, and moved onto the Plains of Abraham. The adrenalin must have been pulsating through his tall, thin frame and he would have experienced a combination of emotions; fear, excitement and anticipation to name but three. Despite the chill of the day, Wolfe did not feel cold, for he was now completely focused on what lay before him and his men. Not only had the army which he commanded apparently managed to achieve the impossible by gaining a foothold on the north shore of the St Lawrence river, within striking distance of their target of Quebec city, but they had also achieved complete surprise over their French adversaries. Wolfe was enveloped by a dawn mist as he walked onto the Plains, which were so soon to become a battlefield, and here he was both delighted and surprised to find that no sizeable French force was present to hinder his deployment. Wolfe was, at last, in his element; he knew that he now had the luxury of deploying his men as he saw fit and, after months of uncertainty and frustration, he must have relished the knowledge that he was now master of the moment and his old confidence would have flooded through his veins. He was sure of both his own ability to win the forthcoming battle and even more certain that his troops would smash any force that the French could send out from Quebec. He must have felt that, within hours, the British would be in control of Quebec and, with the annihilation of the French army, the way would be open for the British to journey on to Montreal so as to finally remove the French presence from Canada.

The French–Indian War (1754–60) is largely remembered in Britain, and to a degree in Canada, for the isolated encounter at Quebec between Major-General James Wolfe and the French commander, the Marquis de Montcalm. Although, in simple terms, the French–Indian War can be viewed as a war between Britain and France, it was far more complicated than that for it was a conflict in which the British Thirteen Colonies, as well as Nova Scotia, fought against New France, which comprised Louisiana, the Ohio river valley, Quebec (Canada) and the Cape Breton and Saint-Jean islands. British troops fought alongside American and Indian allies, while French regulars stood shoulder-to-shoulder with French-speaking Canadians and Indian allies against the invaders of New France. For French Canadians, the war is remembered as the War of Conquest; for many Americans the war is little known, lost as it is in the shadow of the American War of Independence (1775–83).

For many anglophiles, the pictorial images by such artists as Edward Penny and Benjamin West of the dying Wolfe are iconic ones, which have helped, over the proceeding years, to perpetuate almost a romanticism around the battlefield. Certainly, ambiguities surrounding Wolfe's siege of Quebec have resulted in numerous half-truths, or speculations, becoming ascribed as fact and it is no exaggeration to state that myths now surround both Wolfe and the events of 13 September 1759. The importance of Wolfe's victory can be, and has been, overemphasized, but there is no doubt that the siege of 1759 was seen at the time to be central to the conflict, for both Britain and France, in North America. However, it was just a small part of a wider world conflict, the Seven Years' War (1756–63). Although the war was centred on Europe, its European protagonists fought each other in the Caribbean, Asia and India, as well as in Canada. For many historians, including Tom Pocock and even Sir Winston Churchill, the worldwide nature of the Seven Years' War, which claimed nearly a million lives, is viewed as the first true world war.

Within North America, it was a continental war, fought over immense distances of trackless wilderness by small armies, whose commanders were in precarious communication with their home governments. In 1754, Horace Walpole, a British member of Parliament and the future fourth Earl of Orford, wrote: 'A volley fired by a young Virginian in the backwoods of America set the world on fire.' The young man who ordered that volley to be fired was George Washington and it was that action which effectively began the conflict, the French–Indian War, that preceded the greater conflict by a year. Although Walpole's comment was certainly an oversimplification, for there were many other sparks of tension which would combine to make the outbreak of the Seven Years' War inevitable, there is no doubt that Washington's volley was a major contributory factor in the outbreak of the larger, wider conflict. This war would see the capture of Quebec as a central requirement for Britain, as her armies marched on the road to Montreal with the aim of expelling French influence from North America.

To some, the British victory in North America, as part of the Seven Years' War, seems a foregone conclusion; however, this was far from the case. Although the British may have enjoyed a military numerical advantage, this was most certainly outweighed, initially, by the French control of the interior and their knowledge of the tactics required for victory on the continent. Armies could only reach the centres of French authority by three routes and thus the basic strategy was imposed on the protagonists by geography. There were only three strategies for taking New France open to the British colonies. One was to re-establish a presence on the Great Lakes, across the Ohio valley or along the river Mohawk and then strike east to Montreal. The second was to advance north up the Hudson valley and along the length of Lake Champlain, again to Montreal, and the third was to capture Louisbourg and thrust up the St Lawrence river, past Quebec and then again on to Montreal. The first route was protected by a series of positions easy to defend, the second was restricted by a long chain of dangerous rapids and the third route was guarded by a fortress that had been made almost impregnable by nature. Although all three approaches were tried by the British, it was to be a combination of these options that would prove to be ultimately successful. To add to the protracted nature of the conflict, reports and requests for supplies and reinforcements often took six months to cross the Atlantic and receive a response. It was to be a long, bloody and difficult war for all those engaged.

Like many wars, before and since, the seeds of the French–Indian War were sown in an earlier conflict, the War of the Austrian Succession (1740–8). This conflict was primarily one that was restricted to Europe, in which such famous battles as Mollwitz (April 1741), Dettingen (June 1743), Fontenoy (May 1745) and even Culloden (April 1745) were fought with Britain (a participant from 1743 to 1748) and Austria in alliance against France and Bavaria, to name the major combatants. The war did, however, spread across the Atlantic to North America, where the two Empires of France and Britain had earlier established their own territorial sovereignty over vast areas of the continent. Small clashes of arms frequently occurred along the frontier borders between French and British settlers, and their respective Indian allies. Fighting was particularly common in the Ohio valley and in Nova Scotia. This latter region had been ceded to Britain from France by the Treaty of Utrecht (1713), which had formally ended the earlier War of the Spanish Succession, and the French settlers there maintained a strong affinity to France. This loyalty led them to accept direction from the French commander at the coastal fortress of Louisbourg, Count Raymond, to incite violence towards British settlers in Nova Scotia and, in particular, to encourage the local Indian population to hostile actions against the British. French settlers were also secretly invited to migrate from Nova Scotia into the adjacent region of Acadia, which was controlled by France, and there were clashes between British troops and settlers, particularly in and around the settlement of Beaubassin, as the settlers tried to flee. When a British naval operation, combined with New England militiamen, succeeded in capturing the French fortress of Louisbourg on 16 June 1745, further disturbances occurred. The following year, the French, with local support, launched a major expedition to recapture the fortress. The attempt failed, even before it reached Louisbourg, due to storms, disease and Royal Navy attacks upon it. The Treaty of Aix-la-Chapelle, of 18 October 1748, formally concluded the War of the Austrian Succession and accordingly Louisbourg was returned to the French and a commission was appointed to settle the question of boundaries between Britain and France in North America.

The work of the commissioners, meeting in Paris, continued for three tortuous years, during which time the tensions among the settlers of the Ohio valley, Nova Scotia and Acadia simmered dangerously. It seemed apparent, to those in positions of power in North America, that the Paris talks would be unable to achieve any sort of settlement that would be acceptable to either of the participating countries and indeed the talks foundered in an atmosphere of recrimination and indecision. It became more and more clear that any long-term peace would have to be achieved by the sword rather than the pen. Even while the commissioners were meeting in Paris, the French were determined to establish their territorial claim on the Ohio valley and, in the summer of 1749, Captain Céléron de Blanville, with a mixed force of around 200 soldiers, militiamen and Indians, roamed the Ohio and Allegheny valleys, burying lead plates along the river shoreline, by which a French claim to the lands was made. Neither were the British slow to assert their desire to exploit the Ohio valley. In 1747, a group of mainly Virginian landowners formalized their interest in extending the settlements of Virginia westwards into the disputed area by establishing the Ohio Company. In 1749, George II granted the company a royal charter of 200,000 acres of land around the forks of the Ohio river, so as to encourage settlers to the area.

In 1752, Paris despatched the Baron de Longueuil as the newly appointed Governor-General of New France. He arrived in North America with firm instructions to secure the Ohio valley, and, furthermore, he was tasked to establish a series of forts from Louisbourg in the north to New Orleans in the south, to defend the frontiers of New France from the encroachment of the British colonies. The French began their fort-building programme in earnest in 1753, when Longueuil despatched a substantial force of 300 regulars, 1,200 militiamen and 200 Indian allies from Montreal to *La Belle Rivière*, the 'Beautiful River', and throughout the summer and autumn of that year the French hastily constructed Fort Presqu'Île, Fort Le Boeuf and Fort Machault in the Ohio valley. In the north, the French constructed Fort Beauséjour in the disputed area of Acadia and this further increased the tension between the two countries. It now seemed that a small spark might ignite hostilities.

To the Governor of Virginia, Robert Dinwiddie, the French fort-building programme in the Ohio valley was intolerable. Their occupation would, in effect, legitimize the French claim to the area, an area in which Virginia had already, via the Ohio Company, invested much. The French needed to understand that the British claim was significant and that their action was unlawful. The man that Dinwiddie tasked with delivering this firm message was a twenty-one year old militia major called George Washington. In October 1753, Washington, and a small party of Virginians and Iroquois Six Nation Indians, set out on the long journey to the French Fort Le Boeuf. Arriving on 11 December 1753, Washington was able to deliver Dinwiddie's ultimatum to the commandant of the Fort, the elderly Legardeur de Saint-Pierre. In the letter, Dinwiddie expressed his astonishment that the French should build forts upon lands 'so notoriously known to be the property of the Crown of Great Britain'. Furthermore, Dinwiddie impressed that 'it becomes my duty to require your peaceable departure; and that you would forbear prosecuting a purpose so interruptive of the harmony and good understanding which His Majesty is desirous to continue and cultivate with the Most Christian King [Louis XV]'. Saint Pierre delayed his response for three days, at the end of which he informed the young Washington that he would refer the letter to the Governor-General in Quebec for his consideration, but that in the meantime he would remain at his post. Washington could do nothing but accept both the reply and the commandant's hospitality. Saint-Pierre was particularly generous towards the Indians in Washington's party, apparently in an attempt to encourage their defection to the French cause.

Dinwiddie's ultimatum was viewed by both protagonists as a spur to their respective occupations of the disputed territory. The Governor of Virginia ordered the newly promoted Lieutenant Colonel Washington back into the Ohio valley in the early spring of 1754, at the head of a force of 200 militiamen and Indians. Washington's party reached the fork of the Allegheny, Monongahela and Ohio rivers in early April and a detachment of Virginians were left to construct a fort upon a spot which would later become the city of Pittsburgh. Washington moved on with the remainder of his force and established Fort Cumberland at Willis creek. In the meantime, a substantial French force, under the command of Claude Pécaudy de Contrecoeur, arrived at the river fork and surrounded the small party of Virginians, ordering them to withdraw from their half-built fort immediately. Heavily outnumbered, the Virginians had no choice but to comply with the French demand. The French continued the fort's construction and named it Fort Duquesne. When news of the French intimidation reached Dinwiddie, in late April, it was effectively viewed as an act of war.

Other colonies soon offered their support to Virginia. Pennsylvania voted to grant money towards the cost of a fresh expedition, while militiamen marched from North Carolina and a Regular Independent Company moved from South Carolina to Virginia. However, instead of waiting for the arrival of these reinforcements, Dinwiddie ordered Washington to embark upon a new incursion into the Ohio valley. From an assembly point at Redstone creek, approximately 70 miles from Fort Duquesne, Washington was obliged to cut a road through the mountain wilderness and this arduous task took several weeks. By late May, Washington finally forced an opening through the mountains at a place called Great Meadows, and here he established a temporary camp, which he was to name Fort Necessity. At around the same time, the French had completed Fort Duquesne and Indian scouts sent out by Contrecoeur had reported Washington's presence at Great Meadows. The French commandant considered that Washington's force was, in all likelihood, preparing for an attack upon his fort, but, not wishing to be seen as the one who started a war, Contrecoeur refrained from launching a surprise attack upon the Great Meadows position. Instead, Contrecoeur decided to send Ensign Joseph Coulon de Villiers, Sieur de Jumonville with an ultimatum to the force at the Great Meadows to request that they 'leave in peace'. Ominously, the ultimatum included the claim that the British would receive no more warnings.

Jumonville left on his mission from Fort Duquesne on 23 May, with an escort of 32 troops, plus an interpreter and a drummer named La Batterie, who, in strict compliance of protocol, was needed to formally deliver the ultimatum to Washington. The presence of La Batterie would seem to confirm that the party of Frenchmen had no warlike intent. On 24 May, Washington was informed of the approach of the French force by his Indian allies, led by a man named Half King or Tanaghrisson, and he moved to ambush, or at least intercept them. On 27 May, Half King told Washington that the French had encamped in a nearby gully. Washington led forward a force of 40 Virginians and between 20–30 Indians and a short, but brisk, fire fight broke out. There are several contradictory claims as to what actually happened; Washington's own account was remarkably sketchy, surviving Frenchmen claimed that Jumonville was fired upon while reading out the ultimatum, but whoever, or whatever, started the exchange, the direct result was that ten French soldiers were killed, including Jumonville and La Batterie and twenty-one were taken prisoner. One evaded capture and was able to report back to Contrecoeur at Fort Duquesne. Thus the first shots were fired of the French–Indian War.

Washington led his victorious force back to the sanctuary of the Great Meadows where he hastened the construction of Fort Necessity, a simple, small, circular log palisade, in the face of likely French retaliation. Commandant de Contrecoeur wasted no time in reporting to the Governor-General in Quebec the news of the ambush and he also quickly assembled a force of 500 French soldiers and militiamen, along with Indian allies, ready to advance upon Washington's position. With the arrival of Captain de Villiers, and with additional troops and supplies, the force was ready to march against the Virginians. Command was given to Villiers, who was the older brother of Jumonville. On the morning of 3 July, the overwhelming French force had reached and surrounded Fort Necessity and began to pour fire into the fort from the shelter of the surrounding forest. After nine hours of battle, the Virginians had suffered considerable losses to both French fire and desertion and it was clear that the badly sited fort could not withstand the French attack. By the early evening, Villiers began negotiations for the surrender of the fort, stressing that no state of war existed between France and Britain, for he had simply launched the attack so as to avenge the death of his brother. The surrender document was signed by Washington at midnight and, early on the following morning, the garrison marched out of the fort, back towards Wills creek. The French later razed Fort Necessity to the ground. The Virginians had been effectively forced out of the Ohio valley by an enemy superior in both numbers and tactics.

The defeat galvanized the British into a response. In October 1754, the British Prime Minister, the Duke of Newcastle, ably supported by the Secretary of State, William Pitt, ordered the despatch of British regular troops to reinforce the Thirteen Colonies. The 44th and 48th Regiments of Foot, along with a company of Royal Artillery, were transported to Virginia from Cork, under the command of the sixty year old Major-General Edward Braddock. He had seen very little action in forty-five years of army service, and was now, rather surprisingly, to assume overall command of all forces in North America. The British regiments were under strength and Braddock decided to supplement their numbers with locally recruited American colonials and, in addition, two regiments, the 50th and 51st were to be raised entirely in North America. Upon learning of the British reinforcements, the French responded in kind and despatched 3,000 regulars to New France. The early months of 1755 saw frequent trans-atlantic crossings, as both participants ferried reinforcements to this new theatre of operations. Attempts by the Royal Navy to intercept both French troop and supply ships were largely unsuccessful and only two vessels were so detained.

The combatants varied enormously in style and quality. There is no doubt that, in the early exchanges of the war, the French had the upper hand. By the start of the war, the population of New France was largely native-born and most men had experience of at least one campaign. All Canadian males between the ages of 16 and 60 were automatically enrolled in the militia company of their home parish or city neighbourhood and, in 1750, for example, the militia comprised a total force of 13,000 men. Many had experience of the frontier life; they were experts at paddling canoes, some of which were over 30 feet long, and were capable of carrying 5,000 pounds of supplies quickly across vast distances; they frequently had experience of fighting in the terrain of the wilderness and many adopted Indian tactics, clothes and customs. Furthermore, the *Troupes de la Marine*, who were recruited in France and encouraged to settle in New France on completion of eight years' service, were led by mostly Canadian officers, as a result of which they soon mastered the forest warfare tactics of their Indian allies. The French could also rely, much more than could the British, on the help and support of Indian warriors from numerous tribes. The staunchest Indian allies came from a confederation of seven tribes in the St Lawrence valley and included Iroquois people, particularly those of the Mohawks and Onondagas, as well as Abenakis, Hurons, Algonquins and Nippissings. Several hundred warriors from these tribes accompanied the French in the expeditions in the Ohio valley in 1753–4, along with more than 1,000 militiamen and several hundred *Troupes de la Marine*. The arrival of six battalions of French regulars, *Troupes de Terre*, from the regiments of La Reine, Artois, Guienne, Languedoc, Bourgogne and Béarn, in 1755, boosted the available forces for the defence of New France. Trained to fight in a linear fashion, in which the troops were deployed in line and would deliver synchronized volley fire from their flintlock muskets to maximum effect, these French regulars performed admirably in the first two years of their service in North America, when they were largely deployed behind defensive positions or were used to besiege British forts. By 1759, however, battlefield losses, desertion and the infrequency of fresh supplies had reduced both the effectiveness and professionalism of the French regulars.

Like their Canadian counterparts, the American militia compelled males between the ages of 16 and 60 to be enlisted into their local militia company and attend the company musters and regimental training days. Unlike the Canadian militia, the majority of Americans were resident in settled areas; fishing villages, farms and towns scattered along the Atlantic seaboard. The majority of these Americans viewed the forest wilderness of the interior as the domain of the French and the Indians, as a result of which they rarely, if ever, ventured there. Consequently, the skills needed to fight in this environment were largely lacking among the American militia. Support was received from provincial troops, raised by the individual Thirteen Colonies. Uniformed normally in blue or green, so as to distinguish themselves from regular troops, these men were usually reserved for garrison duty, although as the conflict went on, and these soldiers gained more experience, they were to see more action. By 1759, British forces in North America included 16,835 provincial troops, which was a very significant contribution to the total force. Such troops were frequently the front line of defence, which offered protection to the frontier settlements from French and Indian raiding parties.

Provincial troops from Virginia were much more prominent in the defence of the Thirteen Colonies, largely because of the frontier nature of the colony and the additional burden this presented in its defence. It was Virginians, under the command of Washington, that had been involved in the initial skirmishes of the war and, despite Governor Dinwiddie's low opinion of their fighting abilities and their 'want of a martial spirit', Braddock did not hesitate to use Virginian troops to form six companies of Rangers and a company of Light Horse in his advance on Fort Duquesne in 1755. The British were, initially, at a disadvantage in that they possessed little help and support from the Indian population. With the exception of the tribes of the Iroquois Six Nations, who were found in the Ohio valley, it was not until much later in the conflict, as the tide of war shifted away from the French, that the British gained significant numbers of Indian allies.

At the outbreak of hostilities in 1754, the British had just 2,500 regular troops in North America. To defend the vast area stretching from Lake Champlain, Lake Ontario and New York there were just four independent companies. Three more were based in South Carolina, and one of these offered support to Washington in the Ohio valley. A further three regiments were to be found in Nova Scotia, to counter the threat from both the French settlers and the powerful French fortress at Louisbourg on Cape Breton Island. The quality of these troops was generally low for the men had been used for little more than garrison duties for a number of years. As the war progressed, men from these independent companies found themselves drafted into newly raised regiments; for example troops from the South Carolina companies were amalgamated into Shirley's 50th Regiment. Attempts to raise regiments of local troops met with mixed success. In the autumn of 1754, Governor William Shirley, of Massachusetts, and William Pepperell were appointed by the Crown to each raise an infantry regiment along the lines of the regular British establishment. Although both managed to raise regiments by the summer of 1755, each was half under strength. Similarly, the 60th (Royal Americans) could only raise a quarter of its strength from Americans, the remainder being filled with European and British recruits. Despite these recruitment problems, all the locally raised regiments served with distinction throughout the war; the Royal Americans fought at both battles of Quebec and Shirley's and Pepperell's regiment bravely resisted the French siege of Fort Oswego in 1756, before being forced to surrender.

The British regulars, who arrived in North America in 1755, were professional soldiers of high quality, but they were totally unprepared and ill-trained for the fighting they would soon face in the wilderness. Training in the British Army of the eighteenth century had centred on the need to fight in large set-piece battles in the open countryside of Europe. Success in such continental warfare depended upon being able to form and manoeuvre regiments in rigid close-order lines and columns. The continual practice of close-order drill was, therefore, the most important part of training. It trained the officers in the precise execution of the various complicated movements and the control of the firings, and it taught the private soldier to become so accustomed to implicit obedience of orders, and to maintaining his place in the ranks, that, under fire, the instinct to do as he was told was stronger than the instinct to run away. No thought was given to the bush-warfare training that would be an essential tactic to achieve success in the forested interior of North America and, although a limited number of troops and officers had some experience of irregular warfare in Scotland, the sheer size and scale of the task confronting them in North America proved daunting. Adam Stephen, a provincial officer in the Virginia Regiment, wrote of the British regular serving in North America in 1755 that, 'You might as well send a Cow in pursuit of a Hare' – for the British soldier was loaded down with 63 pounds of clothing, arms and equipment, and was therefore completely ill-equipped for rapid movement through the wilderness.

Braddock's strategy for the 1755 campaign season was for a four-pronged assault upon the fortresses of New France. Braddock himself would lead the 44th and 48th, along with provincial units, to seize Fort Duquesne in the Ohio valley. His second-in-command, Governor Shirley, was to march the 50th and 51st, again with support from provincial units, to attack the French forts at Niagara. At the same time, Colonel Johnson was to lead a small force from Albany to Lake Champlain, to storm Fort Saint-Frédéric at Crown Point. Finally, Lieutenant Colonel Robert Monckton was to command 200 regulars and a force of 2,000 militia against Fort Beauséjour in Nova Scotia. It was an ambitious plan that displayed little awareness of the logistical problems that the attacking forces would face.

After a delay of three months, in which Braddock had, with difficulty, assembled sufficient supplies and provincial troops, the Commander-in-Chief led his force out from Fort Cumberland, at Willis creek, on the first stage of the journey to Fort Duquesne. Braddock was forced to cut and build a road to allow for the passage of the 200 wagons and artillery train, which made up his advancing column of more than 2,000 troops and camp followers. Progress was painfully slow, averaging only four miles a day and, when on 16 June the expedition reached Little Meadows, it was clear to Braddock that he must split his force and change his plans in the light of the extreme terrain over which the British were advancing. Braddock himself would now lead a force of 1,200 troops, which was to advance ahead of the baggage and wagons, while a specialist unit of Rangers, provincial troops who were lightly dressed and equipped and who served as scouts and intelligence gatherers, under the command of Lieutenant Colonel Thomas Gage, was to move forward of the column so as to protect it from surprise attack.

Very soon Braddock's men came under sniping and harassing attacks from an unseen foe, for the French and their Indian allies proved skilled in the use of forest cover. There were almost daily incidents in which British troops who wandered from the safety of the column would be killed or wounded. However, Braddock pressed on and, by 25 June, the British had passed the site of Fort Necessity. The French garrison at Fort Duquesne, composed of 100 regulars, 200 militia and around 1,000 Indians, received regular reports of the British column and, with the enemy approaching ever nearer, it became clear to the Commandant, Contrecoeur, that the fort itself was indefensible against such a large attacking force. He and his second-in-command, Captain de Beaujeu, devised a plan in which the Captain would lead roughly half the available troops in an ambush attack upon Braddock's column as it neared Fort Duquesne. On 9 July the two opposing forces clashed and, in the opening few volleys, the British vanguard killed Beaujeu and scattered nearly all of the Canadian militia. Command fell upon Captain Dumas, who effectively rallied the panicky French troops and inspired all to move forward, making full and effective use of the forest cover. Dumas later claimed that he advanced 'with the assurance that comes from despair, exciting by voice and gesture the few soldiers that remained. The fire of my platoon was so sharp that the enemy seemed astonished.' Soon the British were falling to the fire of an invisible foe and it was their turn to lose cohesion. The French were rejoined by their comrades who had earlier fled and, with these extra troops, Dumas was able to attack both sides of the British column at close quarter. The forest reverberated with the sound of musket fire and Indian war cries. None of the British regulars had ever experienced warfare like it before and soon their usually disciplined volley fires became ragged and ineffective. Lieutenant Leslie of the 44th, who survived the battle, wrote three weeks after the event that 'I cannot describe the horrors of that scene, no pen could do it. The yell of the Indians is fresh on my ear, and the terrific sound will haunt me till the hour of my dissolution.' Only the Virginians, firing from behind the cover of trees, offered any concerted resistance.

Braddock himself, leading reinforcements forward, was soon in the thick of the fighting, but even he was unable to coordinate a defence against a hidden enemy, and the French force was able to infiltrate along both sides of the British column. Braddock was a prime target for French and Canadian sharpshooters and in no time he had four or five horses shot from under him and his clothing was peppered with shot, leaving him unscathed. Two of his three aides-de-camp were wounded and only the third, George Washington, was untouched. Braddock's luck, however, could not last, and after two hours of confused, vicious fighting he was mortally wounded in the shoulder. With the majority of the British officers dead or wounded, and the Indian and Canadian militia now wreaking a dreadful revenge on the wounded or captured British, with both scalping knives and tomahawks, the British began their retreat. Washington, with instructions from the dying Braddock, was able to form an improvised rearguard and the surviving British were able to retreat back towards the Monongahela river.

The Battle of Monongahela had lasted nearly three hours and had claimed the lives of 450 of the advancing British, with a further 550 wounded. The French, in comparison, had suffered little; only 23 were killed and 20 wounded. It was a comprehensive defeat and one of the worst suffered by the British army in its long history. James Smith, a British prisoner who had been captured by the French earlier and held at Fort Duquesne, witnessed the return of the victorious French force and the fate of British troops captured on the battlefield. Smith recorded that he saw both Frenchmen and Indians carrying bloody scalps as well as a small party [of Indians] coming in with about a dozen prisoners, stripped naked, with their hands tied behind their backs and their faces and parts of their bodies blacked; these prisoners they burned to death on the bank of Allegheny river, opposite the fort. I stood on the fort wall until I beheld them begin to burn one of these men; they had him tied to a stake, and kept touching him with firebrands, red hot irons, etc., and he screamed in a most doleful manner, the Indians in the meantime yelling like infernal spirits.

Of course, it was not just the British regulars who had suffered; Washington commented that 'our poor Virginians behaved like men and died like soldiers', and generally the colonial troops had displayed greater discipline than the British troops, whose reputation had taken a terrible beating.

Braddock's death and defeat saw an end to British activity against the French in the Ohio valley in 1755. Elsewhere, the British suffered further disappointments. Shirley's expedition against Fort Niagara stalled due to logistical problems and the desertion of troops. This gave the French time to strengthen their defences and bring in fresh troops from Fort Frontenac. Aware of these additional troops in front of his advance, Shirley decided to build up his defensive positions in the Oswego area and await the next campaigning season. Lieutenant Colonel Johnson led a force from Albany to Lake George. He was then tasked with attacking the French at Fort Saint-Frédéric, known to the British as Crown Point, at the southern end of Lake Champain. The French, under the command of Baron Dieskau, strengthened their position in the south of Lake Champain by building Fort Carillon at Ticonderoga. On learning of Johnson's advance, Dieskau led a substantial force against the British camp on Lake George. The two armies clashed on 8 September and the battle soon became a stalemate, in which the French regulars, according to Johnson, 'kept their ground and order for some time with great resolution and good conduct'. The arrival of a British relieving force from Fort Edward caused the French to withdraw. Each side lost more than 200 men in the battle at Lake George; the British now halted and contented themselves with the construction of Fort William Henry.

Of Braddock's initial four-pronged assaults upon New France, the only one which achieved its objective was that led by Lieutenant Colonel Monckton against the French Fort Beuséjour in Nova Scotia. The British spent the first weeks of the campaign clearing the area surrounding the Fort of Acadians, who were providing support to the French. Later the British were to forcibly remove the Acadians from the region, many of whom later settled in Louisiana. By 14 June the British artillery was in a position to begin their bombardment of the fort and, within two days, the French had surrendered, as did the nearby fort at Gapereau. The French strategy of a continuous line of defensive positions, running from Louisbourg to New Orleans, had been broken and, aside from the water route towards Quebec, Louisbourg had been completely cut off.

Despite these losses, the French could look back at 1755 with some satisfaction. For the British, and in particular the regular troops, hard lessons would have to be learnt rapidly if the war were to be brought to a swift and victorious conclusion. French commitment to New France was reinforced by the despatch of the Marquis de Montcalm-Gozen de Saint-Véran as the new Commander-in-Chief in April 1756, along with the 2nd battalions of the La Sarre and Royal-Roussillon regiments. Montcalm, a veteran of the War of the Austrian Succession, was a professional soldier of good reputation, but was also a proud and arrogant man. He soon clashed with the Governor-General, Pierre de Rigaud, Marquis de Vaudreuil, who was appointed in 1755 and remained Governor until the French capitulation in 1760. Vaudreuil was in constant disagreement with Montcalm over the strategy required to defend New France, for the Governor favoured a guerrilla-style campaign against the British along the frontier, while Montcalm believed that regular troops would determine the outcome of the conflict. Montcalm resented, sometimes publicly, what he saw as civilian interference in operational matters and there is no doubt that both men had nothing but contempt for each other. Later their personal animosity was to impact seriously upon the successful defence of the colony.

During Montcalm's transit of the Atlantic, war was formally declared between France and Britain on 17 May 1756. While the French home government viewed the conflict in North America as very much secondary to the wider Seven Years' War in continental Europe, the British took a contrary strategic approach. Under the Secretaryship of William Pitt, from late 1756 onwards, this belief was reinforced, for he was sure that the conquest of New France, and thus its seizure for a growing British Empire, was in Britain's long-term strategic interests. Pitt believed that this could be achieved not simply by reinforcing and strengthening the

British military position in North America, but also by keeping France fully occupied in continental warfare in Europe. A new British Commander-in-Chief, John Campbell, Earl of Loudoun, was despatched to North America, along with such senior officers as Major-General James Abercromby and Major-General Webb, and two further regiments of the line.

The arrival of the new Commander did little for British fortunes in 1756. Conflict was largely restricted to the three British forts at Oswego – Fort Oswego, Fort Ontario and Fort George. Montcalm made good use of his regular units, as well as captured artillery from Braddock's ill-fated advance, and all three forts fell to the French over the summer months. The British seemed incapable of either mounting an offensive or sending reinforcements in time to save their fortress positions. At the end of the campaigning season, Montcalm concentrated his regular force of 5,300 troops at Fort Carillon, while Loudoun was at Fort Edward. His force of 10,000 regular and provincial troops were scattered along the frontier, but their presence did little to deter French raids throughout the winter, in which civilians largely suffered.

As in the previous year, 1757 would be marked by only one major clash between British and French troops, but it did see a renewed determination from the British home government to destroy New France. More than 11,000 British regulars sailed across the Atlantic to join their comrades and, by the end of the year, 21 battalions of regulars and seven independent companies were operational in North America. In contrast, Montcalm received the last major reinforcements from France with the arrival of two battalions of the Berry Regiment. Montcalm had only eight regular battalions with which to counter the British threat. Of equal significance for the British was the formation of the coalition government of the Newcastle–Pitt ministry, which resulted in a major strategic shift in British military policy. The British focus was now to move away from the Ohio valley and the northern lakes to an attack on the French fortress of Louisbourg. Once this was captured, the British would be able to sail a force up the St Lawrence to attack Quebec and from there proceed to Montreal, so as to destroy French power in North America.

To meet this new military requirement, Loudoun sailed with a large force of regulars from New York to Halifax in April 1757, where he was joined by further British forces. British designs upon Louisbourg became well known and, to counter the threat, the French despatched a squadron of vessels, under the command of Admiral Dubois de la Motte, so as to deny the Royal Navy command of the seas around Louisbourg, and thus, hopefully, guarantee the safety of the fortress and its garrison. French ships-of-the-line sailed from Brest and Toulon to converge off Louisbourg by June. Sailors strengthened the garrison, and Acadian volunteers and Indians were positioned in likely landing places so as to deter the British. On 19 August, a British squadron approached the fortress from the direction of Halifax, in the hope of luring the strong French fleet out of the harbour. However, Dubois de la Motte would not take the bait and his ships remained firmly in the harbour. The British naval commander, Admiral Holburne, knew that the presence of the French ships made any landing impractical, but he continued to remain off Louisbourg for a number of weeks in the hope that either the French could be drawn into battle or that their ships would be forced to return to France. Neither event happened and violent storms on 25 September led to the return of the British fleet to Halifax. With the British now dispersed, Dubois de la Motte was able to return to France, safe in the knowledge that he had foiled British attempts to seize Louisbourg for the time being.

Montcalm was kept abreast of the situation off Louisbourg and was fully aware that the frontier had been stripped of a large number of British regulars, who had been sent to Halifax in preparation for the planned assault. Montcalm was too skilled a soldier not to take advantage of this opportunity, and he amassed his regulars at Fort Carillon [Ticonderoga] for an assault upon the British position of Fort William Henry. Montcalm led a force of 7,500, including six regular battalions, against the 2,000-strong garrison at Fort William Henry in early August. The Fort, under the command of Lieutenant Colonel George Munro, was besieged from 4 August and, within a few days, French cannons and mortars had inflicted over 300 casualties upon the garrison. In the face of overwhelming French firepower, Munro, with no apparent hope of relief, was forced to surrender on 9 August. As the British left the smouldering fort, with full military honours, Montcalm proved unable, or reluctant, to control his Indian allies and they entered the fort to murder those British wounded left behind. Furthermore, on the following day, as the British column retired towards Fort Edward, the Indians attacked again, killing a further 50 men, women and children. Once more, the French had difficulty in controlling their allies and Montcalm was forced to provide an escort for the remainder of the column until it reached the safety of Fort Edward.

The 1757 British campaign had been a shambles; Fort William Henry had been lost, the planned attack upon Louisbourg cancelled and the conflict, already violent, had entered a new depressing phase of brutality which shocked the British public. Decisive action would be needed in 1758 and Pitt clearly felt that Loudoun was not the man capable of taking such action. In addition, the colonials were disgruntled by both the lack of pay and command opportunities in Loudoun's army. Benjamin Franklin likened Loudoun to a painted soldier on a tavern sign, always on horseback but never moving, and Loudoun proved to be the scapegoat that Pitt needed. He was replaced by Major-General James Abercromby, who largely adopted Loudoun's three-pronged strategic plan for the 1758 campaign. Abercromby would himself lead the largest British army ever assembled in North America to take Fort Carillon at Ticonderoga and thus secure the Lake Champlain region. A further substantial force, under the command of Major-General Jeffrey Amherst, was tasked with finally taking Louisbourg, while smaller expeditions would be sent against Fort Duquesne and Fort Frontenac.

History has judged Loudoun somewhat harshly for it was the reforms that he initiated which would help seal British victory in later years. Loudoun centralized a system of supplies, for both regular and provincial troops, with store depots at Halifax, New York and Albany, which ensured that British troops, serving in North America, were able consistently to receive sufficient arms, food and uniforms. The difficulties of transporting armies across the vastness of the continent was also, to some extent, addressed, with the formation of a corps of army wagons, a road-improvement scheme and much greater use of the internal waterways.

However, the most radical improvement, which would reap the greatest benefit, was to change the dress, equipment and training of the British soldier in North America, so that he was able to fight the French, their Indian allies and the Canadian militia effectively in a theatre of operations which the enemy had so dominated. Loudoun ensured that regular units received training in woodland conditions, which included newly developed tactics and firing sequences, so as to reduce the fear of fighting in a forest environment. The weight the troops were expected to carry was greatly reduced, coats were cut short and all carried lighter backpacks, which helped to improve mobility. In addition, Loudoun saw that the army would specifically require a group of soldiers who had been trained in the art of skirmishing, scouting and forest-fighting. Although the

Rangers' units of provincial troops largely met these requirements, they were notorious for their lack of discipline, and consequently Loudoun created units of regulars which received Ranger-style training, as well as instruction in the linear fighting methods of the day. Such units gave their commanders troops who could adapt their fighting methods to the terrain in which they fought.

Loudoun's initial transformation began with the formation of the 62nd Regiment, which was raised from troops recruited from the frontiers of Pennsylvania and Virginia. Trained in the skills of both Rangers and regular forces, the 62nd had the discipline of regular troops. Lessons learnt from the formation of this unit were later used to introduce 'light infantry', whose men were, initially, recruited from the fusilier companies of the line infantry battalions. All had to be extremely fit and marksmen, and some had already served for a time with Ranger units. The men were issued with lighter and more accurate carbines, rather than the standard flintlock and, although their training and tactics varied between each unit, as none were the same, the troops were expected to be able to fight in forest terrain, be adaptable to any circumstance and be able to take the fight to the enemy. A number of officers readily took to the flexibility offered by the light infantry. For example, Henri Bouquet, who was second-in-command in the 1758 expedition to take Fort Duquesne, armed and clothed his men in the style of their Indian enemies and trained them by sending them off in small columns into dense forest, where they were expected to deploy swiftly into line formation. The men soon came to view themselves as 'chosen men' and their contribution was vital to Britain's success in North America.

Abercromby received confirmation of his promotion and appointment to overall command of British forces in North America on 7 March 1758 in a letter signed by William Pitt. The new Commander wasted no time in summoning the provincial governors to recruit and place on service 20,000 provincial troops for the coming campaigning season. It appears to have been common knowledge to all, including the French, that Abercromby would lead a huge force against Fort Carillon at Ticonderoga. Thus, in the months it took for the British to assemble their force of 17,000 regular and provincial troops, the French had been able to prepare their defences in and around Ticonderoga. Montcalm arrived at Fort Carillon at the end of June and, although reinforcements were sent by Vaudreuil from Montreal, he quickly realized that, with the limited forces he had at his disposal, an attack upon the advancing British would be at best foolhardy, at worst suicidal. Montcalm believed that, in an entrenched, raised position, the French might stand a chance of beating back the British attack and he used the final days before the appearance of Abercromby and his army to see to the last details of the defences. Montcalm could only hope that Abercromby would rush an attack before he had brought up his artillery.

The scale of Abercromby's army can be demonstrated by the fact that, by 5 July, he had assembled his force at the southern end of Lake George so as to be ferried north along the lake to attack the French position at the southern end of Lake Champlain. The armada required to carry the British forces, and its supplies, consisted of 900 bateaux and 135 barges which, once on the lake, was a mile wide and seven miles in length. It must have presented the French scouts with an overwhelming sight and, as the British neared their destination, the enemy gradually withdrew to the sanctuary of their defensive positions.

The French made no attempt to harass the British advance and, by the morning of 6 July, the advance British units were only two miles from Fort Carillon. Finally, at Bernetz Brook, the advancing British columns clashed with French troops in a confused and fierce twenty-minute fire fight, which saw the death of Lord Howe, one of Abercromby's best and most trusted officers. Pitt had placed much faith in Howe's abilities, which he had hoped would make amends for Abercromby's shortcomings. This clash saw an end to the British advance and, as dawn broke on 7 July, Abercromby's army was scattered and disorganized. With some difficulty Abercromby was able to regroup his forces and begin to move slowly forward once more. Lack of intelligence as to what was ahead stalled the advance, and this provided Montcalm with more crucial hours in which to strengthen his entrenchments. Late in the day, the senior British engineer, Lieutenant Clerk, was able to climb the nearby Rattlesnake Mountain to gain a view of the French position. He incorrectly reported to Abercromby that they looked to be weak, a mistake that was exaggerated on the following morning when British scouts concurred that the defences did not appear to be elaborate.

The following day, 8 July, was characterized by a series of ill-coordinated frontal assaults upon the French position. Abercromby gained intelligence that Montcalm was to receive reinforcements and the possibility of additional French troops seems to have spurred Abercromby into action. He never seems to have had a full grasp of events, and he was undoubtedly badly served by some of his subordinates, men such as Bradstreet and Gage. Upon Howe's death, all sense of leadership seems to have disappeared from Abercromby's army. Regiment after regiment bravely, and recklessly, threw themselves at the French entrenchments, to no avail. Despite the strength of the position, a small group of Highlanders, under the command of Captain John Campbell, did manage to penetrate the abatis and scale the breastwork, only to be bayoneted by the defenders. After about five hours of continuous fighting, the shattered British columns withdrew. Despite losses of around 1,000 killed or missing and a further 1,500 wounded, Abercromby's force still vastly outnumbered Montcalm's men and he could have either awaited the arrival of his artillery or entrenched a position surrounding the Fort, so as to starve the French into submission. However, Montcalm was both surprised and delighted to find that the next day the British force had melted away. Abercromby shouldered the blame for the humiliating defeat and it is clear from an account left by Captain Charles Lee, of the 44th, that the army maintained little confidence in Abercromby's abilities, for he was to write of his indignation that the public had been so grossly abused, ' in having a person appointed to the Head of an Army, who is so utterly destitute of all accomplishments necessary for that high station'. Montcalm ensured that his victory, which meant that New France had avoided conquest for yet another year, was widely publicized in France, much to the anger of Vaudreuil, who felt that the role of provincial troops in the French victory had been minimized by his rival.

The British did achieve some success in August 1758, when Lieutenant Colonel Bradstreet led a force of 2,500 provincials and Royal Americans against Fort Frontenac on Lake Ontario. The poorly defended fort fell at the end of August, as a result of which the French not only lost control of Lake Ontario, but also communications were cut between Canada and Fort Duquesne. This was at a crucial moment for, in the Ohio valley, a British expedition, under the command of Brigadier John Forbes, was heading from Philadelphia to capture Fort Duquesne. This campaign also met with a setback, when, on 13 September, the British vanguard force of 800 men was ambushed within five miles of the Fort and forced to retire. On 12 October, the French even had the confidence to launch an attack from Fort Duquesne on the British position at Fort Ligonier, although they were beaten back. By November, the troops within Fort Duquesne were suffering from low morale and inadequate supplies. As a consequence, the commandant, Ligneris, decided to blow up Fort Duquesne and withdrew his garrison to Presqu'Île and Le Boeuf. The French were, gradually, losing their hold upon the Ohio valley.

Jeffrey Amherst first experienced battle at Dettingen (1743), when he was aide-de-camp to Major-General John Ligonier, and Amherst was also present at the battle of Fontenoy. However, his early career centred upon staff duties and it was in this role that he made a number of useful contacts that were to benefit his advancement in later years. The outbreak of the Seven Years' War found Amherst on the Commander-in-Chief, the Duke of Cumberland's, personal staff. However, after the British humiliations of 1757, in which the French had completely outmanoeuvred the British, Cumberland was recalled and Ligonier was promoted to Commander-in-Chief. Amherst was summoned back to London in January 1758, where Pitt presented him with a great challenge, and opportunity, to command the expedition to seize Louisbourg. Although it is very likely that Ligonier advocated Amherst's appointment, it was still an enormous leap of faith on Pitt's part, for the competent, methodical staff officer had never held any field commands. In accepting the challenge, Amherst was rewarded with the local rank of major-general.

It seems clear that, despite Amherst's rather dour personality, he was a slow but effective communicator; his years of staff work enabled him not only to work effectively with his colleagues and subordinates but also gave him an ability to spot talent and use it effectively. His relationship with Admiral Boscawen, who was to land the British force at Louisbourg, blockade the harbour and ensure that French vessels were kept out of the surrounding waters, was both harmonious and businesslike. Amherst quickly saw that Brigadier James Wolfe was his most able and ambitious senior officer and used Wolfe to his full advantage. Like Amherst, Wolfe's first battle had been at Dettingen and, also like Amherst, he had a number of connections, particularly among his immediate family, which were to ensure his rapid advancement. He was aide-de-camp to General Henry Hawley at Culloden (1745) and, by 1750, he was a lieutenant colonel in the 20th Foot, at the age of just 23 years. He was one of the few officers to emerge from the shambolic British foray upon Rochefort (1757) with any credit and, with his reputation for both competence and bravery now assured, he was offered, in January 1758, the position of brigadier-general in North America for the expedition against Louisbourg.

The French officers in Louisbourg, under the overall command of

Governor Drucour, knew that the fortress would again be targeted by the British in 1758. Much work had been done over the winter and spring months not only to strengthen the existing fortifications, but also to build field fortifications, in the hope that this would either deter a British landing or prevent them from establishing a beach-head. Crucially, however, the French navy was increasingly under pressure from the British, both in European waters and in the Gulf of Mexico. The result of such harassment meant that the French were unable to despatch a sufficient naval force to deter the British designs against Louisbourg in 1758, as they had the year before. Amherst's army converged on Halifax and, by 2 June, Boscawen had transported the bulk of the force into the Louisbourg area. Drucour was adequately warned of the approaching armada by a detachment of French troops, who were posted all along the coastline. Amherst was keen to attempt a landing at once, although he had to wait impatiently for six days until the weather was favourable to launch an assault. Amherst decided to split the invasion force into three groups, each under the command of a brigadier, Lawrence, Whitmore and Wolfe. At 4 a.m. on 8 June, a rocket was fired into the still dark sky to announce that the assault had begun.

Under cover of fire from warships, which bombarded the French shore defences, numerous boats were filled with troops, who rowed vigorously towards the general landing spot of Cormorandière Cove. As the first boats neared the shore the French unleashed a murderous crossfire of both musket and cannon and, to make matters worse, a strong wind suddenly rose, which whipped up the surf on the shoreline, making landing even more hazardous. Wolfe was leading the left division and, seeing the mayhem in front of him, ordered his boats to row further to the left of the cove, towards the smaller cove of Anse aux Sables. The ploy worked and boatloads of light infantry scrambled up the rocks. Wolfe, standing high in his boat, directed as many boats as he could towards the new landing area and the British were able to consolidate the landing, despite some French opposition. Wolfe waded through the surf, armed only with a cane and quickly formed his men into a firing line. A successful landing had been won.

Wolfe was to write that the successful landing was 'next to miraculous' and indeed the French engineers thought that a landing was impossible. Both Amherst and Drucour knew that the successful assault was the decisive moment of the campaign and all that remained was for the British to batter the French into submission. Drucour must have hoped that either assistance would arrive from France or that he might be able to hold on for so long that the British would be forced to withdraw for another year. He must have also realized that each day the fortress defied the British was one day less for the enemy to launch an attack upon Quebec.

Over the next weeks, Wolfe was at the forefront of all British attempts to secure positions from which to place batteries, so as to destroy the French defences. He led forces to take Lighthouse Point, by the middle of June, and Green Hill by the end of the month. French gunners, firing from both the fortress's batteries as well as from warships anchored or partly sunk in the harbour, inflicted numerous casualties among the British gun crews. However, gradually the British closed the net around Louisbourg and their fire claimed more and more victims among both the military and civilian population. As the siege moved into July, the British bombardment became more ferocious. Wolfe, again, was at the forefront of the assaults; on 9 July he led an attempt to capture the French advanced post at Barachois, only 250 yards from the Dauphin Gate and, despite a desperate French counterattack, the British secured the position. The British were destroying the city's defences faster than the French could repair them and, by 25 July, of the 52 cannon that opposed the British batteries, only 12 were offering any reply to the constant British fire. Terms for surrender began to be discussed, but Amherst refused the defenders the 'honours of war' and Drucour was informed that all French troops would be considered prisoners of war. Outraged, Drucour and most of his officers were for fighting on, but Commissaire-Ordonnateur Jacques Prévost managed to bring some sense to the discussion and persuaded Drucour to accept the terms, so as to ease the suffering of the civilians still within the fortress. On 27 July, the battered doors of the Dauphin Gate were opened and the fortress formally surrendered.

Certainly, Wolfe felt that, with the surrender of Louisbourg, the way was now open for Amherst to lead his force down the St Lawrence and seize Quebec before the end of the campaign season, although, in reality the British would have been unlikely to have arrived at Quebec until the end of August, which would have left only a matter of weeks before the onset of winter forced the abandonment of a siege. That it is not to say that a squadron of British warships anchored in the Quebec basin might not have resulted in the early surrender of the city. However, Admiral Boscawen was adamant that an advance onwards to Quebec, so late in the season, was out of the question and resolutely informed Amherst of his opinion. Amherst had little choice but to accept Boscawen's advice and the General clearly felt that his duty was now to establish a firm British position in the area and to secure the region from the French and the Acadian rebels. Amherst ordered Wolfe to embark with three battalions, bound for the Bay of Gaspé, where he was given the objective of destroying the local fishing industry, which had been supplying both the Acadian partisans and the city of Quebec. By 11 September, Wolfe and his men had destroyed everything of value at Gaspé; nets, boats, stocks of fish and buildings, and he was able to inform Amherst that he had 'done a great deal of mischief [spreading] the terror of His Majesty's arms through the whole gulf'. Although this particular expedition has been viewed as rather barbaric and needlessly harsh, it can be easily argued that the fishing fleet presented a legitimate strategic target, for, just before Wolfe's arrival, 26 vessels had left to supply Quebec, and as Wolfe wrote to Pitt 'a material article of subsistence to the Canadians [was now] in a great measure ruined'. Wolfe also ordered Colonel Murray as far south as the settlement of Miramichi and this was likewise destroyed. To nullify the Acadian threat in Nova Scotia, Amherst despatched a force, under the command of Brigadier-General Robert Monckton, to the mouth of the St John river. Here Monckton constructed Fort Frederick and secured the area for the British. Forced deportation of Acadians, along with the destruction of dwellings that were to provide winter shelter for those that escaped the British soldiers may now seem harsh, but such acts certainly eliminated any further threat to Nova Scotia.

At the end of August, Amherst felt that he should reinforce Abercromby's broken army and sailed, with five battalions, to Boston. Quebec would have to wait for another year, much to Wolfe's evident frustration. Despite Abercromby's crushing defeat at Ticonderoga, the campaign of 1758 had firmly shifted the momentum, and balance, of the war in favour of the British. The three vital French positions of Louisbourg, Frontenac and Duquesne were now firmly in British hands, leaving open the real prize of Quebec, and the possibility of Montreal, in 1759. After his poor performance, Abercromby was sacked and Amherst was given overall command. It now remained to be seen who would lead the important British assault upon Quebec.

On his return to Louisbourg, Wolfe considered, under the terms of his original service agreement with Pitt, that, with the fortress captured, he could now return to England. Wolfe wasted no time in securing a passage aboard the *Namur,* and he arrived at Spithead on 1 November. The Secretary of State for War, Lord Barrington, was angered by what he considered to be Wolfe's unauthorized return, for Barrington claimed that Pitt had exceeded his authority by granting Wolfe such liberal terms. Wolfe, never one to avoid an argument, was happy to fight his corner with a mere member of the Cabinet. He was, however, careful in his dealings with the Commander-in-Chief, Sir John Ligonier, and Wolfe soon contacted him in the hope of obtaining a position in the British contingent which was operating alongside the Hanoverians, Brunswickers and other German allies against the French, along the Rhine frontier. Ligonier confirmed that no suitable vacancies, at present, existed. Denied his first choice of military theatre, Wolfe pressed for service in America and, writing to Pitt on 22 November, he left no doubt of his readiness to serve there again, ' I take the freedom to acquaint you, that I have no objection to serving in America, and particularly in the river St Lawrence, if any operations are to be carried out there.' From Ligonier, Wolfe discovered a plan had been agreed for the 1759 campaigning season which settled on two major fronts; one by way of Lake George and Lake Champlain and another via the St Lawrence, to Quebec. To Ligonier, Wolfe stressed his 'desire to go up the River'.

By December, Wolfe's persistent lobbying of Pitt finally bore fruit, although the extent of his success shocked even the ambitious Wolfe. With the news that Amherst was to replace the defeated Abercromby, and then lead the army in the Lake George theatre, Wolfe discovered that Pitt had put his name forward to George II for the command of the Quebec expedition, with the local rank of major-general. Wolfe agreed to take the job, although he does seem to have accepted it with some genuine reservations, for he was to write to Amherst that 'they have put this heavy task upon my shoulders, and I find nothing encouraging in the undertaking, but the warmest and most earnest desire to discharge so great a trust to your satisfaction as my general, and to His Majesty and the publick'. Amherst made it clear to Wolfe that his expedition to Quebec would be a self-contained, distinct force, under Wolfe's sole command. Wolfe had shown by his past actions that he was a master tactician. Now, with his first independent command, he would have to prove that he also had the strategic vision necessary to take Quebec.

Wolfe spent the latter half of December in exhaustive and detailed planning of the operation and he stressed to Pitt that an early presence of the Royal Navy in the St Lawrence would be crucial to its success. Wolfe considered that 12,000 troops would be required, all, apart from 600 Rangers, to be regulars, drawn from those units already stationed in North America, along with an artillery train. The newly appointed major-general was adamant that he alone would be responsible for his choice of officers and he largely got his way. While he was delighted that he could advance the careers of some of his officer friends, men such as Captains William De Laune and Hervey Smith, and was pleased that Brigadiers Robert Monckton and James Murray, both of whom had considerable experience of fighting in North America, were to be his immediate subordinates, he was less happy with his third brigadier. Wolfe had hoped that Ralph Burton would be the last appointee, but this choice was overruled and the position went to the Honourable George Townshend, a long-term devotee of Pitt, who used his influential contacts to gain a brigadier's position on Wolfe's expedition. Despite the fact that Townshend had been present at many earlier battles, such as Dettingen, Fontenoy and Culloden, he had only ever served in staff roles and had never commanded a company in action, let alone a brigade. The aristocratic Townshend possessed an arrogance and pride that was only to be matched by Wolfe himself and, although the major-general initially welcomed Townshend, and expressed his satisfaction with his brigadiers, a clash of personalities was inevitable.

Wolfe was extremely fortunate in that he was to work alongside Vice Admiral Charles Saunders, a veteran of the War of Austrian Succession, and the relationship between the two men was vital for the success of the combined army/navy operations in and around Quebec. Wolfe was less certain of Saunders' second-in-command, Philip Durell, for he had worked alongside Durell during the Gaspé raid and found him to be less than determined. Wolfe raised his concerns with Pitt, but was unable to convince the Secretary of State to replace him. Durell was to command the North American squadron, which was tasked with gaining an early entry into the St Lawrence, in the spring of 1759, as far as the Isle of Bic, so as to intercept any French attempts to supply Quebec, and much would depend on his steadfastness and reliability.

On 14 February 1759, after weeks of intensive planning, Rear Admiral Holmes' squadron left Portsmouth, bound for New York, where it was to collect British regulars before sailing north to the expedition's rendezvous at Louisbourg. Just three days later, Saunders left with the remainder of the fleet, including HMS *Neptune*, which carried aboard James Wolfe. When not laid low by seasickness, for Wolfe suffered terribly from this affliction, he used the voyage to mull over his tactics for the coming campaign. He was already much concerned that his expedition had been starved of troops; of his original request for 12,000 regulars he was finally to see less than 9,000, as men were withheld for Amherst's expedition and an influx of troops from the Caribbean garrisons was not forthcoming. As early as 6 March, Wolfe was contemplating the possibility of failure. In a letter to Amherst, which also illustrates some of the ruthlessness that Wolfe would bring to the campaign, he wrote 'If, by accidents in the River, by the Enemy's resistance, by sickness, or slaughter in the army, or, from any other cause, we find that Quebec is not likely to fall into our hands (preserving however to the last moment), I propose to set the Town on fire with shells, to destroy the Harvest, Houses, & Cattle, both above and below, to send off as many Canadians as possible to Europe, & to leave famine and desolation behind me ...'

The protracted nine-week Atlantic crossing had placed much strain upon Wolfe's fragile health and he must have been greatly relieved when, on 21 April, Saunders' squadron was within sight of Louisbourg. However, Wolfe was cruelly disappointed to discover that the harbour was blocked by ice and, despite Saunders' best efforts, the naval vessels had to admit defeat and sail on to Halifax. Wolfe's joy at finally reaching land must have been short-lived for, to his horror, he discovered the fourteen ships of Durell's squadron still in the harbour, when they should by now have been blockading the entrance to the St Lawrence. Wolfe must have realised that it was likely that French vessels would evade interception and be able to pick their way through the melting ice so as to deliver vital supplies and intelligence from France.

Durell, apparently, had the false impression that the entrance to the St Lawrence remained icebound, and made no attempt to establish whether this was so. The arrival of Saunders and Wolfe spurred Durell into action and he led the Halifax squadron into the Gulf, which was surprisingly free of ice. Although two French vessels were intercepted, Durell learnt, much to his embarrassment, that the first of the French ships, the *Chezine*, had already arrived safely at Quebec. Over the next ten days, a further 23 vessels, mostly supply ships, reached the sanctuary of Quebec. Their crews not only brought vital supplies to a garrison on the brink of starvation, but also 300 recruits and a few gunners and engineers. Among them was Louis-Antonie de Bougainville, who had been sent by Montcalm to Paris on a three-fold mission; first, to obtain as many additional troops and supplies as possible, second to impress upon the French government the imminent dangers to New France and finally to try and establish, once and for all, the command structure of the colony. Bougainville returned with limited supplies and men, which paled next to the mountain of stores and ships the British had committed to the conquest of New France. Via an intercepted letter, Bougainville was able to brief his Commander-in-Chief with details of Amherst's campaign plans, which included the news of Wolfe's imminent arrival in the St Lawrence. Bougainville informed Montcalm that the French government viewed the defence of Quebec as the main priority for the coming season and he was also pleased to inform Montcalm that he had, at last, been appointed to overall command of all military affairs, much to the disquiet of Governor Vaudreuill.

On receiving Bougainville's news, Montcalm rushed from Montreal to Quebec, where, with an energy verging on desperation, he personally supervised improvements in the city's defences, which would ultimately frustrate Wolfe for so many weeks. It appears that, during the long weeks of the Atlantic crossing, Wolfe was able to give much consideration to his plan to besiege, and ultimately capture, Quebec. Much of his thinking appears to be based upon the limited intelligence about the city's defences that was then available to the British. This intelligence seems to have been gleaned largely from a report by Major Patrick Mackellar, of the Royal Engineers, who had been captured at Oswego in 1756 and had spent some months held captive in Quebec. Mackellar had used his imprisonment productively and, with the eyes of an engineer, had, upon his release, submitted a report, and detailed plan, of the city's fortifications to the Office of Ordnance in London. Wolfe, naturally, had access to Mackellar's work and in a letter to his uncle, Major Walter Wolfe, written on 19 May 1759, the Major-General outlined his initial thinking as to the assault upon Quebec. He wrote:

To invest the place [Quebec], and cut off all communication with the colony, it will be necessary to encamp with our right to the River St Lawrence, and our left to the river St Charles. From the river St Charles to Beauport the communication must be kept open by strong

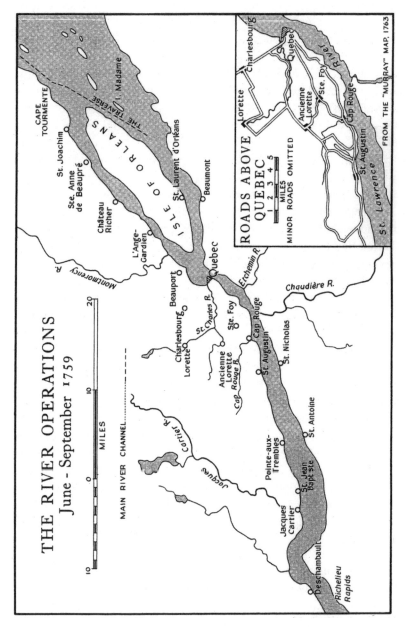

THE RIVER OPERATIONS
June - September 1759

MILES

MAIN RIVER CHANNEL

Montmorency R.

CAPE TOURMENTE

St. Joachim

Ste. Anne de Beaupré

Château Richer

L'Ange-Gardien

ISLE OF ORLEANS

I. Madame

THE TRAVERSE

St. Laurent d'Orléans

Beaumont

Quebec

Beauport

Charlesbourg

Lorette

St. Charles R.

Ste. Foy

Cap Rouge

Cap Rouge R.

Ancienne Lorette

St. Augustin

St. Nicholas

Etchemin R.

Chaudière R.

St. Antoine

Pointe-aux-Trembles

Cartier R.

Jacques Cartier

St. Jean Bapt Ste.

Jacques

Deschambault

Richelieu Rapids

ROADS ABOVE QUEBEC
MILES
1 2 3 4 5
MINOR ROADS OMITTED

Charlesbourg

Quebec

Lorette

Ancienne Lorette

Ste. Foy

Cap Rouge

St. Augustin

St. Lawrence River

FROM THE "MURRAY" MAP, 1763

Map by C.C.J. Bond from Stacey, *Quebec 1759*, by permission of the publisher.

entrenched posts and redoubts. The enemy can pass that river at low water; and it will be proper to establish ourselves with small entrenched posts from the point of Léviz to La Chaudière. It is the business of our naval force to be masters of the river, both above and below the town.

Wolfe would not have needed Mackellar's report to realize that the vital preliminary to the capture of the city would be to attack it on the weak landward face, which lacked natural defences. His initial thoughts led him to believe that this could be best achieved by a landing on the Beauport shore and then advancing across the St Charles river. Wolfe, of course, had not yet had an opportunity to reconnoitre his target and, when he was able to, he would be bitterly frustrated.

Montcalm and Vaudreuil decided upon a show of unity and both worked to strengthen the city's defences. The Governor-General, upon his arrival in the city, approved all the initial measures taken by Montcalm. Waterside batteries had been positioned in the Lower Town and, with the arrival of regular troops from Montreal on 27 May, work was begun on defences around the St Charles. A bridge of boats was constructed across the river and a fortified bridgehead was placed on its northern bank. French efforts were concentrated upon the Beauport shoreline, stretching east of the city, between the St Charles river and the Montmorency river. Five battalions of the *troupes de terre*, under the command of Bourlamaque, began work on the entrenchments there and they were joined by several hundred Canadians. By 11 June, Montcalm was able to write to Bourlamaque with some satisfaction, 'We now have three bridges across the River St Charles; on Wednesday we shall have three large redoubts and many small works completed between Beauport and the Chadière, defences at the head of our bridges, and entrenchments along the River St Charles.' Montcalm's energy and Bougainville's timely warning had meant that the French defences had been much improved. In addition, five of the recently arrived larger vessels, along with three small craft, were ordered to be converted into fire-ships, to be unleashed against Saunders' squadron at an appropriate moment.

Despite such activity, some simple measures were either overlooked or not taken. No gun batteries were constructed to oppose the British fleet as it sailed down the St Lawrence, nor were any placed upon the vital Lévis heights, on the southern shore of the St Lawrence, directly opposite Quebec. A battery here would have prevented British ships from passing above Quebec and would have denied them the position from which they could threaten the city's weak landward defences. As a result, the British were later free to use the position to pour down a tumultuous fire upon the city. Attempts to frustrate the British passage along the St Lawrence were also limited; although marker buoys were moved so as to confuse the British pilots, the river was found to be too deep to sink a ship to block the British passage. It seems that the French were convinced that the city's best defence was the difficulty that navigation along the St Lawrence presented to any attacking force. On 25 June, when British ships were successfully navigating through the Traverse, which was believed to be one of the most dangerous stretches of the river, Montcalm wrote to Bourlamaque that 'our best seamen or pilots seem to me to be either liars or ignoramuses'.

The safe defence of the city was also jeopardized by the decision of Montcalm and Vaudreuil to order provision ships up the St Lawrence to Batiscan, over fifty miles from Quebec, where they would remain to form a safe depot for supplies and munitions. The city was thus to be dependent on a long supply line from the west, with supplies being sent to Quebec by either riverboat or overland in carts. Once the British closed the river to French traffic, the city became dangerously reliant on the overland route, which would seriously affect the city's ability not only to keep itself fed, but also to maintain its resistance.

Saunders' fleet of 22 warships and 119 assorted supply vessels assembled off Louisbourg by 6 June and headed eastward. Favoured by strong northeasterly winds, the force made steady progress and, by 18 June, the fleet anchored near the Isle of Bic in the St Lawrence. Here it rendezvoused with Durell's vessels and confirmation was received that indeed the majority of the French supply squadron had evaded the British. Although Durell had made some amends for his earlier inactivity by navigating as far as the Ile aux Coudres, the continued passage of the combined fleet would now depend upon the expertise of the British navigators and pilots. Ever since the fall of Louisbourg, two navigators in particular, a Dutch engineer officer, Samuel Holland, of the Royal American Regiment, and James Cook, the future maritime explorer, had been making studies of the St Lawrence and it is clear that the British knew more about the successful navigation of the St Lawrence than their French counterparts. James Cook, master aboard the *Pembroke*, had been sent by Durell as far as the Ile aux Coudres and, on 8 June, he encountered the dangerous Traverse. The British spent two days sounding the passage and, by 10 June, Cook was satisfied that the dangers and secrets of the river were now known. Buoys were positioned and, on 25 June, the lead division of the fleet successfully sailed through the Traverse. The main fleet soon followed and not a single British vessel foundered. The British had, with apparent ease, conquered Quebec's first defensive line.

By 27 June, the attacking fleet had assembled in a deep water channel to the south of the Isle of Orleans, which is opposite the Beauport shore. The first brigade made an unopposed landing on this fertile island. The agricultural inhabitants of the pretty hamlets and isolated farmhouses to be found on Orleans had deserted their homes and most of the men folk were now in Montcalm's army. At last, Wolfe had his opportunity to fully reconnoitre his objective and he hurried to the island's West Point. From there, just four miles across the St Lawrence's extensive Basin, was Quebec. Immediately, his trained and anxious eyes told him that his plan of landing upon the Beauport shore would have to be reconsidered, for in front of him he could view the enemy's occupation of six miles of the opposite shoreline, from the Falls of Montmorency to the St Charles river. Four miles were blessed with natural defences of a steep and high river bank. The remaining defensive line, although 'low and level', was deeply entrenched, with numerous gun batteries. In addition, the presence of the Beauport Bank, a wide expanse of shallows, meant that it would be impossible for the fleet to venture too close to shore and thus the effect of any bombardment upon the French defences would be reduced. Although Wolfe must have been disappointed at this discovery, he was, apparently, not distracted from the matter in hand, for he quickly saw what Montcalm and Vaudreuil had missed, that his first objective would have to be the occupation of Point Lévis. Wolfe realised that from this point he could bombard the city with impunity.

That night, a violent storm whipped up the river and the British fleet lost seven transports, driven ashore, and a number of flat-bottomed landing craft were smashed to pieces. The following night, the French unleashed five fire-ships on the ebbing tide, with the aim of damaging and scattering the invasion force. However, the British had been warned of this likelihood by escaped British prisoners, and the threat was easily deflected. The crew of the *Sutherland* fired upon the approaching vessels, thus panicking the Frenchmen to light their fuses too early. Once alight, the fire-ships either drifted harmlessly to shore, or were snagged by grappling hooks and towed out of harm's way. Wolfe praised the vigilance of the navy. For the French, the sight of their ships burning furiously, to no end, must have been a bitter one.

Brigadier Monckton, with four battalions, landed from Orleans at Beaumont to seize the prize of Point Lévis on 29 June. The British were harassed by both militiamen and Indians, and this slight opposition seems to have troubled Monckton, who became uncharacteristically hesitant. It required a visit from Wolfe to settle British nerves, and he supervised the construction of the batteries, gaining a closer view of Quebec, which, from the Pointe aux Pères, was only a mile away. Wolfe could now concentrate not only on the destruction of the city, but also how he could defeat the army that was defending it.

For the British, each day was precious, for the reality was that, at most, they had just three months to capture Quebec before the onset of snow, and river ice, forced them to withdraw to winter quarters. Despite now being in poor health, for Wolfe was crippled by recurring attacks of the gravel (kidney or bladder stones), the British commander was firmly focused upon an attack on the city. Brigadier Murray had been sent with a detachment along the south bank of the St Lawrence to the Chaudière river so as to identify possible landing sites on the north shore. He returned on 5 July and reported that an attempt could be made at Saint-Michel, just three miles above Quebec. Wolfe, however, had to dismiss this option for, as yet, he was not in a position to move more than a small force across the river and he feared that such a force could be beaten piece-meal by the French before he could reinforce it. With the idea of a strike below the city for the moment dismissed, Wolfe again concentrated upon the enemy's defences on the Beauport shore. After consulting Saunders, a plan of sorts began to take shape. He resolved to deliver a substantial force on the north shore, to the right, or east, of the Montmorency Falls. On the night of 8 July, 3,000 troops were embarked from Orléans and by dawn all had been landed safely at L'Ange Gardien, just the other side of the Falls from the French. To their astonishment, the French awoke to look across the gorge of the Montmorency river at the strong British force. At this point, so early in the day, the French lost an opportunity to ford the river further upstream, outflank and attack the British. However, the French commander on the spot, Lévis, vacillated and, although a number of Indians did attack the British in the woods, claiming thirty-six scalps, the British were able to further reinforce their newly claimed position and had survived the immediate threat.

From their new position on the north shore, the British contemplated their next move. The Montmorency river flowed swiftly before it plunged over the Falls. Its banks, particularly on the French western side, were very steep and the defenders had placed breastworks which made an assault impossible. Although the river could be forded three miles upstream, the position was guarded by Montcalm's army and the heavily wooded nature of the terrain made the movement of a large British force difficult, if not impractical. Wolfe almost certainly hoped that, by placing his troops on the north shore, he would provoke Montcalm into an attack, and a number of raids were sent against the French throughout July. However, it was often the case that the French, and in particular their Indian allies, came off better from these frequent skirmishes, for they were more adept at fighting in such terrain. Although some of his subordinates favoured a bold attack upon the British position, Montcalm decided upon a defensive attitude towards the British at Montmorency and he was recorded as saying, 'Let him [Wolfe] amuse himself where he is. If we drive him off he may go to some place where he can do us harm.'

Although Wolfe's move had been a bold one, it brought him no closer to his goal of drawing Montcalm's army into battle. Furthermore, the strain on both him and his brigadiers in defending the exposed Montmorency position led to the beginning of a deterioration in relations between the Major-General and his immediate subordinates, particularly Townshend. The remainder of July was characterized by an increase in ferocity of the warfare. From 12 July, the British mortars at Pointe aux Pères began an almost continuous shelling of Quebec and a further three batteries were brought into play later in the month, causing widespread devastation, particularly of the Lower Town. Of course, it was not just destruction that Wolfe was aiming for, he also hoped to terrorize both the garrison and the city's inhabitants. In this, the British had some success, for one survivor of the siege recorded that, after the first day and night of shelling, 'the people all fled from their Homes and sought for refuge upon the Ramparts, on the side next to the Country. When day appeared, and the Gate was opened, Women and Children were seen flying in crowds along the fields; and the damage done to the Town ... was very considerable.'

While Wolfe's efforts were firmly concentrated on the capture of Quebec, other British expeditions were marching against the remaining outposts of New France. Amherst was to lead the major force against Fort

Carillon, and the new Commander-in-Chief decided upon a further two attacks upon French positions. Although independent of each other, Amherst wished to exert the maximum geographical pressure upon New France and all the operations can be viewed as a concerted strategic action. He ordered Brigadier Prideaux, with a force of two regular regiments, as well as 3,000 provincial troops, and, for the first time, a significant number of Iroquois Indians, to take Fort Niagara. The capture of this fort would cut any links between French outposts in the west and would put an end to any French hopes of mischief in the Ohio valley. By mid-July, the British had surrounded Fort Niagara and a formal siege began. Unfortunately, Prideaux was accidentally killed early in the siege, but command fell upon Sir William Johnson, who was able to rally his new command effectively to rout a French relieving force, sent from settlements along Lake Erie. This bloody encounter, of 24 July, combined with a failed attempt by the besieged forces to storm the British trenches, brought an end to French resistance and the fort surrendered on 26 July. With this success, the British had secured both Lakes Ontario and Erie and had destroyed the western frontier of New France. A small force of the 60th Foot was tasked with securing the British position at Fort Pitt and reopening communications between it and Fort Ligonier in the Ohio Valley. This was to be a prelude to an attack upon the final French forts in the Valley, at Presqu'Île and Venango. Although there were skirmishes between British and French troops throughout June and early July, the French were forced, due to the loss of Fort Niagara, to abandoned their forts. The Ohio valley was now firmly in British control.

With knowledge that there were to be two major British offensives in 1759, against Quebec and Fort Carillon (Ticonderoga), Montcalm knew that he would have to concentrate his meagre forces to meet and deflect the challenge of one of these expeditions. The French Home government had made it clear that they believed the security of Quebec was the real prize and Montcalm gambled that, although Amherst's offensive might well be ultimately successful, the Commander-in-Chief would be likely to be ponderous in his advance. Thus, if Montcalm's available forces could defend Quebec, New France would survive for at least one more year. There was always hope that, as long as Quebec could be held, the situation in Europe would dramatically swing in favour of the French and, therefore, the long-term future of the colony could be secured.

Montcalm was correct in his assessment of Amherst's advance. It was not until the end of July that the British expedition marched against Ticonderoga; Amherst had spent the initial weeks of the 1759 season in the construction of forts to cover the rear of his advance, as well as in acquiring intelligence on the French defences. Montcalm had placed the Chevalier de Bourlamaque, with 4,000 regulars, to face the British attack. However, with Wolfe's arrival at Quebec, he was now ordered to withdraw the bulk of this force back to the city and use the remainder to delay and harass Amherst's troops. As the British slowly advanced, the French destroyed Fort Saint-Frédéric and eventually abandoned Fort Carillon, before establishing a fresh defensive line at the Île aux Noix. Amherst settled down to a summer of construction; the forts at Ticonderoga and Saint-Frédéric (to be named Crown Point) were rebuilt, and Amherst devised a scheme to build a number of vessels from which he hoped to gain superiority over the French on Lake Champlain. Although rangers were sent on various scouting missions, including the infamous raid upon the Indian village of St Francis, in which Major Robert Rogers was to gain widespread notoriety, as well as infamy, Amherst's force became largely static. The advance finally continued on 11 October, well into the season, and was almost immediately overwhelmed by a combination of strong gales and extreme cold, which made the transit along Lake Champlain impossible. Amherst was forced to draw back his forces and winter in the newly rebuilt forts. The advance on Montreal would have to wait until the following year.

Once Amherst's advance had slowly ground to a halt, British offensive efforts centred on Wolfe's attempts to wrest Quebec from Montcalm's control. For much of July, the contest had become, what has been termed, something of a 'phoney war', with envoys regularly trading letters, containing threats and taunts, between the two adversaries. Clashes were restricted to brief naval exchanges and to frequent skirmishes in the forests surrounding the British position at Montmorency, mainly involving Indians allied to France and Anglo-American Rangers, although British regulars were caught up in some of these incidents. Wolfe announced that a bounty would be paid for every Indian killed and the Rangers seemed to relish the taking of scalps just as much as the Indians did. The danger to Quebec dramatically increased on the night of 18–19 July when *Sutherland* and the frigate *Squirrel*, along with two transports and two armed sloops, succeeded in passing the guns of Quebec to enter the upper river. Now Wolfe had the ability to move his forces above and below the city, which would divide the defending forces which had so far been concentrated upon the Beauport defences.

On 19 July, Wolfe himself reconnoitred upriver, accompanied by Captain Bell and the engineer Samuel Holland. The Major-General was able to confirm Murray's earlier assessment that a landing at Saint-Michel might well be possible. Also, during the day, Wolfe first set his sights upon the small cove of Anse au Foulon, which was eventually to be the key to unlocking the French defences. According to Holland, writing some years after the event, upon reaching the Etchemin river, on the south shore, Wolfe looked directly across at the ascent at the Anse au Foulon. The British party observed a number of Indians and Canadians walking on the cliff top and others bathing in the river, with their canoes beached upon the shoreline. Holland recorded that Wolfe showed great interest in this position and stated that, if all other plans failed, this pathway up would be his last resort to try and gain a footing for his army on the north shore. There are numerous theories as to how Wolfe either discovered, or was told of the possibility of, an ascent at Anse au Foulon, and Holland's claim is just one more to be added to the list. However, what is certain is that Wolfe did reconnoitre along the upper river on 19 July and there is no reason to doubt that, with his strong eye for a tactical advantage, he would have taken a mental note of the possibility that the Anse au Foulon might later offer.

The direct consequence of Wolfe's journey of 19 July was that a new plan was considered to land a substantial force, under the command of Monckton, upon the north shore, near Saint Michel. On 20 July, Wolfe gave Monckton his orders to be ready to embark a thousand troops for the initial landing, much to the annoyance of Murray, who felt badly aggrieved that he had not been chosen to lead the assault, having completed the first reconnaissance of the area. Wolfe pacified the fiery Scot by stating that he would command the next wave of assault troops, but Murray would continue to harbour his resentment towards his commander, which grew throughout the siege. After two days of planning and preparation, the assault was postponed for Saunders felt that, at this stage, he could not guarantee the safety of the vulnerable flat-bottomed landing craft as they passed the guns of the city. Adverse weather, and the difficulty in navigating in the confined space of the river, now affected Wolfe's plans and it was not until 23 July that additional vessels, including the frigate *Lowestoft*, could pass upriver. By now the plan had lost its momentum and, with the arrival of the British ships in the upper river, the enemy had reinforced the Saint-Michel area. This included the establishment of a battery at Samos. Wolfe himself was to experience the accuracy of the French gunners on 21 July, when the barge he was in had its mast severed by a well-aimed French shell. In the face of such opposition Wolfe abandoned the assault. However, with ships now in the upper river, Wolfe had won a tactical victory, although as yet they were of insufficient number and strength to be a strategic threat to the French. Wolfe has been criticized for his indecision during the planning for a possible assault in the upper river during July; he clearly issued contradictory orders and can be criticized for taking no counsel other than his own, but he realised that he required additional naval support in the upper river before he could be satisfied that an assault would be likely to succeed. British attention now turned, once again, to the Beauport shore.

With his latest plan abandoned and the majority of his force now stationary at Montmorency, the pressure was beginning to mount upon Wolfe for a decisive move that would force Montcalm from behind his defensive walls. On 23 July, Wolfe called a rare meeting with his brigadiers and Saunders to discuss the options now open to them. In his journal, Wolfe recorded at the meeting that there existed 'Resolution to attack the French army. Debate about the method,' and it is easy to see the frustration Wolfe was feeling with his subordinates and the situation in which he found himself. On 26 July, Wolfe joined a reconnaissance force, consisting of the 35th Foot and a company of Rangers, through the forests of Montmorency and towards the river ford which was guarded by the French. His troops were repeatedly attacked by Indians and, in a number of sharp clashes, the British suffered more than forty killed and wounded. Despite this opposition, Wolfe was able to get close enough to the ford to realize that the defences were too strong to contemplate an assault. Again frustrated, Wolfe had to consider other options.

On the night of 27 July, the French launched a fire-raft, packed with all measure of combustible materials and explosives, against the British vessels in the Basin. This attempt again met with failure, as British sailors simply grappled the raft and dragged it out of harm's way. This desperate French assault seemed to match the equally desperate thinking coming from the British camp. It seems that Wolfe was now seriously considering a frontal water-borne assault of the Lower Town, despite the obviously formidable entrenchments and the danger of crossing the Basin under fire. However, Major Mackellar apparently convinced Wolfe of the dangers and impracticality of such a plan. Wolfe now focused on an attack upon the two westernmost redoubts of the Beauport shoreline, close to the Montmorency Falls and below the left flank of the furthest French encampment. By 28 July, Wolfe had expanded his thinking as to the likely operation; with just four companies of grenadiers, Lieutenant Colonel Burton would lead the first assault to take the redoubts and hold them until they could be reinforced. The Navy would come close to shore to provide covering fire. By the next day, the limited excursion had become a major operation; the initial attack would now involve all the grenadiers, as well as two hundred Royal Americans. Monckton's troops would be ferried across from Point Lévis for the assault and additional support would come from Murray's and Townshend's brigades, who could join the assault from the British positions at the Montmorency Falls, using a ford only accessible at low tide. Colonel Howe, with a body of light infantry and Rangers, would make a divisionary attack upon the ford further up the Montmorency Falls. When the attack was under way, naval cannon fire, as well as field pieces and howitzers from the Montmorency position, would provide supporting fire.

The assault, scheduled for 30 July, had to be postponed, due to lack of wind to fill the British sails, and it was not until 8 a.m. on the following day that the grenadiers, based on the Isle of Orleans, and the 15th and 78th Foot, from Point Lévis, boarded the flat-bottomed boats to sail across to the northern shore. At 10 a.m., the armed transports, *Russell* and the *Three Sisters*, ran aground on the Beauport shore and began to fire upon the French positions. Almost at once the attack encountered problems; the water was much lower than thought, which forced the landing craft to deposit their human cargo much further from the redoubts than expected and it also meant that the covering fire from the British warships, particularly the fifty-gun *Centurion*, was much less effective than hoped. However, the most worrying discovery was that the French entrenchments, behind the western redoubts, were much closer than Wolfe and his colleagues had assumed. This meant that if the British did capture the redoubts they would be under a heavy fire of musketry from the French above. From his position aboard the *Russell*, Wolfe was exposed to French fire and even had his cane knocked out of his hand by a French cannon ball, but he was able to make a quick assessment of the new obstacles that now faced the assault. Apparently undeterred, Wolfe was resolved to continue with the full-scale attack.

However, more difficulties were to now strike Wolfe's operation. Much time had been lost in gathering the landing craft and in waiting for sufficient water to enable the troops to be landed and it was not until the early afternoon that Wolfe ordered the first wave of grenadiers ashore. As the landing craft approached the northern shore many of them grounded upon a previously unknown ledge, which may have been a barrier of boulders placed, unseen, by the defenders. Wolfe was forced back and it was not until 5.30 p.m. that Wolfe found a suitable spot on which to recommence the landings. The prolonged nature of the operation meant that the French in this sector, under the effective command of Lévis, were fully alerted and ready for the assault.

The thirteen companies of grenadiers, along with two hundred Royal Americans, led the assault. The troops, frustrated by the delay, stormed ashore and, momentarily, discipline was lost. Instead of forming on the beach and waiting for Murray's and Townshend's brigades to join them from Montmorency, the troops of the first wave simply made a mad and rash charge for the enemy. In his journal, Wolfe wrote of the men's 'disorderly March and strange Behaviour'. At the sight of the rushing grenadiers, the French simply abandoned the redoubt and decamped to join their alerted comrades positioned in entrenchments on the heights above. From the security of this position, the French, many of them Canadian militiamen who later received much praise for steadfastness under fire, poured down disciplined volleys upon the grenadiers and soon claimed many victims. Fate, in the shape of a sudden downburst of rain, intervened and this soddened the powder of both the French and British troops, no doubt saving many British lives. The discipline of the bayonet may now have gained an advantage for the attackers, but the rain had made the slope up to the heights too slippery to climb, and the attack stalled.

Wolfe now became conscious of the turning tide, which would make the retreat of Murray's and Townshend's troops back along the beach to Montmorency impossible. With no apparent likelihood that a fresh assault by these troops would be successful, Wolfe decided upon a withdrawal while the tide still permitted. Monckton's troops and the wounded were re-embarked, while Wolfe joined Murray and Townshend as they led their commands back to Montmorency. The sounds of *Vive le roi* filled the air as the British retired, in the face of jubilant and victorious Frenchmen.

The defenders had behaved admirably and had been well led by Lévis. Montcalm seems to have been happy to reinforce the threatened position, but otherwise left local command to Lévis. Wolfe was to write that the failed assault had been a 'foolish business' and he was particularly critical of the behaviour of his grenadiers. The British had lost 210 dead and a further 230 wounded. It was a bloody lesson for the British commander.

It appears that Wolfe was determined not to let this setback dent his own morale, or that of his troops. The following day he wrote to Monckton, 'This check must not discourage us.' Wolfe maintained the respect of both his officers and men, although there were now rumblings that Murray and Townshend were discontented with Wolfe's impulsive attack and his lack of consultation with them. That Townshend was a 'malcontent' seems to have been fairly general knowledge, at least among the officers. The unhappy brigadier even made his frustration known in a series of well-drawn, but ultimately childish, sketches of Wolfe that did nothing for his reputation among Wolfe's more loyal junior officers. Perhaps in part to deflect the combined plotting of his two unfaithful brigadiers, on 3 August Wolfe ordered Murray, with around 1,200 troops, far up the St Lawrence. Murray was to aid Admiral Holmes in the destruction of enemy shipping and settlements along the shore and to journey as far as Deschambault, forty miles above Quebec, to eliminate the stores and munitions there. The brigadier was also instructed to try and establish contact with Amherst's expedition.

On 6 August Murray's force embarked aboard twenty flat-bottomed boats which were to carry them beyond Quebec to join Holmes' squadron, including the powerful *Sutherland*, upriver. Under cover of darkness, the mission was successfully completed and Murray even had an opportunity to survey the French position at Saint-Michel, which he found to be well fortified. He also discovered that the enemy now had a post at Cap Rouge, just eight miles from the city. As the combined force moved up the river, their movements were shadowed by a mobile enemy force, 1,000 strong, under the command of Colonel Bougainville. This contingent included the best of Montcalm's regulars and a corps of cavalry. The quality of these troops is a reflection of the importance Montcalm placed upon the maintenance of his lines of communication. Of course, by trailing the British movement, Montcalm stretched his limited defensive capabilities even further and the absence of these troops from the city would later be critical.

The early British operations up the river were not successful. On 8 August Murray attempted two landings at the Pointe-aux-Trembles, twenty miles from the city. The first amphibious operation, launched at low tide, was slowed when many of the landing craft grounded on a shallow reef. The second attempt, begun at high tide, was beaten back by determined resistance from around 300 of Bougainville's men, who had had time to assemble. Although the operation had been a failure, and 140 British troops were either killed or wounded, it demonstrated to Murray the need for greater planning; for Wolfe the failure at Pointe-aux-Trembles indicated the need to use the tides effectively and that even a small force of determined defenders could deny a superior British landing force. Such lessons would prove to be invaluable.

Frustrated at Pointe-aux-Trembles, Murray and Holmes resolved to land a substantial force upon the south shore at Saint-Antonie. On 10 August the advance party, under Major Dalling, came under sniping fire from the local militiamen. In retaliation, Murray burnt all the houses in the neighbouring village of Saint-Croix. Despite Murray's warning that all attacks upon the British must end, a number of marines were butchered and Murray himself led a force to Saint-Nicholas, which was also torched. This had the desired effect and resistance ceased. The local civilian population were gradually becoming sucked into the 'total war' that was to encircle Quebec over the next few weeks. Murray's greatest success came on 19 August, when he led a surprise landing on the north shore near Portneuf and from there marched his force to Deschambault. Everything here was burnt and destroyed, including a large store house, containing spare clothing and equipment, including gunpowder, as well as Montcalm's personal baggage. Despite Bougainville having recently had his command increased to 1,600 troops, he was over twenty miles away when Murray struck and arrived too late to deter or harass the British. The British were rapidly learning that planning, good intelligence and, crucially, the element of surprise were essential prerequisites to a successful amphibious operation.

Murray's absence was now causing Wolfe some concern, for he considered that he could not launch any fresh assault upon Quebec without both Murray's troops and Holmes' ships. Wolfe issued a number of recall letters to Murray and, in the meantime, the British commander rigorously oversaw the continued training of his troops. Frustratingly for the British flotilla, the French supply ships managed to keep one step ahead of their pursuers and, when Murray finally returned to Quebec on 25 August, he could only report the partial success of his mission. He did, however, bring news of Amherst's successes at Ticonderoga and Crown Point and also of the capture of Fort Niagara. Wolfe must have been delighted with this information, for he could now hope for some cooperation from Amherst, with the expectation that the Commander-in-Chief would be pushing vigorously towards the St Lawrence. Of course Wolfe was not to know that Amherst's advance had now stalled upon the shores of Lake Champlain. Amherst was apparently nervous of advancing further into French territory until he knew of Wolfe's success or failure at Quebec.

News of the fall of Fort Niagara had reached Montcalm long before it reached Wolfe and the French commander felt obliged to despatch 800 troops, that he could ill-afford to lose, under the leadership of Lévis, to try and shore up the crumbling western theatre. Perhaps even more damaging to Montcalm than the loss of the troops, was to be the absence of his able second-in-command, Lévis, who, at the crucial moment of the siege, might well have been a calming voice of reason. He might even have been able to deflect Montcalm from his chosen, and ultimately fatal, course of action.

The month of August was a difficult one for Wolfe. Not only was he in extremely poor health, which was no doubt exaggerated by the stress he was under, but his personal relationship with his brigadiers had soured still further. Frustrated, and almost certainly depressed, Wolfe decided to unleash a 'reign of terror' against the local population sheltering in villages and isolated farm dwellings along the St Lawrence. Although Wolfe might well have been led to such a course of action by what he perceived to be the atrocities carried out against his troops by the Canadians and Indians, it seems clear that he hoped that by targeting their homes and families he might induce those Canadians fighting behind Quebec's defences to either desert or perhaps even sally out from behind the walls to fight the British. In retrospect, Wolfe's brutal policy against civilians, women and children, as well as property, demonstrates both the frustration he was now feeling and the bankruptcy of his ideas.

The scale of operations during this, frankly, depressing stage of the siege, is almost beyond imagination. Starting with the burning of the settlement of St Paul's Bay on 4 August, whose inhabitants had had the affront to fire upon British shipping, revenge and retribution visited every settlement between the Etchemin river and La Chaudière. While the Ranger units were at the forefront of the operations, and Indian-haters such as Joseph Gorham seemed to relish their task, British regulars were also involved. Major George Scott led a mixed force of regulars and Rangers on a fifty-two mile march of devastation, in which his men destroyed 998 buildings, killing five Canadians and taking fifteen prisoners. Throughout August the sky surrounding Quebec was blackened by the numerous fires along the shores of the St Lawrence. The final tally of destruction during this month-long campaign of terror was in excess of 1,400 buildings torched, along with crops ruined and farm animals captured or slaughtered. On top of this, it is now impossible to calculate the number of incidents of murder and rape that befell the local population. Such action was, of course, counter-productive, for, by his endorsement of such a brutal campaign, Wolfe gave the locals no alternative but to offer resistance to the British aggressors. When Wolfe's despatch to Pitt was published in the *London Gazette*, details of the operations to lay waste the countryside along the St Lawrence were suppressed, as they were considered unsuitable for the British public to read.

Towards the end of August, Wolfe had gained sufficient strength to pen a memorandum to his brigadiers which contained his own views on how the operation to take Quebec should proceed, along with a request that they should 'consult together for the publick utility and advantage; and to consider of the best method of attacking the enemy'. Wolfe listed his own three options for an attack upon the French defences; two were of similar design to that which had failed at Montmorency on 31 July, although some details differed, but Wolfe's preferred plan was to send a substantial force from Montmorency on a long, looping march through the forested wilderness, so as to cross another ford through the Montmorency river, nine miles further up. The force would then march on to Beauport with the aim of a dawn assault on the rear of the French defences. After two days of consultation, the brigadiers, along with Admiral Saunders, signed a joint response in which they rejected all three of Wolfe's plans. They considered another attack from the Montmorency position, against the strong Beauport defences, unlikely to succeed, while the looping march was dismissed because it was 'exposed to certain discovery, and to the disadvantage of continual wood fight'. A fourth option was offered by the brigadiers, which envisaged an operation above the town, in the upper

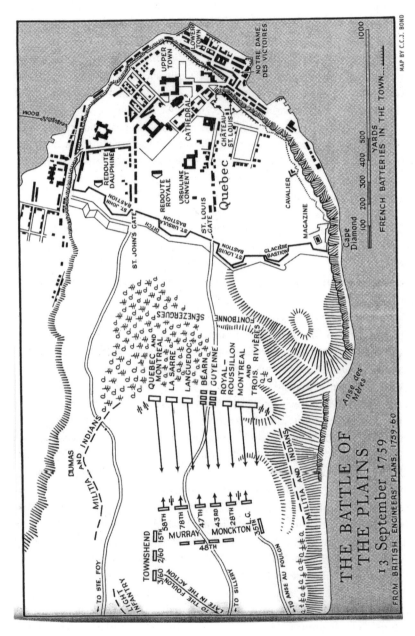

THE BATTLE OF THE PLAINS
13 September 1759
FROM BRITISH ENGINEERS' PLANS, 1759-60

Map by C.C.J. Bond from Stacey, *Quebec 1759*, by permission of the publisher.

46

river, in which troops were positioned on the south shore for an amphibious attack upon the north. Once a force had been landed, the British would be between the city and its supplies and between Montcalm troops and Bourgainville's force. The brigadiers believed that Montcalm would be forced out of the city to oppose such a British landing and could be beaten in a general action.

Along with their suggested change of direction, the brigadiers also presented a 'Plan of Operations', which envisaged that the camp at Montmorency should be evacuated and, apart from sufficient troops to secure the bases on the Isle of Orleans at Point Lévis and Pointe aux Pères, the remainder of the army should be moved to the south shore, above the Etchemin river. From there, a night-time landing could be made on the north shore, and the brigadiers advised that a suitable spot could be found 'half a league' above the Cap Rouge river. Whether Wolfe was reluctant in his acceptance of the brigadiers' plan is unclear, but he must have surely realized that, in the face of their united opposition to his suggested options, he had little choice but to comply with their thinking and work to find a suitable location, and opportunity, for a landing on the north shore. Although he was still clearly sick, Wolfe now threw himself with renewed energy at this latest plan of attack.

Wolfe perceived that any British landing upon the north shore would require two elements. First, the need for surprise, for, if any of Bougainville's roving force were in a position to oppose a landing, it was likely to repulsed; and second, naval control of the river above Quebec. Even as late as 27 August, French naval forces were operating in the area of Pointe-aux-Trembles, with the aim of threatening the small British naval presence above the town. However, any French aspirations to attack the British ships disappeared on the night of 27/28 August when the British, on their fourth attempt, were able to reinforce their naval power above Quebec with five more of Saunders' ships, including the frigate *Lowestoft*. The plan of the brigadiers, to land a force above Quebec, could now take full advantage of the strong British naval contingent there. As the easterly winds continued to blow, Saunders was able to transfer more of his fleet into the upper river and, on the evening of 31 August, the frigate *Seahorse* strengthened, still further, Wolfe's options.

Although, for Wolfe, the British withdrawal from their Montmorency position was an admission of failure, the commander attempted to turn the situation to his advantage by trying, one more time, to entice Montcalm out from behind his entrenchments. The evacuation began on 1 September, with the sick and wounded placed in landing craft. The army's tents had been struck overnight so as to give the impression that the bulk of the forces had already left. In reality, the battalions remained behind, lying low and silent, with Wolfe hoping that Montcalm might finally unleash his troops on the embarking British wounded. Even now, Montcalm was not to be fooled and the French remained solidly behind their defences. By 3 September the last British soldiers left their position at Montmorency, in an orderly and disciplined fashion, although many must have regretted the loss of comrades in the heavy skirmishes that had been such a feature of the last eight weeks. Indeed, during this period, Wolfe had suffered 850 casualties, seriously depleting his already inadequate force.

After a day's rest, the British troops began the move upriver on the evening of 5 September, with Murray's four battalions joining Rear Admiral Holmes' fleet. Townshend's and Monckton's commands, along with Wolfe, completed the assembly the following night. With the movements of the enemy, Montcalm was forced to adjust his own dispositions; troops were moved from the left flank at the Beauport shoreline to the right and Bougainville received even more men into his command, pushing his contingent to around 3,000, of which around half formed a mobile reserve, the rest being placed in a series of guard posts stretching from Sillery to Trois Rivières. Bougainville, in an attempt to deter the British, ensured that his troops were very visible to the British positioned in their ships or on the southern shore.

Despite the strength of the French positions, Wolfe was determined to launch an assault and, following the geographical guidelines issued in the brigadiers' 'Plan of Operation', the region of Cap Rouge Bay was chosen for an assault on 7 September. That afternoon, 1,500 British troops had climbed into the assembled landing crafts, but French naval activity and a turning tide stymied any possible landing on this occasion. Another attempt was planned for the night of 9 September, this time further up the river, near Pointe-aux-Trembles, but this too had to be cancelled due to poor weather. As the apparently never-ending rain poured down, Wolfe continued to reconnoitre the river in an attempt to find a landing spot on the north shore. Whether he chanced upon the position at Anse au Foulon, was led to it by a French deserter or recalled the location from his earlier mission with Holland, is now uncertain. What is clear, is that the decision was his alone and, from 9 September, Wolfe was resolved to launch a landing at Anse au Foulon and he set about planning his attack.

On 10 September Wolfe returned to view the Anse au Foulon again, this time with Brigadiers Townshend and Monckton, Admiral Holmes, the engineer Major Mackellar, Colonel Howe and Captain Chads of His Majesty's ship *Vesuvius*. Chads, who had been the landing officer during the Montmorency landings of 31 July, would have a vital role to play in a successful landing on the north shore. Mackellar was optimistic in his engineer's analysis of the slope rising up from the shoreline and he considered that an ascent at the Anse au Foulon would be difficult, but practical. Such a conclusion must have cheered Wolfe, who now had to hope that the French position at the top of the slope was lightly defended and that, once upon the cliff top, Montcalm would meet the British in a general engagement. Although a landing at this position on the north shore presented many difficulties and dangers to an assault force, it offered crucial advantages to the British. First, it would certainly achieve the surprise that would be essential so as to avoid the unwelcome presence of Bougainville's opposing forces and second, by landing so close to the town and British positions across the river at Point Lévis, Wolfe would be able to bring a substantial force of regular troops within one mile of the thinly fortified city walls, and upon ground which his army could line to face an onslaught from Montcalm's men. A landing further up the river would risk intervention from Bougainville, and, perhaps crucially, it would be some time before the initial British landing force could be reinforced from troops on the south shore. By landing at Anse au Foulon, Wolfe would be able to quickly concentrate his whole force, with the exception of a detachment to guard the Island of Orleans.

Having made the decision, no time was to be lost for, if the British were to take full advantage of the tide and the moon, Wolfe had calculated that the assault must take place on the night of 12/13 September. Even Wolfe's sternest critics admit that his awareness of the tide and moon in the decision to launch his attack when he did verged on the brilliant. The troops were re-embarked aboard the ships off Saint-Nicholas on 11 September and they then sailed further up the river to give the impression of a landing there. While the naval vessels retained their presence, and hopefully diverted Bougainville, the troops in landing craft were to drift silently down the St Lawrence on the ebb tide, so as to arrive at the Anse au Foulon at around 4 a.m. on 13 September. In calculating such a move,

Wolfe would have to deal with three separate problems; the distance that the landing craft would have to travel, the strength of the tide and the darkness of the night. The troops would have to travel 7.6 nautical miles from embarkation to disembarkation and the time taken to travel these miles would depend on the exact time the tide turned and the speed of the current. Knowing that he did not want his men to spend more than two hours in the landing craft, Wolfe calculated that the night of 12/13 September would see the tide turn at just after midnight and it would carry the landing craft at a rate of around 5 knots. Thus, if the troops entered the landing craft at around 2 a.m., they would arrive at the Anse au Foulon at the desired time of 4 a.m. Once the initial landings had taken place, there would still be time to use the landing crafts to ferry the remainder of the army across from the southern shore. The direction of the large quarter-moon in the eastern sky would also benefit the assault, for it would illuminate the river for the landing flotilla, outlining the northern shore, but French sentries looking up river towards the British warships would be able to see little. Such conditions of tide and moon would not be repeated until much later in the month. For Wolfe, the assault had to be on the morning of 13 September.

The troops aboard the British ships must have sensed that, after many frustrations and disappointments, something important, and dangerous, was about to happen. It appears that Captain Chads, at almost the last moment, began to worry greatly about his ability to land the men in the correct location on such a fast tide. Wolfe had to reassure Chads and stated that, if the mission failed, the commander himself would shoulder the blame. In addition to this worrying last-minute interruption by Chads, Wolfe had to pacify his brigadiers. Although Wolfe repeatedly stressed the need for secrecy, there was no excuse for him failing to brief his brigadiers properly, especially as he had taken his old friend Colonel Burton into his full confidence. In desperation, the brigadiers demanded to know Wolfe's full intentions and their precise roles in the forthcoming operation. However, it was not until nearly 9 p.m. on 12 September that Wolfe, in a rather exasperated manner, responded to their written plea for more information. This incident clearly demonstrates how low relations had fallen between Wolfe and his brigadiers. Wolfe may have had confidence in his troops and junior officers, and they in him, but on the eve of battle he plainly had little regard for his immediate subordinates.

At around 2 a.m. on 13 September, with the troops already embarked in the landing craft, two lanterns were swung high above *Sutherland* as the signal for the boats to be untied. Caught in the ebb tide, the landing craft began their journey towards Quebec. Wolfe was among his men as they were silently carried along. They were soon joined by armed sloops and craft carrying ordnance stores and munitions. At around 3 a.m., Holmes followed with three frigates and two transport ships which carried the troops of the second wave. Despite his earlier nerves, Chads steered the landing craft superbly, but the whole operation nearly floundered within one mile of its destination when the landing craft approached HMS *Hunter*, which was anchored off Sillery. Earlier that night two French deserters had swam out to *Hunter* with the information that a French convoy of provisions was expected down the St Lawrence at any moment. The men aboard *Hunter* were on the lookout for the convoy and, as the British landing craft emerged from the darkness, there was an anxious moment before the identity of each party was confirmed. The meeting was to benefit Wolfe's assault, for the likely presence of a French convoy was now known by the advancing British.

In fact, due to the large British naval presence in the upper river, the provisions convoy had been cancelled. Bougainville, however, had failed to tell his sentries along the northern shore of the cancellation and, when an alert French sentry challenged the drifting British landing craft, a quick-thinking officer, named Captain Fraser, was able to turn this failure of communication to his advantage. Fraser had previously served in the Dutch army and spoke French fluently. He was able to answer the sentry by claiming that they were the French provisions convoy and Fraser even had the guile to tell the sentry to keep quiet for fear of drawing fire from *Hunter*. The ploy worked and no alarm was raised. Minutes later Chads turned the first landing craft into shore and grounded his vessel. Seconds later, British troops were piling out and running towards the cliffs that rose up in front of them.

As the first boats ran ashore onto the narrow gravel beach at Anse au Foulon the British officers in the vanguard, Captain Delaune and Colonel Howe, immediately realized that, despite Chads' effort's, the strong current had placed them below their objective. Frustratingly, although Delaune did record the precise time of the landing as 4.07 a.m., neither he, nor Howe, nor of course Wolfe himself, left a record of the initial events of the landing. What is clear is that, as soon as Delaune and Howe ascertained they were slightly adrift of the prescribed landing spot, they led their separate commands by example; Howe ordered Delaune and his twenty-four 'volunteers' of the 'forlorn hope' back along the beach so as to scale the path, while Howe himself led three companies of his light infantry straight up the 175-foot cliff that rose in front of them. The cove of Anse au Foulon was formed by a geological fault which runs across the St Lawrence at this point. A rivulet, coming from the west, descends the cliff here and cascades into the river. From the stream's east bank a path transversed up the face of the cliff. A French officer named La Pause inspected the path in the early summer of 1759 and described it as a path 'on which two men can descend abreast'. That the path was fit for the purpose was demonstrated throughout 13 September, and in subsequent days, when the British were able to haul supplies and artillery pieces up the slope. It seems slightly incredible that, despite the diligence shown at Beauport and Montmorency, the French did not realize the vulnerability the slope presented to their defensive line.

Howe's light infantry literally threw themselves at the shale cliff face and sought purchase on whatever piece of vegetation was available to them. Although it is not known how long this ascent took, it must have been fairly quick, for the climb did not seem to disturb the French sentries on top of the cliff. Once on the summit, Howe led his men to the left to attack the rear of the pickets that were guarding the path. Their success owed much to surprise, the darkness of the hour and an element of guile. Apparently, another French-speaking officer, Captain McDonald, was able to respond to the challenge of a sentry by stating that he was bringing reinforcements to guard the path. This deceit bought sufficient time for the British to overwhelm the defending picket. While the light infantry had been able to complete their ascent without a shot being fired, the landing craft immediately behind them, carrying battalions led by Monckton and Murray and including Wolfe himself, were met by musket fire from a scattering of militiamen and Indians as well as cannon fire from the four guns of the Samos Battery. As light dawned, these guns began to inflict some casualties upon those still in boats and did slight damage to the frigates *Lowestoft* and *Seahorse*. Fortunately, the light infantry soon dispersed both the militia and Indians and the battery was abandoned by the French at the first sight of Murray's advancing battalions. Quartermaster Sergeant John Johnson recorded in his journal of the siege that Wolfe, in the second wave, 'leaped out upon the beach' and, although there is no certainty as to the means by which he assailed the cliff, it is probable that he climbed the path behind Delaune's advance party. Wolfe must have been jubilant to find that the path was so poorly defended and there is some evidence that, before he joined Howe and Delaune on the summit, he helped to marshal some of the landing craft onto the narrow beach.

No one is sure who fired the first shot at the summit; whether it was a French sentry, one of Delaune's party or a light infantryman is unclear, but the silence of the earlier morning was certainly shattered and it took only a few moments for the British to secure their immediate objective. At the sound of musket fire, and the screams of terrified and dying soldiers, the French officer in command at Anse au Foulon, Captain Vergor, dashed from his tent wearing only his nightshirt and fired his pistol wildly into the air. He then fled with the majority of his detachment towards the walls of Quebec. He was, however, shot in the ankle and fell to the ground, where his cries of agony joined the rising cacophony. The light infantry were soon joined by the Highlanders and a company of Grenadiers, and gradually the British force began to assemble.

With the immediate opposition now either silenced or in headlong retreat, Wolfe was afforded the luxury of being able to study the terrain over which he soon expected to fight. The Plains, or Heights, of Abraham, named after Abraham Martin, a river pilot who once grazed sheep there, was undulating ground, rising slightly towards the city walls. Although there were patches of corn scattered across it and some scrub growing around its fringes, it was effectively an open field, which provided Wolfe sufficient space so as to deploy his troops. Wolfe sent pickets to the west, beyond Sillery, to ascertain the proximity of Bougainville's force. They reported that there appeared to be no immediate danger from that direction and, with this reassurance, Wolfe began to deploy his troops across the Plains, facing towards Quebec.

As the battalions reached the summit, Wolfe first formed them in line with their backs to the river, with the city to their right and Saint-Michel on their left, so as to defend the army's possible line of retreat if circumstances dictated a withdrawal. With a light rain now falling, Wolfe, accompanied by his aide-de camps, made a reconnaissance towards the city. Crossing right over to the St Charles declivity, Wolfe looked down at the bridge of boats. There were no signs of activity; nothing to indicate that Montcalm was rushing troops to meet the British threat. It appears that Wolfe gave some consideration to placing his front line upon on a rise known as Buttes à Neveu, just eight hundred yards from the walls, but which would have given the British some advantage in restricting any French advance. However, the position was within range of the cannons sited upon the city walls and Wolfe rapidly rejected this option. About five hundred yards further west there was a small hillock, about fifty feet high, on the St Lawrence side. In line with it, and near the St Charles slope, was a small group of farm buildings belonging to a family named Borgia. Wolfe decided to form up his army on the mile or so of uneven ground between these two points, which provided good flank positions.

By 6 a.m., once it had become clear that the British would not receive an immediate response from the French defenders, three battalions, and the Louisbourg Grenadiers, were marched onto the Plains and were placed facing Quebec. A detachment of light infantry occupied Borgia's farm and the remainder was sent to form a screen at a wood to the rear of the position. The third battalion of Royal Americans was left to guard the landing place, while below on the beach, the sailors were earnestly engaged in manhandling guns on to the shore and up the narrow cliff path.

The rest of the force was marched straight across the plateau, until they came to the road from Quebec to Sainte-Foy, where, with the town about two miles distant, they turned right, reaching the Borgia farm. They then wheeled right again and marched back across the plateau to form up in battle order. By 8 a.m., Colonel Burton's command had been ferried over from their position at Point Lévis and, as the army was concentrated and more men had ascended the cliff, Wolfe was able to extend his line and placed his forces in a horseshoe formation. Monckton, as the senior brigadier, was given the right of the line, facing the city, while Murray was notionally in charge of the centre. Townshend was responsible for the left wing, which comprised the 15th and two battalions of the 60th, and this was moved back so as to face northwards on a line parallel to the Sainte-Foy Road. This deployment was initially done to counter a growing threat from French militiamen on that flank, but it also had the added advantages of depriving the French of access to the road while, at the same time, offering some protection to the rear if Bougainville's flying column should suddenly arrive. Similarly, on the right flank, Monckton had placed the 35th on the far right of the line, again moved back, to offer protection against more militiamen who were gradually infiltrating the bushes lining the cliff top.

The main battle line in the centre comprised the Louisbourg

Grenadiers, drawn up on the right, then the 28th, 43rd, 47th, 78th and 58th Foot, with the 48th, under Burton, as a reserve behind this central line. Howe's light infantry were given the task of offering further protection to the army's rear. Soldiers and sailors combined to haul two light six-pounder field pieces up the Anse au Foulon and these were placed in the front line. Wolfe made himself visible to his men and seemed to be everywhere during this initial deployment. He finally decided to post himself with the Louisbourg Grenadiers on the right flank, nearest to the city walls, yet conveniently placed to quickly call upon Burton if the reserve was required. Wolfe's deployment was very broad and this forced him to adopt a two-rank formation, rather than the customary three. Furthermore, the men were placed three feet apart, with a forty-yard interval between battalions. However, Wolfe's disposition meant that, apart from nuisance attacks on his flanks by Canadian militiamen, it would not be possible for Montcalm and his French regulars to offer anything more than a frontal attack upon the British line. Wolfe's broad line took full advantage of the natural limits of the plain and the short distances involved.

Conspicuous in the centre were the Highlanders, wearing kilt and plaid. Wolfe's first line consisted of just 3,111 men. While it has been frequently recorded that the British troops, dressed as they were in their scarlet frock coats and scarlet breeches with white gaiters to above their knees, made a handsome sight, the reality would almost certainly have been very different. These men had been repeatedly ordered in and out of landing craft, in which they sometimes had to spend many uncomfortable hours, they had been engaged in battle at Montmorency and had lived for many weeks in tents, and their appearance can hardly be considered the parade-ground look that some historians would have us believe. However, their undoubted resolve would have made for an impressive, and worrying, sight in the eyes of their French foes. The troops were armed with sword, musket and bayonet, while their the officers and sergeants would have carried pikes. The red line of British troops was indeed a thin one.

The success of British forces in launching an amphibious operation, scaling a cliff-top and deploying in line went remarkably smoothly and is worthy of some comment. The professionalism of the soldiers and, particularly, the sailors involved justifies high praise. The careful use of the tides and the skill of Captain Chads to place the landing craft so near to the Anse au Foulon, and the control and discipline of naval beach masters not only to shepherd the first waves of landing craft, but then ferry Burton's men from the Point Lévis was all quite remarkable. Although the French can be criticized for their subsequent actions, the British, and their commander had won the right to be at the walls of Quebec and it was an opportunity that was now seized.

Wolfe had given Admiral Saunders the task of directing French attention well away from the landings at Anse au Foulon and in this Saunders succeeded well. Throughout the night of 12/13 September, Saunders had led a feint directed towards the Beauport lines. The vessels of the main body of the fleet assembled off Point Lévis with orders to distract the French forces positioned along the Beauport lines. According to James Cook, master of *Pembroke*, all the rowing boats in the assembled British ships 'made a feint to land at Beauport in order to draw the enemy's attention that way'. The log of *Stirling Castle* records that 'Att 11 they put off from thence and kept rowing between Bow port [Beauport] and mouth of Charles River'. This deception continued until 4 a.m. and provided the French, and their commander, Montcalm, with an anxious, sleepless night, with the expectation that the British would attempted a landing at Beauport. Once dawn broke, it became clear that the anticipated attack would not be forthcoming and the exhausted French troops retired to their tents to grab some much-needed rest.

When a southwesterly breeze brought Montcalm the sound of the guns at Samos, he thought that the British had attacked the French provision convoy and that the battery was endeavouring to cover it. Saunders also heard the Samos guns, and, knowing the real reason for the cannon fire, immediately recommenced his own barrage to further distract the French. As dawn broke, the French could see no threatening movement in front of them. Crucially, all the British tents at the Orleans and Point Lévis camps were still standing, with guards apparently patrolling as usual. A relieved Montcalm, convinced that the bulk of the British Army was still east of Quebec, retired to his command post in the village of Beauport for a cup of tea. Saunders' deception was complete

Refugees from Vergor's overwhelmed command at Anse au Foulon were the first to bring news of the British landings to Quebec. On hearing the news that the British had established themselves on the heights west of town, Montcalm could not believe that this was the main British army, for he is reported to have said, 'it is but a small party come to burn a few houses and retire.' For the French commander the news was hard to credit and at first he, and other French officers, struggled to comprehend how they had been so outwitted by Wolfe. Montcalm was now forced to believe the reports, as he was appalled to see to the south-west, two miles across the St Charles, the motionless red line of British soldiers drawn up across the plateau. Montcalm is reported to have exclaimed, 'I see them where they have no business to be! This is a serious state of affairs.' Once he had recovered his composure, Montcalm knew that he must assemble the army immediately to counter this new and dangerous threat to the city. French troops, sleeping in their tents along the Beauport lines, were rudely awakened by the sounds of drummers beating the call to arms. Rubbing the sleep from their eyes, pulling on their recently discarded uniforms and grabbing their muskets they began to form into their units.

Ordering his regular battalions to concentrate west of the city walls, Montcalm also sent an urgent dispatch to Bougainville to come to his assistance. Montcalm then put spurs to his horse, galloped across the bridge of boats and up the steep streets to the far side of the town, with such troops as he could gather round him. Those who saw him say he rode with a fixed look, uttering not a word. He was accompanied by the Chevalier Johnstone, a Scottish officer who had gone to France after the Jacobites' defeat at Culloden and had obtained a commission in the French army. The two men viewed the British line with a combination of despair and disbelief. All Montcalm could do was send Johnstone to the Beauport lines to call up all available troops and request as many artillery pieces to be sent forward as possible. The dual command of Vaudreuil and Montcalm caused confusion to the end. When Johnstone arrived at the left of the camp he found that the commander there, Colonel Poulariez, had already received orders from Vaudreuil that under no circumstances was he to move, in case the British carried out a second landing on the Beauport position. In spite of Johnstone's frantic expostulations the matter was referred back to the Governor-General.

Out beyond the ramparts, Montcalm rode back in person to remonstrate at the slowness with which the troops were coming up. The battalion of Guienne had moved up from their encampment near the St Charles and formed a precarious cordon on the Buttes à Neveu. As the other regiments slowly debouched from the town they were sent to join them. There is no evidence that Montcalm was denied his request for cannon from Quebec. He did eventually move onto the battlefield with at least three field pieces, although Montbeillard stated that there were four and another French officer claimed that five pieces were used during the battle. Whatever the final number, it reflected only a small portion of what was available within the city. When the British finally entered Quebec, an anonymous British officer recorded that the British 'found 180 pieces of cannon, from 2 to 36-pounders; a number of mortars with a large quantity of artillery stores'. Even if Montcalm had been forced to manhandle some of these weapons onto the Buttes à Neveu, the French could have possessed a huge artillery advantage over the British and smashed the British line at will.

In the confusion surrounding the British landing, Montcalm obviously gave no consideration to this possibility and he clearly felt that the few field pieces he took onto the field would be sufficient. He could not believe that the British Army before them represented Wolfe's whole striking force. His one thought was to sweep them down the cliff again before reinforcements could arrive. 'Since they have got to the weak side of this miserable garrison, we must give battle and crush them before midday,' he told his staff. Apart from a brief discussion with Johnstone and Vaudreuil very early in the morning, Montcalm seems to have been in no mood to discuss the issue with his staff. If the able Lévis had been present, Montcalm might have sought his advice and acted differently, but as it was Montcalm knew what he had to do and that was to act decisively and quickly. Despite Johnstone's claims that Vaudreuil tried to hold back troops for the defence of the Beauport lines there seems to be little evidence that this was the case, although confusion over the joint command may have delayed the departure of some of the troops from Beauport. Certainly, Montcalm advanced with virtually all his available regulars. He had little more than 3,500 regulars and marines with which to form his line of battle. A further 1,500 Canadians and Indians, primarily from the Ottawa and Abenaki tribes, were out on the flanks in the bushes and many were already harassing the British line. Thus the French had a numerical superiority in troops and a slight advantage in artillery over the British. Of course, if Bougainville's 2,000 troops, plus artillery and cavalry, could return to Quebec in time then the advantage would certainly lie with the French.

By about eight o'clock the main French force had assembled and, when their field pieces started to open fire, Wolfe ordered most of his men to lie down, in order to better escape the cannon shot and snipers' bullets. As the morning advanced Townshend's men on the left and Monckton's on the right came under an increasingly galling fire from the Canadian militia and Indians, who were endeavouring to infiltrate along the flanks, sniping with some effect from behind trees and bushes. Company-strength sorties by the British succeeded in keeping them at a distance and skirmishers were thrown out in front of the lines to hold the militia back. At one point some more enterprising militiamen succeeded in flanking Townshend, by running along below the St Charles declivity, but a brisk sortie by the light infantry drove them off. Fearing that these brisk exchanges might indicate a British threat upon the St Charles bridge, so as to cut off a French retreat, Montcalm sent over a few companies of colonial marines as reinforcements.

Just after 9 a.m. Montcalm led his army over the crest of the Buttes à Neveu and began their deployment from three columns into line. Captain York, of the Royal Artillery, upon Wolfe's order, began to place a steady and deadly fire down onto the French line from the two 6-pounders, which delayed Montcalm's final deployment. Wolfe now ordered his whole line to advance one hundred paces, where he halted them. The two forces were now only a quarter of a mile apart. The rain that had steadily fallen since the landings now disappeared and a weak sun broke through the clouds to illuminate the two opposing lines. Both armies despatched sharpshooters to cover their fronts and harass each others' flanks and musket shots intermittently struck home. Wolfe was again amongst his men; at around 9.30 a.m. a trooper in the 28th saw Wolfe move towards a platoon of grenadiers on the right and talk to them. Although there is no record of what was said in this exchange, the trooper did record that all men smiled ruefully and some of them laughed. Wolfe was clearly relaxed and very much in his element as the battle approached.

While the deployment of the British troops is well recorded, how Montcalm deployed his men is not so clear and is open to dispute. However, the best calculations appear to place a large number of militiamen and Indians on the right, in advance of the French line. These men were harassing the British left flank from the scrub and tree-line. Vaudreuil later claimed that next were units of militia, from both Quebec and Montreal, in the actual battle line. Then, right to left were placed the five battalions of French regulars; La Sarre, Languedoc, Béarn, Guienne and Royal-Roussillon, all clothed in white uniforms, now rather grey from months of service. The battalion colours, two to each, flapped in a slight breeze. To the left of these regulars were militiamen from Montreal and Trois Rivières and a number of Canadian and Indian snipers. Even the French regular battalions were not as strong as they appeared, for Montcalm had earlier decided to bolster these units, and to forge links between his diverse army, with the inclusion in their ranks of approximately 600 militiamen. Clothed in the same uniforms, these men had spent barely three months with the regulars, which was insufficient time for them to learn the essential battlefield manoeuvres with which to present a unified front to an enemy. Additionally, Montcalm's best troops, the grenadiers, were not on the battlefield, for these men had been transferred to Bougainville's flying column. As an experienced soldier, Montcalm must have surely known of the weakness of his troops and that they could hardly be expected to defeat an army of well-trained and disciplined British regulars, yet he was now to risk all in a desperate advance.

Fire from Canadian sharpshooters began to claim some victims. As men fell, wounded or dead, the British line would extend slightly to fill the gaps in the ranks. On the British right, a Captain, standing near Wolfe, suddenly fell, shot through the lungs. Wolfe instinctively cradled the officer's head in his hand, thanked the stricken officer for his service and promised him a promotion. Wolfe sent an aide-de-camp to Monckton to ensure that, if he fell in the coming battle, the promised promotion would be approved. It was soon after this incident that Wolfe was hit for the first time: shot through the right wrist, a wound which tore the sinews. Wolfe must have been in agony, but he seemed, to those around him, hardly to flinch. He simply bound up his wrist with a handkerchief and continued to offer encouragement to his men as he walked up and down the line.

Montcalm was convinced, probably even before he had seen Wolfe's army on the Plains, that he could not afford to wait any longer, for he apparently felt sure that the British were entrenching their position and growing stronger by the minute. Two cannons were now firing at his troops and he surely feared that it would not be long before the British brought up more troops, as well as heavy 24-pounders and mortars to pulverize the city walls. Indeed, such weaponry had already been landed at Anse au Foulon, and the British sailors were now struggling to drag them up the slope. A French officer, Montbelliard, spoke with Montcalm just before the latter gave the order to advance and the conversation was later recorded. 'I [Montbelliard] paused a moment with M. le Marquis de Montcalm, who said to me: "We cannot avoid action. The enemy is entrenching. He already has two pieces of cannon. If we give him time to establish himself, we shall never be able to attack him successfully with the sort of troops we have." He left me without giving me time to say anything in reply.' Montcalm was correct in that the French could not avoid action; Wolfe's army were astride the Sainte-Foy road, thus cutting a vital communication link through which supplies had been brought into the city. With limited food supplies available, the city would either have been starved into submission or blasted by British cannons. However, although the French advance was inevitable, it could have been made at noon, or even later, when the French army could have concentrated more troops and artillery pieces.

That Montcalm should have delayed his attack until Bougainville and his troops, the best in Montcalm's army, were attacking the rear pickets of Wolfe's army, is an easy and obvious statement to make. If he had so delayed, Wolfe's army would have been positioned between two opposing forces and, although a British defeat would have been far from certain, for Wolfe's troops were so superior to those of Montcalm's army, the French chance of battlefield success would have been significantly enhanced. But Montcalm had had no news of Bougainville's whereabouts and thus had no idea if and when he could expect support from that direction. However, if Montcalm had felt unable to delay his advance on the chance of Bougainville's return, he should surely have considered waiting until sufficient cannon had been brought from Quebec to be placed upon the slope of Buttes à Neveu to pound away at the British line. Although such guns would probably have had to be manhandled onto the field, and this might have taken some hours or more, Wolfe, and his thin line of British troops, were simply waiting, hoping that the French would attack them, and were not about the leave the field. A delay for the guns would have allowed the Canadian militia to continue their successful harassment of the British flanks and the arrival of a significant number of artillery pieces would have certainly swung the advantage to the French, by which time Bougainville's troops might have entered the battle.

Of course such hypothesizing does nothing to alter the true course of events, for the still undamaged great clock in the Quebec basilica was marking five minutes past ten when Montcalm, upon a huge black charger, waved his sword above his head and ordered the French to began their final advance. Colonel Williamson, a British veteran of the battle, later wrote 'they marched towards us in three columns M. Montcalm at the head of the centre one.' Wolfe must have been both relieved and delighted that Montcalm had taken his bait. The expression upon his face at this moment was recorded as being 'radiant and joyful beyond description'.

With a cry of *Vive le Roi!* the French regulars advanced at a brisk pace. Major Malartic, a French survivor of the battle, later wrote that his comrades advanced at a run, 'much too fast'. It appeared to the British that the French were grouped into three massive columns; however, only the centre of the advancing line, composed of the Béarn and Guienne battalions, had been organized into an assault formation. The presences of short, tough, undergrowth, particularly clumps of alder, forced the remaining troops to squeeze together to avoid this natural obstacle and all attempts to advance in extended line formation failed. So compressed did the French advance become that a British sergeant-major later wrote that the French had attacked six deep. Malartic stated that the formation of the advance soon fell to pieces; 'We had not gone twenty paces when the left was too far in rear and the centre too far in front.'

According to Lieutenant John Knox, of the apparent three columns, two moved on the British left, the other the right. The men began firing obliquely and unsteadily while still out of range. The French, shouting as they ran, finally halted at about half musket range, 125–150 yards, and the regulars at last fired the only concerted platoon volleys. The French continued to fire as they moved forward in ' a wild scattering manner', as recalled by Knox. Many of the musket balls flew harmlessly over the British line and, although some of the British did fall, casualties were relatively slight due to large spacing of the line.

For all the bravery and apparent splendour of the initial advance, the French soon fell into disorder. The flank units, in the ever-constricting space, struggled to move from column into line and the confusion was increased when a group of militia, who had been harassing the British flanks since the deployment, tried to withdraw through the advancing French lines. The advance became further disordered when the militia, who had been placed among the regular troops, threw themselves on the ground to reload, after their Canadian fashion, and refused to rejoin the ranks. Malartic, again, recorded that 'the Canadians who formed the second rank and the soldiers of the third fired without orders, and according to their [Canadian] custom threw themselves on the ground to reload. The false movement broke all the battalions.' While Knox reported that the French continued to fire as they advanced, right up until the moment of the first British volley, some French accounts suggest that many troops did not move any further forward after they stopped to fire for the first time. Despite the efforts of Montcalm, and his officers, all attempts to regroup their men failed and all cohesion was lost.

To add to the mayhem, Captain York's guns raked the masses with grapeshot. Colonel George Williamson wrote, 'We had two field pieces which kept an incessant fire upon them. The Canadians did not relish it. They turned most of their fire on the two guns, and lest we might get up any more, prevailed on their General to attack us.' Men continued to advance and to fire, by companies and platoons and as individuals, but such a piecemeal movement towards the British guaranteed that their shots would be without collective effect. There is no doubt that the French fire was ineffective, and much less of a danger than that of the skirmishers earlier. The British line was never significantly threatened by such a disorganized French assault.

Wolfe was fully aware of the devastation that the musket could reap among advancing troops, especially at close range. The balls were three quarters of an inch in diameter and Wolfe ordered that two should be put in every charge. As he walked along the line, Wolfe gave instructions to all to hold their fire until the French were only forty yards away. Quartermaster Sergeant Johnson later recalled that 'General Wolfe had given positive Orders, not to fire a Shot until the Enemy should be within Forty Yards of the point of our Bayonets.' The General was sure of his men and their discipline. The British stood tall, their muskets ready.

Wolfe had by now positioned himself with the Louisbourg Grenadiers, commanded by Colonel Guy Carleton, on the right of the line and upon a slight rise to afford a better view of the advancing French. Montcalm and his officers did their best to urge on their men, who it seems continued to stop to reload, before firing and then continuing their march towards the motionless British. John Knox wrote that despite a steady reduction in their numbers from the French fire, the British troops demonstrated 'the greatest intrepidity and firmness'. As the French line reached the desired forty yards distance, the British battalion officers screamed out the orders, 'Make ready. Present. Fire!'

One of the many myths that settled around the battle of the Plains of Abraham was that a concerted, concentrated volley from the British line enveloped the French. This was not the case. No single commander could scream loud enough to coordinate a volley fire along a whole line of troops. Individual battalion commanders would have judged the distance themselves and shouted the order to fire when they thought the distance correct. However, there is some evidence to suggest that the troops on the left and right flanks may have been ordered to fire when the French were still sixty yards away, angling their fire against the sides of the French advance, as they had been trained to do by Wolfe throughout the summer. Indeed, it seems highly probable that Wolfe gave Carleton the nod to order the Louisbourg Grenadiers, on the right flank, to fire first. This initial volley was the cue for the other battalion commanders to unleash their volley fire at the advancing French. Thus while the two initial volleys were not continuous, each was probably completed in only 30–40 seconds, in which time Carleton's men would have reloaded and been ready to fire again. Those in the centre, the men of the 43rd and 47th Regiments, stood fast and fired last, when the French were at their closest. Then, according to Knox of the 43rd, they delivered as

> close and heavy [a] discharge, as I ever saw performed at a private field exercise, insomuch that better troops than we encountered could not possibly withstand it: and, indeed, well might the French Officers say, that they never opposed such a shock as they received from the centre of our line, for that they believed every ball took place, and such regularity and discipline they had not experienced before; our troops in general, and particularly the central corps, having levelled and fired – *comme un coup de canon*.

The dense columns of the Béarn and Guyenne regiments were devastated by such fire.

As the smoke from the British musket fire cleared, it could be seen that the heads of the French columns had been literally swept away like wheat by a scythe and that the remainder had become a static, gesticulating, screaming mob. The British line advanced and battalion volley fire again rolled across the Plains. The line advanced once more, to escape the swirling fog of gunpowder smoke, and a final coordinated volley, which was described as 'a general fire' and 'like a cannonshot' tore into the French at between 20 to 30 yards with murderous effect. When the smoke cleared the British could see that those Frenchmen who were not lying either dead or rolling in agony upon the ground, were in full retreat. With a loud 'hurrah' and a spine-chilling Highland yell of 'Claymore', the British line broke into a run, some still firing, some relying on their bayonets, and Fraser's wild Highlanders, wielding their dreaded broad swords, pursued the fleeing French in the direction of the city walls.

The whole battle had lasted little more than ten minutes. Two or three controlled volleys from the British line had been sufficient to blow Montcalm's army from the field. In truth, it was not much of a battle, and indeed the next encounter between the British and French armies, over the same ground, which was to occur the following year, was to be a much bloodier affair. However, the battle of the Plains of Abraham, or the first battle of Quebec, was much more than just a victory of disciplined musketry. The battle was the culmination of years of planning and hard work which had been able to place a British army at the gates of Quebec. Wolfe, whose performance in the three months leading up to the battle is open to some criticism, cannot be faulted on the crucial day. He certainly viewed the encounter as the means by which the British would not only gain access to Quebec, but also destroy the French army in the field, thus depriving France of the ability to resist and continue the conflict. The result of the battle was that the British achieved Wolfe's first objective, but not his second, and this was to mean that the conflict would continue for another weary and bloody year. A tactical victory had been won, a strategic opportunity lost.

It can at least be argued that, if Wolfe had survived the battle, or his last orders had been carried out, then the complete annihilation of Montcalm's army might well have been achieved and the war would have then been brought to a more rapid conclusion. This was not to be for Wolfe was fatally wounded just at the moment of his victory. As the regulars of the Guienne and Béarn had reeled from the first volley, Wolfe, on the right wing, had led forward, for a few paces, both the Louisbourg Grenadiers and the 28th Foot. As the British, with Wolfe near the front, emerged from the smoke of the volley fire, Canadian marksmen were still firing from the cover of scrub and bushes that lined the cliff top above the St Lawrence and, early in the advance, he had been shot in the breast, possibly by two simultaneous shots. Again, another of the 'myths' that surround Wolfe was that, on the day of the battle, he deliberately courted death, for he felt sure he was dying, probably of tuberculosis, and thus sought a gallant death. Such a theory ignores the facts that, if he had survived, he would have received a tumultuous hero's welcome back in London – and he had a fiancée who was waiting patiently for his return. He had much to live for. Earlier evidence shows that Wolfe had been everywhere along the front line, encouraging his troops and that during the French advance he had placed himself upon a slight rise where he had been wounded in the wrist. It seems that Wolfe simply felt he had to lead by example, from the front, and this made him a conspicuous target throughout the battle. It was this that cost him his life.

As Wolfe was hit, he reeled back, falling out of the line of advance. James Henderson and Lieutenant Henry Browne, of the Louisbourg Grenadiers, rushed to his aid and supported him. As he was carried back for about one hundred yards, Wolfe had the strength to wave his hat as a signal to the 35th to advance and flank the enemy. He now begged to be laid down and Henderson discovered that his general's chest was soaked with blood. Browne rushed to dress the wound, but Wolfe was now haemorrhaging and it was clear to all that nothing could be done to save him. The last moments of Wolfe's life are again surrounded by contradictory reports, but John Knox did at least go to some lengths to record the accounts from as many persons present as possible and, according to Knox, as Wolfe slipped in and out of consciousness, someone nearby suddenly exclaimed 'They run, see how they run' and Wolfe reacted, as if roused from a deep sleep, to ask 'Who runs?' Wolfe was answered, 'The enemy, Sir. Egad they give way everywhere.' On hearing the joyous news, Wolfe issued his last order, 'Go one of you, my lads, to Colonel Burton. Tell him to march Webb's regiments with all speed to Charles's River, to cut off the retreat of the fugitives from the bridge.' Knox recorded that the general's last words were, 'Now, God be praised, I will die in peace.' A few moments later, Henderson recalled, with a smile fixed on his face, Wolfe quietly passed away. He had not lived long after his fatal wound, for the master's log of the *Lowestoft* recorded that 'At 10 our troops began a general action with the French. ½ past 10 was brought on board General Moncton wounded and several officers. At 11 was brought on board the corps of General Wolf.'

On the battlefield confusion reigned, not just among the French, but the British too. This confusion resulted in the failure to carry out Wolfe's last order. Several accounts confirm that the French right broke first, then the centre and that the left stood longest. The only regiment which made an effort to holds its ground, encouraged by Montcalm, was the Royal Roussillon, which stood on a shallow ridge to the south of the Sillery Road. However, even their defiance was short-lived and, after a few minutes, the men of the Royal Roussillon too joined the retreat. All but three of the regiment's officers were either dead or wounded and it was at this point that Montcalm received a fatal wound in his lower stomach, perhaps from grapeshot fired by York's guns. Supported on his black charger, he was able to reach the sanctuary of Quebec's walls, where he was to die the following morning. It was chiefly the Highlanders who reduced the French to a state of panic. A British naval volunteer who followed the troops across the field described their work:

> The bullet and bayonet are decent deaths compared with the execution of the sword. Happy in escaping unhurt, I traversed the field of battle while strewed with bleeding carcasses and covered with unemployed arms; a neat silver-mounted hanger, fastened to the side of an apparently headless trunk, and which consequently was useless to its original French possessor, attracted my attention. When the body turned over in order to unbuckle the belt, my astonishment was indeed great; his head lay underneath his breast, one stroke upon the back of his neck having cut through the whole, except a small part of the skin of the throat, by which it remained with the body.

Yet Knox was to write that the speed of the French retreat was such that even the Highlanders could not overtake the main French body and it is significant that the British did not capture one of the French regimental colours, and only two of their cannons.

There had been terrible slaughter and, of course, on both the French and British sides the loss of commanders and senior officers simply added to the confusion. Montcalm was carried from the field, Senezergues, the French second-in-command, was mortally wounded, the third in command, Baron de St Ours, killed. Colonel Carleton was badly wounded and Major Barre, who had been present with Wolfe during the ascent of Anse au Foulon, had half his upper cheek shot away and his eyeball was left hanging out of its socket. On the death of Wolfe, British command fell to Brigadier Robert Monckton, who had little time to use it for, within minutes, he too fell, shot through the lungs. Indeed it is not clear whether Monckton ever received the news that Wolfe was dead, or his general's last order, before he was forced to leave the field. Despite the French panic, the British did not have the pursuit all their own way. Some of the French managed to escape back into the town, but the rest were forced to cascade down the bluff outside the walls, and head for the safety of the St Charles bridge.

In the confusion, Brigadier Murray saw, probably erroneously, that there appeared to be an opportunity to cut off these fleeing French troops from the sanctuary of the bridge and either destroy or capture them. Acting on his own initiative, Murray tried to seize the bridge. The attempt unfortunately floundered, due to the bravery of a group of the Canadian militia who had earlier harried Townshend's men. The militia now took up position in the bushes at the top of the bluff and succeeded in killing or wounding nearly two hundred of the impetuous Highlanders, many of whom had discarded their muskets in their pursuit, happier to rely on their claymores, and were thus unable to return fire. The militia were supported by the cannon from two hulks in the Charles river and by a gun firing grape-shot, brought to bear from the walls of the town. Fraser wrote of how the 78th, after pursuing the French to the city walls, were directed by Murray in a circuit through the woods towards the bridge. Here, however, the Highlanders became engaged in a fire fight which, following a number of British fatalities, 'obliged us to retire a little, and form again'. Two hundred Canadians succeeded in delaying nearly four times their number of Highlanders sufficiently long enough for the bulk of the French force to reach the bridge. It was only with the arrival of the 58th and the second battalion of the 60th that the Highlanders were again able to attack and push the militia back to the bridge.

On the right, the British were also held up by militiamen in a coppice to their front. After about half an hour's delay, the coppice was cleared and Colonel Hunt Walsh wheeled his own regiment, Bragg's and Kennedy's, to the left, parallel to the walls, with the intention of supporting Fraser's men, just as Wolfe had envisaged. It seems clear that Burton, and the reserve of the 48th, never received Wolfe's last order, for it was these men who simply turned around to confront Bougainville when he appeared later in the day. Even though the French army had succeeded in crossing the bridge and despite the fact that the position was heavily defended, there is little doubt that a hard-pressed British advance could have forded the river elsewhere and pursued the panicky French. However, this was not to happen, for, at about 11.45 a.m., Brigadier Townshend, through the confusion of the battle, was finally made aware that command had now fallen upon his shoulders. He inherited a chaotic situation and responded by attempting to restore some order to the British troops; he appeared at the front, called off the pursuit and ordered all the regiments to re-form on the original field of battle.

One of the great arguments that has surrounded the battle has been the view that Townshend's timidity in command allowed the French army to largely escape to fight another day. Certainly, by recalling the attacks of Murray, and those on the right flank, all hope of trapping the fleeing French evaporated. In truth, when Townshend finally realized that he was in effective command, the opportunity had already passed. The delaying actions of the militia had already stalled the British pursuit sufficiently to allow the vast majority of the French army to evade death or capture. If Wolfe's last order had been acted upon promptly, and of course in the confusion this did not happen, there is still no certainty that the French would have been annihilated. Rather it was Wolfe's death, and the lack of direction and coordination that this caused to the British advance, that allowed so many French troops to escape the battlefield. If Wolfe had lived to lead the British advance, then the chances of blocking the French retreat would have been significantly enhanced.

Now, Townshend had to face Bougainville, and his flying column, which appeared on the road from Cap Rouge, at around noon. Any consideration Townshend may have had, and it is not clear that he had formulated any plan, to cross the St Charles and pursue the French further, now disappeared as he was forced to react to this new threat. There is an element of mystery surrounding the delay in the return of Bougainville to the battlefield. It is possible, and perhaps understandable, that his men may have been exhausted from their continual patrolling along the St Lawrence, and therefore slow to react to news of Wolfe's landing. Bougainville was later to claim that he had not heard of the British assault until nearly 9 a.m. and that he then reacted promptly. However, it is inconceivable that Bougainville and his troops were deaf to the sounds of cannon and musketry and, at the very least, he could surely have despatched, post-haste, his detachment of cavalry, 200 strong, to the sounds of the guns. Their appearance in the rear of the British line, at the height of the battle, might have swayed the issue for the French.

By 11 a.m. Bougainville's advance force, commanded by Captain Le Noir, had reached the Samos battery, which was defended by a fifty-strong force of Royal Americans, commanded by Lieutenant Daniel McAlpine. Le Noir lost thirty of his men as he tried unsuccessfully to expel McAlpine's men. On his arrival, Bougainville, with a force of 2,000 men and some artillery, decided to simply bypass the battery and move on to Quebec. It did not take him long to realize that the issue had already been decided. Townshend positioned men of the 35th and 48th, men of Howe's light infantry and two field pieces across the road, blocking the French advance. Although Bougainville's command was twice the size of the force that now opposed him, he decided that, rather than risk his men, he would preserve them, and he retreated northwards towards Lorette and the safety of the nearby Sillery Woods. The British were masters of the field.

The cost of the battle had been heavy; according to British returns, casualties totalled 664 of all ranks, including 58 killed. At least a third of the total had been inflicted upon the Highlanders, as they clashed with militia after the battle. The French casualties are harder to verify. Townshend estimated them at 1,500, while Vaudreuil was later to claim that they amount to 644, including 44 officers. While the British began to bury their dead, entrench their position on the Plains and bring up heavy cannon and mortars in preparation for a siege, the French panic continued behind the walls of Quebec. At this crucial moment in the history of New France, its inhabitants required real leadership and guidance from its Governor-General, but Vaudreuil was at a loss as to what to do. Apparently paralysed by the disastrous situation surrounding him, Vaudreuil could only think to ask the dying Montcalm for advice. The contradiction is evident; the two men had so frequently been at loggerheads, yet in his deepest crisis Vaudreuill turned first to his old adversary.

Montcalm, who must have been in complete agony from his wound, knew he was dying, and Vaudreuil's request for advice could not have been welcomed. However, via his aide-de-camp, Martel, Montcalm promptly responded and informed the Governor-General that, as he saw it, there were only three unpalatable options. First, was capitulation 'for the whole Colony', which seemed a particularly pessimistic choice. Second, Montcalm suggested that a fresh attack could be launched upon the British that instant, but who could inspire an already beaten and demoralized army to victory was unclear. Finally, the remains of the French force could retire from the city to the Jacques Cartier river, where the troops could combine with Bougainville's force and an army led by Lévis. From this base, an assault could be made to try to recapture Quebec in the following spring, which, following the departure of Vaudreuil, would surely fall into British hands. Although perhaps not the most considered options, Montcalm's thoughts did at least inspire Vaudreuil sufficiently to regain his composure and call a council of war of all his remaining officers for 6 p.m. that evening.

The meeting of senior officers, including Johnstone and Poulariez, as well as the Intendant, Bigot, was apparently a brief affair. No serious thought was given to launching a fresh advance against the now entrenched British and it was unanimously decided to march the remains of the army out from the city, under cover of darkness to the Jacques Cartier river. All heavy guns, stores and camp equipment were to be abandoned at Beauport, while the disorganized mass of 2,500 troops, which used to be Montcalm's army, was to escape the city via the only road now open to them. This road, which led north-west for six miles, passed through the village of Charlesbourg to a small cluster of houses at Lorette, where the St Charles river was fordable. Once over the river, the road doubled back, following the river for three miles to a point where it joined the valley road from Quebec. From this junction of roads, it turned south-west for another three miles until it crossed and then followed the upper Cap Rouge river to Pointe-aux-Trembles and then on to the Jacques Cartier river, thirty miles away, and safety.

The evacuation from the city, which began as soon as it was dark, went silently and smoothly enough, although once on the road the army's retreat became something of a flight. Malartic later wrote that it was difficult to maintain discipline among the men and described it as 'a forced march, with little order'. Johnstone was even more damning when he claimed that the beaten troops 'ran as hard as they could'. However, despite the apparent panic and ill-discipline, the night march was a great success and the army was allowed to escape to continue the fight.

Whilst Townshend's actions on the battlefield can be understood, for he clearly needed to restore order to the British army so as to face the dangers presented by Bougainville's flying column, the fact that he did not use his force to close all avenues of escape completely for the French army is less easy to forgive. Not only were the British completely unaware of the departure of the beaten army, but no attempt was made to place a force to cover the junction of the valley road and river road. Here a force of light infantry, perhaps only a few hundred strong, could have thrown the already panicky French into complete disorder, which would have almost certainly forced their surrender, or their flight back into Quebec. Furthermore, Townshend can be criticized for not using his artillery at the earliest opportunity, against the walls of Quebec. If British shells had been raining down upon the city in the afternoon of 13 September, then it is possible that an already vacillating Vaudreuil might have been pushed to the edge and surrendered there and then. However, by not putting the city under the greatest pressure, Vaudreuil, and his senior officers, were given sufficient breathing space to enable them to concentrate their thoughts and organize the retreat of the army.

Before Vaudreuil's departure, the commandant of Quebec, Jean-Baptiste de Ramezay, had demanded instructions from the Governor-General as to what action he should take in the face of the British cannons upon the Plains of Abraham. Vaudreuil had responded that under no account was Ramezay to hold out in Quebec beyond the exhaustion of the available food supplies. During the siege, no stores of provisions had been kept in Quebec, because of the danger from the British artillery fire. Supplies had been brought daily from the camp at Beauport, from the surrounding country and from the supply ships lying further up the river. With supplies for only a few days in sight, Quebec seemed to be on the verge of starvation. Among the civilians were 2,700 women and children and a host of clerks, workmen and domestic servants. In addition to these were the forces in the town, numbering perhaps 2,600.

With Vaudreuil's instructions in mind, on the morning of 14 September, Ramezay attempted to try and solve his most serious problem, that of the scarcity of food. Since the French tents were still standing at Beauport, Ramezay sent men there, hoping to find abandoned provisions. Unfortunately, both the Indians and the local inhabitants had already raided the supplies. That portion of the abandoned supplies which they could not carry off they had wasted, and Ramezay's men found flour and other stores strewn about in the wildest disorder, food which might have saved Quebec for a few days longer. To add to Ramezay's depression on this day, Montcalm died in the early hours. Now very much alone, Ramezay had to consider the diverse requirements for the welfare of those inhabitants under his care and the need to remain defiant towards the British, now happily entrenched in front of the walls. An anonymous British officer did record that on 14 September, the French were able to throw 'shott and shells from the ramparts into our camp'. Such acts of defiance were as much aimed against the defeatism that was now rampant among both civilians and troops alike as it was against the encroaching enemy. Ramezay considered that his only hope was to 'play for time' and pray that Lévis could march to the relief of the city.

The following day, Ramezay summoned the fourteen remaining senior officers of the Quebec garrison to a council of war, at which he asked each of them to give their views in writing as to whether the city should continue its resistance. With the lack of food being the pressing concern, thirteen advised capitulation, with only one officer, Fiedmont, voting to 'reduce the ration again and persevere in defending the place to the last extremity'. Ramezay could not ignore such an overwhelming vote, nor the perilous food situation, but he continued to procrastinate in the hope that relief was on its way.

Indeed, a reorganized French army was marching back towards the city even as the terms of capitulation were being negotiated. François-Gaston, Chevalier de Lévis, the tough Gascon brigadier who had served Montcalm as second in command, was equal to the responsibilities of commanding the army he had inherited. With Amherst's advance now stalled on Lake Champlain, Lévis had been able to answer Vaudreuil's pleas for support and had detached part of his force, so as to make a junction with the Governor-General and the remains of Montcalm's army. He had taken over at Jacques Cartier on 17 September, and at once had stiffened the spines of the refugees he found there. Showing nothing but disdain for their flight, with Vaudreuil's concurrence, he had ordered the troops back down river. Lévis' plan was 'to do and risk everything in the world to prevent the taking of Quebec, and, if the worst came to the worst, to move all the people out and destroy the city, so the enemy will not be able to spend the winter there'. However, Lévis was also plagued by lack of food and a day was lost while his revitalized troops foraged for sufficient supplies. On 18 September, Lévis began a rapid march towards Quebec and, by the end of the day his force had reached Saint-Augustin, less than a day's march from the city.

Vaudreuil was, by now, in contact with Bougainville and he ordered him to send a detachment of cavalry back into Quebec to inform and reassure Ramezay that relief was indeed on its way. On the night of 17/18 September, La Rochebeaucourt led a small cavalry force around the British and reached the city, with his men carrying 'a hundred and some pouches of biscuits' on their saddles for the inhabitants. The efforts of La Rochebeaucourt, and his troops, had been in vain, for Ramezay had already agreed the terms of capitulation with Townshend.

Despite his delaying tactics, the events of 17 September had forced Ramezay to begin surrender talks with the British. On this day, the British had begun to construct batteries to breach the fortifications facing the Buttes à Neveau and, according to Knox, they had in place 60 guns and 58 howitzers, posed to begin a fierce bombardment. Furthermore, it was at noon on this day that Admiral Saunders brought 'eight great ships' close to shore 'in a Disposition to attack the lower Town, as soon as General Townsend was ready to do so by the upper'. Faced by such a formidable weight of weaponry it is not surprising that Ramezay was beset by a clamouring civilian and military population for the immediate surrender of the city. According to his own accounts, at 3 p.m. that afternoon, Ramezay hoisted the white flag upon the city walls and sent the town mayor of Quebec, Joannes, to the British camp to begin the surrender negotiations.

The negotiations were not protracted for, with the strength of the British position and the weakness of the French, there was little to discuss. Furthermore, at this stage Ramezay had no firm knowledge of Lévis' relief mission. Joannes did try to convince the British to allow the remaining troops within Quebec to join their comrades at the Jacques Cartier river, but this was firmly declined. Townshend did show a great deal of magnanimity towards the besieged French. The remaining garrison was to be allowed the full honours of war and was to 'be embarked as conveniently as possible, to be sent to the first port in France', while the Québécois were to have the rights of property guaranteed, and they would be granted the 'free exercise of the Roman religion'. Furthermore, full safeguards were to be accorded to the clergy, to all dignitaries of Quebec society, and in particular the Bishop of Quebec. With men of the garrison deserting more and more frequently, and the inhabitants placing strong pressure upon him to surrender, Ramezay was in no position to decline such terms. When he learnt, just a few hours later, of the approach of Lévis' army, he must have bitterly regretted his acceptance, but, as he wrote to Vaudreuil, 'The thing was too far advanced to be able to withdraw.' Townshend was later to receive some criticism for the generosity of the terms he offered Ramezay, but he defended his actions by the need to conclude negotiations rapidly in the advance of a Canadian winter and the return of a French army. Such criticism soon evaporated in the euphoria of Wolfe's victory and an event that Horace Walpole was to conclude was stranger than fiction and even mythical.

Once he learnt of Quebec's surrender, a disappointed Lévis, lacking both artillery and supplies, had no choice but to order his men back to

Jacques Cartier, where he had them build a fort from which the French could coordinate the harassment of the British garrison over the winter months. Here, on the frontier of New France, Lévis watched for an opportunity to run a ship past the British fleet at Quebec, for he felt sure that, as soon as the home government learnt of the fall of Quebec, reinforcements and supplies would be despatched from France, and he was confident that, so provisioned, he could regain the city for his king. Vaudreuil journeyed to Montreal, where he seems to have spent the winter busying himself with a series of blame-shifting memoranda back to Paris, in which the failure to hold Quebec was laid firmly on Montcalm's imprudent decision to attack and Ramezay's lack of resolve to hold out. Despite some clear personal failings, Vaudreuil could comfort himself that he had achieved the minimum required of him by France, in that the army in Canada was still an effective force with which he could continue to oppose the British into 1760. He could only hope that, by the spring, New France would be in receipt of fresh troops and supplies, or the situation in Europe would have greatly swung in favour of the French.

The first British soldiers entered the city of Quebec on the evening of 18 September 1759. Fifty men of the Royal Artillery marched in, pulling a field piece on which the British colours were draped. It was Colonel Williamson, the chief gunner, who was given the honour of hoisting the victorious flag on the walls, and this probably reflects the influence of artillery in the victory of the 13th. Next to enter through the gates were the Louisbourg Grenadiers. Originally drawn from the Grenadier companies of the 22nd, 40th and 45th Regiments, these troops were soon to return to their own detachments, but it was fitting that this unit, which had been formed to fight in Canada and had been led by Wolfe in his last moments, should have been chosen for the first guard-mounting ceremony at the city gates. As the flag was hoisted, Captain Palliser of the Royal Navy landed in the Lower Town with a body of seamen, tasked to begin the unloading of heavy cannon from the ships for the British defence of Quebec, over, what was to prove to be, the long Canadian winter months. Any fears of British retribution that the Québécois might have had soon disappeared as the near-starving inhabitants were served provisions from the British stores. As one anonymous British officer wrote, 'Upon our taking possession of Quebec we found everything in the greatest disorder, the upper town very much shatter'd and the lower town quite destroy'd, such effect had our batterys at Point Lévi.' The task of defending such a broken shell of a city was to call for the greatest exertion, and sacrifice, from those troops who had been victorious upon the Plains of Abraham.

On 23 September 1759, the field of battle was the scene of a thanksgiving service and, on 27 September, the Ursuline Chapel, the only one left intact in Quebec, was used for a similar purpose. A naval chaplain, the Reverend Ely Dawson, preached a sermon which shows how the glory of Wolfe was already regarded. 'Ye Mountains of Abraham, decorated with his trophies, tell how plainly ye opposed him when he mounted your lofty Heights with the Strength and Swiftness of an eagle: Stand fixed upon your rocky Base, and speak his Name and Glory to all future generations!' The legend of Wolfe and Quebec had already begun and would continue even to this day.

2

Hold at All Cost

Even as the victorious British troops entered the ruins of Quebec, there was some consideration as to whether it would be better to simply destroy the city, for to defend such a shattered fortress, without support from the fleet, in hostile country and in the face of the harshness of a Canadian winter, was certainly no easy task. A council of war, held between Townshend, Monckton, Murray and the British admirals, Saunders and Holmes, concluded that a city so hard won was not to be abandoned, and it is certain that the British realized the importance of their prize and the sacrifices made to win it; it would be held at all cost.

However, it must have looked to many of the British troops that the prize was not worth all the effort, and loss, to secure it. Brigadier Murray wrote in his diary of 19 September 1759 that 'This day I marched into Quebec, or more properly the ruins of it ...' Indeed, Wolfe's bombardment had been most effective. In the Lower Town, a total of 535 houses had been destroyed, a third of the city's stock, and the rest were uninhabitable. The narrow streets were largely impassable due to fallen masonry and other debris. The Upper Town had fared better although its principal buildings were in ruins; the Governor's Residence, the Castle of Saint-Louis, the Bishop's Palace, the Cathedral and the Jesuit College, had all been in range of the cannon on the opposite shore, and the British batteries had left little but the walls. In the seminary, the college for training priests, only the kitchen buildings remained and even walls six feet thick had not withstood the savage battering. In a macabre display, the British cannon had thrown up the bones and skulls of those long buried in the graveyard of Recollet's church.

Once The Honourable George Townshend had made clear his desire to return to London, after the fall of Quebec, there remained no alternative but to appoint Murray to the role of commander of British forces in

Quebec, for the wound suffered by Brigadier Robert Monckton forced his evacuation to New York for further treatment and recuperation. The Honourable James Murray, the fifth and youngest son of the fourth Lord Elibank, has been described as a forceful, stubborn, if not dire, Scot. His physical appearance was that of a thin man, with tight lips and a sharp, almost hooked nose. He had seen service in Europe and the West Indies, and, in the previous year, had served with distinction during the siege of Louisbourg. Lieutenant Malcolm Fraser, who served under Murray, claimed that Murray possessed all the military virtues except prudence. According to another contemporary, he was 'the very Bellows of sedition; Envious, Ambitious, the very mention of another's merit canker'd him'. Certainly, his relationship with his superior, Wolfe, had not been harmonious throughout the siege of Quebec and, although some of their troubles could be laid at Wolfe's inability to include his brigadiers in the decision-making process, there seems little doubt that there existed in his ambitious character a flaw which led Murray to criticize his superiors and rivals alike.

Aged thirty-nine when he assumed overall command, in many ways Murray was the ideal candidate, for his dourness and stubbornness would be essential if the British were not only to overcome a Canadian winter but also the threat of a French army. In contrast, he could be ardent, high-spirited and fearless. He had fought, and had been badly wounded, at the siege of Ostend, in 1745, during the War of the Austrian Succession, and had served alongside Wolfe at Rochefort and Louisbourg. Although Murray had had considerable experience, promotion had been rather slow in coming and this may have been because his elder brother, Alexander, was a fanatical Jacobite, who remained a close associate of Bonnie Prince Charles in France. The appointment of Colonel Burton, of the 48th Foot, as his deputy, would unite the two men in a common cause and Burton would learn to temper some of his commander's excesses. Unfortunately Murray's overriding ambition, and his thirst to emulate the glories of Wolfe, would result in him jeopardizing the British position at a crucial moment, when battle could easily have been avoided, and his action threatened the loss of Quebec.

Once it was agreed that the British would remain to defend the city, it was clear that Murray would need the help and support of every available soldier. On 24 September, the British muster roll showed a force of 8,504 men, of whom a mere 5,707 were fit for duty. A few grenadiers and artillery men sailed with the fleet, which left Murray with 7,313 defenders of all ranks to face the potential return of the French and the hardship of the winter. The regiments that remained were the 15th, 28th, 35th, 43rd, 47th, 48th, 58th, 60th, and 78th. The 60th contained two battalions of colonial troops, the Royal Americans and approximately 100 Colonial Rangers. Finally, Murray could also rely on the service of 207 officers and men from the Royal Artillery, whose expertise would later be vital to hinder the French siege works.

There was no suitable anchorage where the large ships of the fleet could remain for the winter and avoid the destructive powers of the ice, so Admiral Saunders made ready to sail with the fleet. However, before he did so, a mountain of stores had to be offloaded to supply the troops through the forthcoming winter. Enough salted provisions were unloaded to feed the city, it was considered, for approximately twelve months. With so few buildings left standing in the city, the choice of storehouse was limited. In the Lower Town, Murray chose the Intendant's Palace as the chief supply depot, while in the Upper Town the large Jesuit College was, in part, used for similar purposes. The task of unloading and transporting the stores involved heavy labour, for there were very few horses in Quebec. Furthermore, many of the streets were nearly impassable and much work had to be done to clear a passage for the traffic. Finally, to reach the Jesuit College the troops were forced to drag the stores up a very steep hill. Murray was to write that there was not a man who was not 'constantly employed'.

The British were also forced to remove a large number of cannon from the fleet, as the French guns left in the city were found to be in poor condition and of little use to deter a potential French siege. This work also proved to be difficult and cumbersome, and it was not until 10 October that a portion of the fleet was ready to depart. The ships saluted the garrison with 21 guns and the batteries on shore returned the courtesy. Admiral Saunders journeyed back to England, but he left a portion of the fleet at Halifax, under Lord Colville, with instructions to return to Quebec as soon as the melting ice allowed.

As the last remains of the British fleet departed from Quebec on the morning of 18 October 1759, Brigadier James Murray, now in sole command of the British forces at Quebec, must surely have felt a shiver of fear down his spine as he realized the loneliness of his position and the responsibility upon his shoulders. The British garrison was now cut off from succour by the sea for at least six months. The two sloops, *Racehorse* and *Porcupine*, which Saunders left behind, became embedded as the river froze and were of little use to Murray until the spring thaw, when he found them encased in fourteen foot of ice. Murray and his men were on their own and the men were reliant on each other to survive the dangers that the next months would surely bring.

Before he left for England, Townshend had begun the process by which the local population were shown leniency and clemency by the conquerors, for he knew that the British were too few, and too weak, to impose order upon the city, its surrounds and its inhabitants. Militiamen, who had borne arms against the British, did not share the same fate as the captured French regulars, that of return to France, in British ships, under a flag of truce. The British allowed the militiamen to remain with their families, as long as all weapons were surrendered and an oath of fidelity to the British Crown was taken. By taking the oath, all would enjoy the protections afforded to British subjects and, furthermore, they were assured the right to continue to practise their religion under the care of the Bishop of Quebec. The security of their property would also be guaranteed. Murray continued this policy as soon as he was given command. In obedience to his military order, the inhabitants within a five-mile radius of the city journeyed to Quebec on 21 September to take an oath of fidelity to King George and a promise not to take up arms against His Majesty. The following day, Murray proclaimed a manifesto which informed the locals that the British had not come to conquer them, but to give them mild and just government.

Murray soon discovered that those inhabitants who were to be found on the south side of the St Lawrence proved to be either unwilling or reluctant both to disarm and swear an oath of fidelity. He therefore quickly decided that a British force should be despatched to compel their compliance. However, for many weeks the weather, and the increasing ice floes, meant that a crossing of the St Lawrence proved impossible. It was not until 30 November that a body of troops, 200 strong, under the command of Captain Leslie, was able to mount an operation. The badly frostbitten party did not return until Christmas Day, but they were able to report that most of the inhabitants had been disarmed and oaths of loyalty had been extracted. The success of Murray's policy was demonstrated by the end of January 1760, when he was able to confirm that 6,000 Canadians had taken the oath, which was almost the entire adult male population. The conformity of the local inhabitants would reap dividends for the British when the hardship of the Canadian winter began to take its toll of the garrison.

The British threw themselves into the task of getting the town ready to face the predicted onslaughts of both the winter and the French. The positions at Point Lévis and on the island of Orleans were evacuated. The city's walls were strengthened, as were bastions and batteries, and wrecked houses were sufficiently repaired to provide some shelter for the garrison. On 29 September the work was sufficiently complete, if far from ideal, for the garrison to leave their tented accommodation on the Plains of Abraham and march into the city. Both the Canadians and Murray must have breathed a sigh of relief when the British troops behaved well on entering Quebec, for their were no reported cases of looting or pillaging. The officers drew lots for quarters in ruined houses, while the rank and file made the best of what was left available. Captain John Montrescor secured a roofless house and, by savaging timbers from houses too far gone for repair, was able to make it a refuge from the worst of the weather. Similarly, Captain John Knox, who kept a journal throughout the siege, left details of the particular quarters assigned to him and of the manner in which he made it habitable:

On 5 October I removed to the tenement assigned me for my quarters, which is a cart-house and a stable, called by the inhabitants *Un Hangar*; within it is a spacious, but unfurnished, apartment, with a closet; it has no ceiling, save a parcel of boards laid loose; and it thereby forms a loft, or place for hay; a rack and manger stood at the other end for horses, from which, however, I was separated by a stone partition. I have troubled the reader with this trifling circumstance, to give him some idea of our winter cantonment; several officers, it is true, were better lodged, particularly those of superior rank; yet I was far from being singular: there were a great many who, though they had a more decent entrance to their houses, were much more indifferently lodged; for, with the assistance of a good stove and some carpentry-work, my habitation was rendered tolerably comfortable.

While Murray ensured that both officers and men had at least basic accommodation, he was also concerned that Quebec be made, once more, into a defensive position. It was vital that this was done as soon as possible, for Murray surely realized that once the winter descended upon the garrison all the troops' energies would be directed upon the need for sufficient warmth and food for survival. Murray's actions soon indicated to his officers, if not his men, that their commander had little faith in the walls of the Quebec being able to withstand a French siege, for he concentrated his defences away from the city.

His men were soon erecting a row of blockhouses a musket-shot away from the walls, both to prevent surprise and to stop the enemy gaining the high ground which commanded them. The engineer, Major Mackellar, advised Murray to throw up entrenchments on the Plains of Abraham and these were described by Captain Knox in his journal:

A barrier is erected on the outside of the strong angle near the hangman's redoubt, which covers the lower road leading from the Palace-gate through the suburbs of St Rocque to the general hospital, the river Charles and the adjacent country; a house, conveniently situated without this barrier, is fortified to contain a detachment; as is also a smaller habitation on the inside for a serjeant's guard; the former is on the north side of the road, and the other is on the south. From these posts, entirely round that quarter, we have extended a line of picquets with loop-holes for musketry, which are strengthened, at the extremities of the point, by block-houses; a chain of these timber fortresses are to be constructed on the heights, round the outside of the ramparts, at six or seven hundred yards distance, across the isthmus: these will effectually prevent any attempts of the enemy by surprise.

Knox, like his commander, realized that, despite all the efforts of the British to enhance the defence of the city, it would still remain, in his words, 'an indifferent fortification, and tenable only against light field artillery and musketry'.

Murray's plans for the outlying defence of Quebec were more ambitious than he could realize. To ensure the city's safety, Murray considered it necessary to occupy all the approaches to Quebec and had hoped to extend the British outposts so as to keep the French beyond the Jacques Cartier river. With the limited number of men, and provisions, at his disposal, such a move proved impracticable and Murray was forced to place his farthest outpost at Lorette, just eight miles to the west of Quebec. The church here was fortified and, by holding this position, the British deprived the French of the most strategically important road to Quebec, which led through Charlesbourg. At Saint-Foy, on the plateau a mere five miles from the city, the church was also fortified and thus the most southerly road from the west was also watched. At both positions field pieces were sited and well entrenched. This decision did mean that hostile French scouting parties and Indians, sometimes disguised in animal skins, were kept at a distance from Quebec, thus improving the safety of the garrison.

It was apparent that Murray had decided, within a few days of entering Quebec, that the city was too weak to defend and that, if a French force should attack, he would not stay behind its walls but attack them. Murray's perception that Quebec could not withstand a long siege may well have been a correct one, if he were to face an enemy well supplied with heavy cannons, yet it was far from certain that any attacking force would be so provisioned. However, during the long winter months it seems clear that Murray convinced himself that he would be facing an enemy more numerous and better supplied than his own and this was to fatally determine his actions once the French advance was discovered.

In the meantime Quebec swarmed with British troops. Guardhouses were positioned at twenty different points, squads of armed troops went the rounds of the city, while sentinels paced the ramparts. The military duties were very demanding, and became more so as the harsh winter dragged on. Daily guard duty alone required the involvement of 25 officers and 930 other ranks. In addition, there was always the possibility, and danger, of skirmishes with the French near the outposts of Saint-Foy or Lorette, or of raids upon foraging parties by Indians allied to the French.

The presence of the enemy was not simply restricted to the nearby outposts for, at the appearance of Wolfe's force in late June, a number of French vessels, both frigates and supply ships, had sailed further up the St Lawrence to escape capture. Here they had remained, despite Murray's raids along the shore during the summer. The British were constantly on watch in case these ships tried to escape their self-imposed prison and, on the night of 22 November, the French ships attempted to sail silently past the British guns at night. However, they were detected and fire from the garrison forced the French vessels to desist from their escape attempt. Two nights later, the French tried again and, despite a terrific fire from the guns of the garrison, they appeared to have successfully sailed past the city. The morning light revealed this not to be the case as the British fire had driven five French ships aground. The defenders discovered that the French crews had fled and that four of the vessels were ablaze. Captain Miller of the sloop *Racehorse* sailed with a party of forty sailors to board and survey the surviving fifth ship. It is not clear whether the fleeing French had sabotaged this ship, or if the gunpowder on the vessel was ignited by accident, but a huge explosion shook the ship and many of the British party were thrown into the air. Most were killed outright; the rest, including Miller, received horrific burns and all succumbed to their injuries over the next few days. This tragedy was the single largest loss of life throughout the winter months and must have surely adversely affected the morale of the garrison.

With the death of Montcalm, command of the French forces passed to his second in command, the able, and tough Gascon, Major-General François-Gaston, Chevalier de Lévis. It was he who had rallied the fleeing French army in September and had led them back to Quebec, only to discover that Ramezay had surrendered the city to the British. Lacking sufficient cannons and provisions for a siege, Lévis had had no alternative but to retire to Jacques Cartier and here he ordered a fort to be built from which his men could harass the British garrison throughout the winter. Lévis was determined that Quebec should be retaken for the French king. It seems certain that he considered that the coming winter would serve French interests better than those of the isolated British and Lévis had no hesitation in rejecting Murray's overtures for a winter's truce.

Lévis clearly hoped that the rigours of the winter, disease and the occasional skirmish would so weaken the garrison as to make the retaking of the city possible, before British reinforcements could arrive in the spring. The French commander seems to have been realistic as to the small likelihood of troops and supplies arriving from France and he placed all his energies into creating a force that would be large enough to beat the British. To this end, he was aided by Wolfe's earlier decision to devastate the countryside around Quebec. This resulted in many Québécois seeking refuge in the Trois Rivieres and Montreal districts during the winter. Fortunately, the harvest around Montreal had been both bountiful and early and the authorities were able to feed the refugees who were then available, and eager, to help Lévis expel the British from Quebec. Lévis could spend the winter months training his new army while waiting for the thaw, which would enable his men to march on Quebec. In the meantime the British could only watch, wait, shiver and die in the severe conditions.

While the October weather had largely been kind to the men of the British garrison, the month of November saw alterations of rain, sunshine, frost and snow and, as the temperature dropped, the conditions for the inhabitants worsened, as did the discipline of the troops. The extent of Murray's problems were reflected in his standing orders to the garrison issued as early as 4 November, in which he clearly demonstrated that he was not reluctant to use harsh methods to control the inhabitants. It seems that worries among the troops, as to the adequacy of the provisions, forced Murray to issue this early declaration: 'Every soldier is receiving 2lbs of provisions more than ever was allowed in any of the King's garrisons before, in addition to the gill of rum, which is provided gratis. So every Officer, Sergeant, Corporal and faithful Soldier is asked to discover any man, who shall presume to complain of the said allowance, so that the offender may be brought to trial for sedition, and receive the punishment, which such a notorious crime deserves.' It would appear that Murray was attempting to contain dissent before it spread throughout the garrison.

Desertions, drunkenness and theft were also major concerns and Murray ordered 'those found drunk to receive 20 lashes every morning, till the man acknowledged, where he got it, and to forfeit his allowance of Rum for six weeks'. He ordered that the sale of liquor was to be prohibited and that only the official rum allowance, administered by the officers, would be given to the men. On 21 November, two pairs of army women, who had been found guilty of selling rum contrary to orders, were whipped through the streets.

As morale and discipline declined, Murray adopted firmer punishments. On 17 November a Frenchman was hanged for attempting to entice British troops to desert. A soldier received 1,000 lashes for being absent from duty and for using language to excite desertion and mutiny. Another soldier received 300 lashes for being out of his quarters at night and for wearing a disguise with the intent to desert. A soldier of the 48th Regiment was executed for robbing a Quebec citizen. Furthermore, Murray did not hesitate to expel a number of the local inhabitants from within the city walls whom he suspected of giving information to the enemy, lurking nearby, or for inciting the troops to desert. He learnt that some Jesuit priests had been taking advantage of the hardships the men were forced to endure and had incited them to desert. Soon after this, gunpowder and 15,000 cartridges were found to have been 'artfully concealed' by a Jesuit's valet. Murray could not afford a 'fifth column' and, despite murmurings from the local population, on 26 October, he gave the Jesuits notice to leave the city as soon as possible. A few of those most suspected were held by Murray in confinement.

The Governor also encouraged many of the local inhabitants to journey to Montreal, and he gave them permission to leave Quebec. Again, concern about a fifth column promoted this action, but Murray was also keen to reduce the number of mouths to feed over the winter months. Many of the wealthy, and more prominent, families seized this opportunity, as did the Bishop of Quebec, who abandoned his poorer flock to the deprivations of the winter and British rule. For those locals that remained, Murray seemed determined to administer a firm but just rule. As well as guaranteeing freedom of religion, the Governor instructed his officers to pay 'the compliment of the hat' to any religious procession that passed them in the streets. Although religious meetings were permitted, all other gatherings were forbidden. Furthermore, the inhabitants had to report promptly to the British anyone who had recently arrived in the city. Lights had to be extinguished by 10 p.m. and anyone found out at night was ordered to carry lanterns, to show that they were on a legitimate errand. Intermarrying between British troops and the Canadians was forbidden.

More restrictive measures included the death penalty for any locals who were found to have been in correspondence with anyone in the adjoining countryside, although this does not seem to have deterred an active relay of information between the French population in Quebec and that in Montreal. Murray was not slow in applying his new, self-imposed powers; two locals who were stopped late at night without a lantern were publicly flogged as an example, and a former inhabitant who returned from Montreal but did not report to the British authorities, was imprisoned when his presence was discovered.

By early December the weather was taking a toll upon those unlucky enough to be in Quebec and it was to become one of the severest winters ever experienced in the region. Both Captain Knox and Lieutenant Fraser reported in their respective journals that by December the winter 'had become almost insupportably cold'. Naturally, the garrison, accommodated as they were in ruined buildings, suffered. To avoid some of the worst effect of exposure while on sentry duty, Murray issued the following order on 3 December:

> As the sentries on their posts, and the soldiers otherwise employed on the duty of the garrison, may, from the severity of the weather at this season of the year, be exposed to be frost-bitten, Doctor Russell recommends that every person to whom this accident may happen should particularly to avoid going near a fire, and to have the part frost-bitten rubbed with snow by one who has a warm hand, and, as soon as can be, afterwards put into a blanket, or something of that kind, that will restore heat to that part.
>
> *This order to be read at the head of every company for six days following by an officer.*

Avoiding frostbite was just one of many concerns that faced Murray and his men; the chief worry was the need for warmth. On 1 December, he ordered two weeks' firewood to be issued to the garrison. Previously, the troops, much to the annoyance of the local inhabitants, had torn down damaged houses to provide their fuel. Murray ordered that 'no persons whatever shall pull down houses or fences or carry off any timber belonging to the inhabitants'. Lieutenant Fraser, writing in his journal, thought 'we shall have great difficulty in supplying ourselves with fuel this winter', for it was believed that nearly 20,000 cords of wood would be needed to sustain the garrison and that only about 1,000 cords were on hand. A cord of wood equates to 128 cubic feet. Clearly, more would have to be done to obtain supplies of firewood if the garrison was to sustain itself over the severe winter months.

The British had acted quickly to acquire supplies of wood, for just a few days after the surrender of Quebec two frigates had been sent four miles up the river to procure wood which the Canadians had piled on the heights. The British force was assailed by both Canadians and Indians, but a body of Rangers held them back while the wood was thrown over the cliff into the river and secured by the sailors. Lévis reacted promptly, for he could see the importance that a regular supply of wood would have for the British garrison. He ordered the burning of all available firewood which the French could find on the south bank of the river, as far as Point Lévis, so that it could not fall into Murray's hands.

Murray turned to the local population for supplies of firewood and offered the Canadians five shillings for each cord delivered. Although, at first, the Canadians appeared to have been somewhat reluctant to supply the British, Murray's apparent just rule and magnanimity paid dividends and deliveries from the locals gradually increased. However, it was still clear that, even with this additional source of supply, the garrison was destined to freeze. Murray had to take direct action. First, fuel was brought by boat from the Île Madame and Île Orléans, but, as floes of ice made navigation difficult, and later impossible, Murray was forced to turn to the forests of Sainte-Foy, five miles away, for supplies. At any one time, up to 300 soldiers were employed on a daily basis in the dangerous, difficult and extremely arduous task of felling trees and transporting the wood back to Quebec. With few horses available, the British were forced to work in teams of eight, yoked together in couples, with a ninth man to guide the sleigh. They dragged the wood the five miles to the town through the deep snow and, on occasion, it was necessary to light the road with beacons as the men fought their way through blizzards. Each regiment was issued with nine sleighs and each were obliged to take their regimental turn to cover the ground between Sainte-Foy and Quebec. Many troops suffered from severe frostbite as they struggled to keep this vital supply line open.

It was not only the weather that the troops had to fear for, realizing the importance of the firewood for the survival of the British garrison, Indians, allied to the French, made repeated and often daily attacks upon the exhausted men. The troops were forced to be always on their guard and were obliged to carry the additional burden of a loaded musket slung over their shoulders while struggling with the heavy loads of wood through the snow. The Indians constantly lurked around the foraging parties and any men who became separated from the main body were instantly pounced upon. Their mutilated, and scalped, bodies would make a gruesome discovery for those troops who still battled to collect firewood. By January 1760, the blizzards on some days were so intense that even this much-needed lifeline had to be suspended. However, by the end of the month it became clear that the almost Herculean efforts of these British troops were not in vain, for gradually they were able to create a reserve, or magazine, of firewood near the walls of the city. Thus the immediate danger of freezing to death, or a violent end at the hands of the Indians, was diminished. Captain Knox described the general delight at this news: 'A magazine of wood is now forming on the heights of Abraham, and is supplied by horsesleighs: in a few days the garrison will be inabled to draw from thence, which being so near, and the soldiers being excused taking their arms, they will be able to make two turns per day, a circumstance that affords general satisfaction.'

Despite this now adequate supply of firewood, the intense cold could not be escaped. The troops were forced to cut up blankets to make socks and gloves and they wore anything they could lay their hands on, even French uniforms found in the stores in Quebec, in a vain attempt to keep out the cold. Sentries on duty in the open air were found to be deprived of the power of speech, due to the severe cold, and the guard was changed every half an hour, or less, so as to give some protection to the men. Captain Knox recorded in his journal the almost comical apparel in which the men clothed themselves to try and keep warm. He wrote:

Our guards, on the grand parade, make a most grotesque appearance in their different dresses; and our inventions to guard against the extreme rigour of this climate are various beyond imagination: the uniformity, as well as nicety, of the clean, methodical soldier, is buried in the rough fur-wrought garb of the Laplander; and we rather resemble a masquerade than a body of regular troops; insomuch that I have frequently been accosted by my acquaintances who, though familiar their voices were to me, I could not discover or conceive who they were; besides, every man seems to be in a continual hurry; for, instead of walking soberly through the streets, we are obliged to observe a running or trotting pace. Yet, notwithstanding all our precautions, several men and officers have suffered by the intenseness of the cold, being frost-bitten in their faces, hands, feet and other parts least to be suspected.

The Highland troops, clothed as they were in kilts, suffered disproportionately from the cold. Their officers struggled, largely in vain, to acquire breeches for their men. The distress of these men was communicated to the Ursuline nuns, who still remained cloistered in their convent. The nuns had been forced to relinquish two of the three floors of their convent for the use of a hospital for the wounded and sick of both armies, and they cared for the men there. In addition, Murray held meetings of his council in the building, and even the chapel was used for Protestant services twice a week. In return, Murray guaranteed the nuns' safety, and a sentry was on guard day and night before the doors of the convent. The British repaired the convent, which had suffered considerably during Wolfe's bombardment, and the nuns were permitted to draw supplies daily from the British commissariat department. Murray's conciliatory approach towards the nuns seems to have been appreciated for, upon their own initiative, the nuns knitted hose to cover the bare legs of the Highlanders, thus giving the Scotsmen some protection from the cold. However, despite these acts of kindness the garrison continued to struggle to survive the rigours of the winter, which continued relentlessly. By January, Knox described the city as being just one entire sheet of ice and told of how the troops found it impossible to get down the steep slopes with safety, and were therefore obliged to sit down on the summit and slide to the bottom, one after the other to prevent accidents, as the men's muskets were loaded. By February the temperature fell so low that bottles of spirits left in cellars were found to be frozen.

Sometimes the streets became blocked by huge snow drifts; more snow lodged in such quantity under the walls of the city that any assailants could have walked clear over the walls. To avoid this danger, the frozen, exhausted British were forced, after every snowfall, to dig away the snow from the walls and pile it up as an outer defence. Barrels filled with ice helped to make a glacis of this outer line and a large ditch increased the defence. In such conditions, the British were forced to improvise, and Murray encouraged his men to 'go native'. Mocassins were proved to be warmer than boots, and were less likely to slip. The Rangers from New England taught light infantrymen how to move across the snow and ice on snowshoes. Although the use of such devices proved a little tricky at first, Murray greatly encouraged his troops in their use and by January all guards were issued and trained in their use, so as to effectively pursue French and Indian skirmishers across the snows.

It appears that many of the British officers were at least able to enjoy some comforts while serving in the garrison. Captain Knox recorded that the daily dining routine was that they 'dined every day between eleven and twelve, and afterwards were respectively served with a cup of *laced* coffee; our dinners were generally indifferent, but our suppers (which they call their *grand repas*, or best meal) were plentiful and elegant. The hour for supper was between six and seven in the evening. As we dined so early, I gave myself no trouble about breakfast.' He was also able to enjoy the company of the captured and wounded French officers, and their ladies, and he even played cards with them to pass the time. The harsh reality of garrison life for the British rank and file was very different from that experienced by Knox. After the need for warmth, the chief concern for the British troops was to acquire sufficient, nutritious food.

Whether it was the arduous duty of collecting firewood, or the daily hazard of trying to keep warm, and free from frostbite, while on guard duty, the provision of salted food was insufficient to sustain the men of the garrison. To supplement their diet the troops had to rely largely on their own resourcefulness. For example, they soon learnt from the Canadians how to catch fish through holes made in the frozen river and a barter system quickly developed between the locals and the British, with the former exchanging fresh meat and vegetables in return for biscuits, wine or salted provisions. However, as the harsh winter continued and supplies dwindled, even the barter system collapsed and food prices soared. To reduce the amount of Canadian profiteering, Murray instructed Colonel Young, whom he had earlier appointed to act as a magistrate in civilian affairs, to agree fixed prices for certain foodstuffs with both the British and French traders in the city. All butchers were informed that they were not permitted to charge more than 6d a pound for mutton and 5d for beef and the price of bread was similarly fixed. Of course this did little to alleviate the suffering of the troops, for a black market rapidly developed, and it was those lacking the financial wherewithal to pay for the ever-diminishing food that suffered.

Murray seems to have been powerless to stop the slide into famine, and malnutrition, for both his men and the inhabitants. In February, to ease the suffering of the locals, Murray ordered that one day each week the provisions allotted to all officers and men should be given to the Canadians, despite the fact that many of the soldiers were now reduced to little more than walking skeletons. The soldiers accepted a further reduction in the meagre diet without a murmur. However, this may have had more to do with the fact that Murray renewed his earlier threat that any troops would be charged with sedition if they were heard to complain about the food and the allowance, rather than any generosity on the part of the garrison. In such conditions of stress, hardship and malnutrition, it was no surprise to the British that scurvy broke out among the troops.

Since wine was plentiful, and it was deemed a cure for scurvy, Murray encouraged those who could afford it to buy wine out of their remaining resources. This, of course, meant that there was less to spend on food and the circle of famine continued. This situation was compounded by the fact

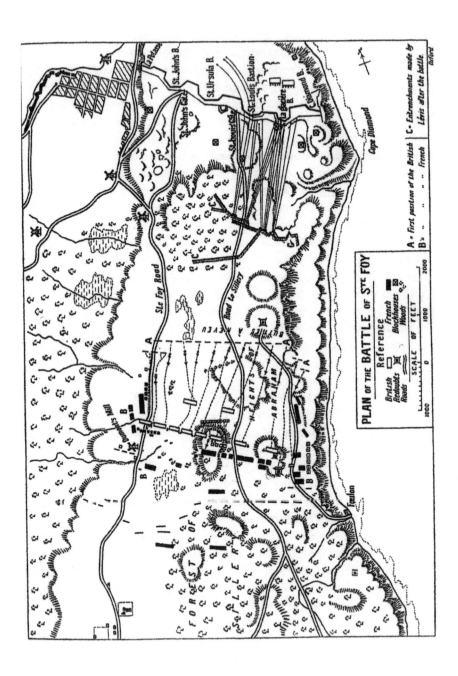

that Murray had no monies with which to pay his troops, for a sloop despatched from Halifax with £20,000 on board was forced to return when ice closed the St Lawrence river. Thus the troops pay remained in arrears from the end of October 1759 until the British fleet returned in May 1760. Murray declined to issue a paper currency and forbade the circulation of the now defunct French paper money, which further hindered the troops' ability to acquire additional food supplies.

Other, less costly, remedies were tried to alleviate the effects of scurvy: ginger and vinegar, tar-water and a liquor made from the spruce tree, which Murray ordered to be mixed with the men's daily rum ration. All these approaches appear to have had little effect for, as the winter wore on and the food diminished, hundreds of troops began to die. Captain Knox wrote:

> Our brave soldiers are growing sickly; their disorders are chiefly scorbutic, with fevers and dysenteries; this is far from being surprising, when we consider the severe fatigues and hardships they have hitherto, and still unavoidably undergo, which, with indifferent cloathing, uncomfortable barracks, worse bedding, and their being intirely confined to a salt provision diet, are sufficient to reduce or emaciate the most robust constitutions in this extremely frigid climate.

By February, Knox again reported the declining conditions of the troops: 'The men grow more unhealthy as the winter advances, and scarce a day passes without two or three funerals; though several do recover, yet the hospitals still continue full: it is, indeed, melancholy to see such havock among our brave fellows, and their daily suffering distress the officers beyond expression.' The harsh winter even affected the disciplinary measures which Murray took against offending troops. Four men who were found guilty of deserting their posts and breaking open the king's stores, were sentenced by the governor, with two receiving the death penalty and the remaining men 1,000 lashes each. However, the severe weather meant that the normal practice of parading the garrison to witness the sentence had to be curtailed; the lashes were reduced to 300 per offender and the death penalty was carried out on only one man, the decision as to who was to be reprieved being decided by the throw of a die between the two men.

Reports from Quebec as to the condition of the garrison reached Lévis in Montreal, where he was gradually building up his force to try to retake Quebec. It must have seemed to him that his tactic of letting the Canadian winter take its toll of the British was working and certainly he was to confront considerably fewer British troops in April 1760 than he faced in September 1759. By April men were becoming stricken with disease at a rate of 200 a week and most of the men had become little more than skeletons. On 24 April, Murray reported that 2,299 troops were sick among the eleven regiments and that he had little over 3,000 troops fit for duty. Approximately 1,000 men had succumbed to the harshness of the winter and various diseases. Of these, 700 bodies still awaited burial in the spring thaw, for the ground was so frozen that graves could not be dug. The bodies were aligned in grotesque lines outside the city walls and there they remained, for many weeks, as a poignant monument to the hardship of the Canadian winter.

While both Murray and his men were desperate for the winter to end, he realized too that the thaw would be likely to bring a French force to the walls of the city. The French activity over the winter months had convinced Murray that a spring French offensive was imminent. The enemy occupied a position at Saint-Augustin, only three miles from Quebec, and French troops actively patrolled close to the city. During February, Murray was forced to despatch a force, composed of the 28th Foot and Fraser's Highlanders, across the frozen St Lawrence to attack, and repulse, a French force which had landed at Point Lévis. Here the use of snowshoes by the British gave them the upper hand. In March, Murray sent an armed patrol to attack the enemy position at Saint-Augustin. Surprise was complete and the British returned with eighty prisoners.

By April, Murray had received enough intelligence reports, both from prisoners and deserters, to be certain that Lévis would imminently lead a force against the city. On 9 April, Murray ordered that the two sloops, *Racehorse* and *Porcupine*, be cut free of ice, and this difficult task was completed by 17 April. He now had two vessels to deter any attempted French landing and he had them anchored before Quebec. On 20 April, with the river now clear enough of ice, a schooner was despatched to Halifax with letters on board for Lord Colville, in which Murray urged that a naval force be sent with all haste to the relief of the garrison. Certain that any French advance would be by river, for the roads had been turned into muddy quagmires by the thaw, Murray ordered the occupation of the mouth of the Cap Rouge river, so as to prevent a French landing there.

Despite having barely 3,000 men fit for duty, Murray spread his force even wider. On 19 and 20 April, he ordered his men to drag two heavy cannon to strengthen the defences at Lorette. This work, for men weakened by scurvy and lacking horses, was extremely arduous and was found to be folly, when Murray decided that the position was too remote and ordered the cannon, and the garrison, to be withdrawn to the entrenchments of Sainte-Foy. The British destroyed all the bridges over the Cap Rouge river so as to impede any French advance.

On 21 April, his sense of paranoia as to the danger of 'the enemy within' led Murray to order all the remaining Canadians, with the exception of the nuns, to leave the city, giving them only three days to comply. To turn out helpless civilians to face the rawness of the April weather was certainly a stern measure, but Murray tried to make the expulsions as lenient as possible. He allowed the people to carry away what property they could and he arranged for the remainder to be stored at the monastery of Récollets, under the protection of the friars. However, Murray was forced to renounce his guarantee of the protection of property for, as his able-bodied troops were busy on other tasks, the collection of firewood was interrupted and he, therefore, allowed his men to use the timbers of the abandoned houses for fuel.

Murray had been correct in his assumption that the muddy roads would force the French to advance by river. Lévis had waited anxiously, and impatiently, for the first signs of the spring thaw and for the ice to break, so that ammunition, cannon and supplies could be carried by river. Lévis planned a rapid action by which to surprise Murray and hoped to take Quebec by the end of April. He knew that he would have to advance as early as possible and, to this end, French preparations began in earnest in Montreal in March, although the attempted replenishment of military stores illustrates that there was a worrying shortage, among other things, of ammunition and powder. There was also a shortfall of bayonets, and Lévis improvised with butcher's knives fastened to muskets. Many officers lacked swords, and warm clothing was also scarce. However, the most crucial deficiency was in artillery. Lévis withdrew what cannon he could from the posts at Île aux Noix and St John's, but he was still left with just twelve pieces, the condition of which was described as 'miserable', to batter the walls of Quebec.

What the French lacked in materials and supplies they made up for in morale and were eager for the fight to regain Quebec. The backbone of the force consisted of regular troops from France; the *troupes de terre* had arrived with Montcalm in 1756 and were by now veterans of Canadian warfare. The regulars consisted of eight battalions including the Languedoc, La Reine, Royal Roussillon Guienne, La Sarre and two battalions of Berry. Although the engagements of the previous years had reduced their numbers, Lévis could still rely on about 5,000 of these combat-hardened troops, of which more than 3,000 were available for the advance on Quebec. He also had at his disposal a small force, about 1,000 strong, of *troupes de la marine*. These regulars were recruited for service in the colonies, with the expectation that they would become settlers once the terms of their service had expired. They knew the country well and were reliable fighting men. The remainder of Lévis' force of 7,000 troops were composed of Canadian militia, whose fighting qualities were considered suspect. Despite Lévis' desire to place a French officer with each unit, to install some cohesion, this had not always been possible and the units were generally lacking in discipline, weak at drill and poorly armed. However, many had been forced to flee from Wolfe's policy of the devastation of the hinterland of Quebec and were eager for revenge. In addition, Lévis had the service of around 300 Indians, who acted chiefly as scouts but were to prove of little military use on the battlefield.

Although officers had been instructed to join their regiments as early as 10 March, the ice was slow to clear and the French advance was stalled. However, 4 April saw the first signs that the ice was breaking and expectations grew that the troops would soon depart on their great crusade to liberate Quebec from the invaders. The army, and its supplies, were to be carried in over four hundred open boats, and two French frigates, *Atalante* and *Pomone*, commanded by Jean Vauquelain, which had remained at the mouth of the Richelieu river over the winter months, were to add their support to the expedition. Before this armada could depart, the French were forced to hew many of the vessels out of the remaining thick ice and drag them to the channel of water that was beginning to open in the middle of the river at Montreal. In such conditions, the embarkation of stores, cannon, horses and men was extremely dangerous and accidents did occur in which men were lost, most notably Montegrou, a militia leader, who was drowned.

By 20 April, the difficult task of loading the numerous flotilla, and the frigates, was completed and Lévis and his men began the arduous, and desperate, journey to Quebec. Those troops in the small boats could not rely on sail and were forced to use oars throughout the whole of the river passage. Although a channel was now navigable, the shores were still littered with ice, which made any landings difficult and dangerous. Each night the men, chilled through, exhausted and hungry, were forced to drag their boats over the ice to the shore to find rest wherever they could, the fortunate ones finding a resting-place next to a fire in one of the many inhabited cottages on route. Each man carried with him eight days' worth of provisions and Lévis insisted that the officers had the same rations, for in this expedition all were to share the same hardship.

By 25 April the French had landed at Pointe aux Trembles and had busily unloaded supplies and men for a rapid march on Quebec. Here, however, the French advance halted. The direct route from the landing zone to Quebec was via the Cap Rouge, but French and Indian scouts reported to Lévis that a British force had occupied the high ground there. All plans for a night march to reach the Plains of Abraham at dawn had to be abandoned and a change of plan became inevitable. Lévis decided to re-embark his force from Point aux Trembles and land again at Saint-Augustin, a little above Cap Rouge, and then march quickly inland. The French could then cross the Cap Rouge river a few miles above its mouth and reach the road which led from Lorette up to Sainte-Foy. From here, it was an easy march to the walls of the city and Lévis still hoped that he might be able to surprise Murray. By 10 a.m. on 26 April most of the French fleet had reached Saint-Augustin where, once more, the men dragged the boats over the ice to unload their supplies, including three cannons, on the shore.

Lévis despatched his second-in-command, Brigadier Bourlamaque, in advance of the main army, with a party of grenadiers and Indians, to clear the route and reconstruct the destroyed bridges across the Cap Rouge river, and so advance on Lorette. Here, Bourlamaque discovered that the British had abandoned the position and they had neglected to destroy the road between Lorette and Sainte-Foy, thus allowing an easier passage for the French. By nightfall on 26 April, the French advance guard were in possession of some houses a few hundred yards from the British position at Sainte-Foy and it appeared that the British had no knowledge of the presence of the enemy. The element of surprise, which Lévis considered so central to French success, still seemed to be holding.

The weather, which had been so severe upon the British garrison, now seemed to favour them, for the main French army was overtaken by a tremendous storm. Having landed with the main body at Saint-Augustin on 26 April, Lévis let his men rest for a few hours before marching out to rendezvous with Bourlamaque in the middle of the afternoon. At 5 p.m. the advancing French column was hit by torrential rain, fierce winds and thunder and lightening. Paths soon became quagmires of mud, which slowed the march to little more than a crawl. Night fell before the vast majority of the French troops could reach the sanctuary of Lorette and most floundered knee-deep in snow and mud. The cold and persistent rain also soaked through their uniforms. Lévis was later to write that the night was 'most frightful' and that the 'army suffered greatly ... Since the bridges were broken down the men had to wade in the water. It was so dark that the workmen could do but little in the way of repairs. Had it not been for the flashes of lightning we should have been forced by the darkness to halt.' Forced to march in single file, in such terrible conditions, it was not until well into the night that the exhausted French troops reached Lorette. Lévis had gone on ahead of the column to discuss with Bourlamaque the prospects of seizing Sainte-Foy in a surprise attack.

Although Murray was now certain that the French had begun their advance, he had, at this stage, no reliable information as to the precise whereabouts of the enemy. This was to change by a piece of sheer luck, for a French soldier, from Bourlamaque's initial scouting party, had been washed overboard from his boat and was carried downstream by the current. He was able to cling on to an ever-diminishing ice flow and he sailed down to the calmer waters below Quebec. Here, his desperate and exhausted cries were faintly heard by a British seaman on board *Racehorse* and the Frenchmen was plucked from the St Lawrence more dead than alive. After two hours of recovery, the soldier was able to reveal that he was a sergeant in Lévis' army which at that moment was just a few miles from Quebec.

The cold and wet French troops awoke, after a dismaying night, to find the rain still falling. Lévis ordered his men to try to dry out their soaked weapons, while the army awaited the arrival of three artillery pieces which had been much delayed by the appalling condition of the roads. Thus, it was not until 10 a.m. that Lévis was in a position to recommence his advance on Sainte-Foy. Again, the weather and the mud impeded the march and it was not until noon that the main body sighted the fortified church of Sainte-Foy. The British position was well sited to command the single road and, as the weary French column appeared, the defenders opened fire with their cannon and were able to inflict a number of casualties. Lévis, still awaiting his own meagre artillery train, was unable to reply and he had no intention of advancing against such a well-defended site without artillery support. He decided to wait for the cover of darkness, when he intended to turn the British left and get between the garrison of Sainte-Foy and Quebec, thus isolating and neutralizing them.

Murray, now fully alerted to the threat to both Sainte-Foy and Quebec decided to withdraw his outpost at Sainte-Foy. Early on 27 April, he assembled a makeshift force of those troops still fit enough to march and set off on the five-mile journey from the city to Sainte-Foy. Although Murray kept some regiments in the city, with orders to march post-haste to his aid if required, it seems clear that this was no simple reconnaissance in force and that he was prepared to fight the French wherever he might find them. As the British approached, Murray, to his disquiet, could see an enemy force, under Bourlamaque, already attempting to work its way around the left side of the British at Sainte-Foy. Furthermore, Murray believed that he might face, at any moment, the real possibility of attack from a French force on the river and this, combined with his impetuous nature, meant that he was eager to give battle. Lévis, however, was too experienced to take Murray's bait, for he was determined not to engage until his whole force was assembled, and he sent a message to Murray that he would gladly seek battle the following day.

Murray, perhaps on the advice of Colonel Burton, or possibly because he realized the danger of his force being outflanked, decided to retire back behind the walls of Quebec. At 2 p.m., Murray ordered the troops in Sainte-Foy to destroy the position and a mighty explosion blew the roof off the church. The British, lacking wagons and horses, were unable to withdraw all their provisions, ammunition and two 18-pounders and these all had to be destroyed. The remaining cannons were dragged back to Quebec by the retiring British, who were harassed by French mounted troops and grenadiers. Despite constant sniping, the British force suffered only two casualties as they marched the five miles back to the city.

Lévis, despite his challenge to Murray, did not expect to face a pitched battle the following day and, once the British had departed from Sainte-Foy, he encouraged his troops to find what rest and warmth they could in order to dry out soaked clothes and equipment. Murray in turn attempted to boost the morale of his troops by issuing an extra rum ration that night. It appears that Lévis now considered the British would simply remain behind the walls of Quebec and would stay there awaiting a French attack. He spent the evening of 27 April in planning how he would bring up supplies, both by road and river, so as to begin his attack upon Quebec on 29 April.

Murray's impetuousness was to now disrupt Lévis' plan of attack. Very early on the morning of 28 April, Lévis and Bourlamaque rode over the ground which the French intended to occupy before Quebec. To the delight of the two Frenchmen they discovered that the British had thought better of maintaining a presence at their last remaining outpost, Dumont's Mill, a mere mile and a half from the city. As dawn broke, Lévis sent five companies of grenadiers to occupy this position, which gave the French a fine rallying point on the left. Away to the right, two British redoubts, built near the top of the ascent which Wolfe had climbed with his army the previous September, were also abandoned by the defenders and, once again, these were occupied by a small French detachment. The forest of Sillery, which stretched from the Anse au Foulon across to the Sainte-Foy Road, offered cover for the French main body as it advanced towards Quebec. At around half-past six, as Lévis was surveying the ground with some satisfaction, he was both amazed and shocked to see that Murray had decided not to wait behind the walls, but was leading a force of two columns out through the gates of the city with the obvious intention of meeting the French in the open.

It is clear that Murray had always intended to attack the French if they appeared on the Plains of Abraham and, like Montcalm before him, he rushed his force out of the city, placing no reliance on Quebec's defences. Murray had already predetermined his position on the Plain, on a rise known as Buttes à Neveu, just eight hundred yards from the walls and here, Murray considered, the British would be able to prevent the French from occupying these heights and thus deny them both an approach to the city and the ability to fire down on the defenders. To this end, Murray's troops left the city, not just carrying arms and ammunition, but also entrenching tools with which they hoped to strengthen the position on Buttes à Neveu. Murray, knowing the French to be weaker in cannon, placed much reliance on his superiority in artillery and the British, lacking horses, dragged 20 field pieces and 2 howitzers onto the battlefield. In their weakened state, and with the ground covered in a mixture of melting snow and mud, this was no easy task.

The force that left Quebec to face the French was not the same army that had beaten Montcalm. Over 1,000 men had been lost to illness and disease over the long winter months, 2,300 were unfit for duty and of the 3,866 men who joined Murray on the battlefield, many hundreds, in their weakened state should by right have been left behind. Quartermaster Sergeant Johnson described them as 'a poor pitiful handful of half-starved, scorbutic skeletons'. Yet the determination and resolve of many of these men was also chronicled by Johnson, in his diary of the siege: 'They went out ... determined to a Man to Conquer or Die. Many of them had laid by their crutches, and would not be prevailed upon to stay behind. They followed us to the gates in the rear, and fell in, when we formed line of battle.'

Despite the condition of his troops, and their lack of numbers, Murray had complete confidence in their ability to beat the French. He was later to try and justify his decision to seek battle to William Pitt thus: 'When I considered that our little army was in the habit of beating the enemy, and had a very fine train of artillery it seemed better to go out boldly and attack the French, than to await attack behind the wretched fortifications of Quebec.' In defence of Murray's decision, it now seems clear that he thought his army outnumbered by the French four to one, rather than the reality of two to one, and he certainly feared the possible arrival of more French troops by river at any moment and thus the real danger of being assailed from both land and water. He must have considered that a quick blow would drive back Lévis' army before it was fully assembled. Murray was resolved to give battle and he must, therefore, be criticized for not realizing the importance of the position of Dumont's Mill, for this outpost should most certainly have been either defended by picked troops or destroyed the night before, thus depriving the French of a crucial rallying point. Additionally, as events would later show, Murray should have been more aware of the condition of the ground over which he was to ask his men to fight, and, most importantly, the difficulty of both entrenching a position and of moving artillery in such conditions.

On sighting the British advance, Lévis immediately realized the danger of his position, for although Bourlamaque was well placed with the grenadiers at Dumont's Mill, the main army was approaching only slowly and the British might be upon them before they could form in line to meet an attack. Lévis thus hurried back to his troops, so as to hasten their march. With some difficulty, due to soft conditions under foot and their weak constitutions, the British troops reached the assigned position on top of the elevated Buttes à Neveu and began to entrench. However, even this task proved to be arduous for the British soon discovered that under the top layer of mud, the ground remained frozen.

If Lévis had been amazed by the British advance, Bourlamaque was alarmed. By seven o'clock, from his position at Dumont's Mill, he witnessed Murray lining up the British troops, two deep, as Wolfe had done, so as to make his weak force look more formidable, and he recorded the surprise he felt at this moment: 'No one believed that the enemy would dare to advance and the army was resting ... We were all worn out and wet. We had no thought of moving forward until daybreak on the next morning when we should have boats at the Anse au Foulon to support our advance guard on the right.' Murray wasted no time in unleashing his artillery at Bourlamaque's grenadiers, which, for a time, caused confusion and even panic among the French. However, Bourlamaque quickly regained control and despatched more troops to strengthen the position at Dumont's Mill, whilst assembling three brigades in line. Meanwhile Lévis was frantically hurrying forward the main body of the French force.

It was now that Murray, without consulting Colonel Burton or his staff, made a fatal choice. Whether Murray's decision was influenced by the difficulties which the troops were experiencing in entrenching their position or if, as is more likely, he saw that the moment was right for an attack, for the French, on the left, were still in column and a rapid advance might catch them unprepared to face the British onslaught, is now not certain. What is clear is that Murray believed an opportunity now presented itself for a quick victory to be won and for a man of such impetuous character this was simply too good to miss. Quartermaster Sergeant Johnson was later to recall that Murray, at this decisive moment, was too full of 'mad enthusiastic zeal'. Captain Knox was more diplomatic in his use of language to describe the events which led to the British advance:

Upon coming to our ground, we described the enemy's van on the right marching along the road of St Foy, inclining, as they advanced, in order to conceal themselves. Upon this discovery, and our line being already formed, the troops were ordered to throw down their entrenching tools and march forward, this being deemed the decisive moment to attack them, in hopes of reaping every advantage that could be expected over an army not yet thoroughly arranged.

Thus, instead of simply remaining on top of the Buttes à Neveu, and using his vast superiority in artillery to harass an enemy attack and keep the French at bay, Murray risked all in a general advance. The battle of Sainte-Foy, or the Second Battle of Quebec, was much bloodier than Wolfe's victory of the year before. Initially, it appeared that Murray had succeeded in catching the French off guard and the British had some success. Knox left a detailed description of the advance: the right brigade, under Colonel Burton, was composed of the 48th, the 15th and the second battalion of the 16th, 'advanced with great alacrity'. The left, under Colonel Fraser, consisted of the 28th, 27th and 47th, and met little resistance at first, while Colonel James in the centre commanded the 58th. A second line, composed of the 35th and the third battalion of Royal Americans, was drawn up, to appear more numerous, two deep. The right flank was covered by Major Dallings' corps of light infantry, and the left by the company of volunteers and Rangers, under their respective commandants, Captains McDinell and Hazen. The artillery, commanded by Major Godwin, assisted by Major M'Kellar, the chief engineer, did, as Knox records, 'amazing execution'. Knox wrote that:

> as soon as we came within the range of musketry, the light infantry attacked the French grenadiers on the left of the army, and routed them: at the same instant the volunteers and rangers engaged their right, repulsed them in like manner, and possessed themselves of a redoubt occupied before by the enemy; the center posts, seeing their right and left give way, fled without firing a shot.

During the advance, the apparent panic among the French, which Knox reported, was in danger of becoming widespread. It would appear that Lévis believed, at this moment, that he would be unable to bring the majority of his army into line for battle and he did indeed panic. He ordered Bourlamaque to withdraw from Dumont's Mill and regroup around a house named La Fontaine. As Bourlamaque rode forward to carry out this order, he was caught in a murderous volley from a detachment of British light infantry; his horse was shot from under him and he received a bullet in the calf, causing him much pain. The British regained Dumont's Mill and Bourlamaque was carried by his troops from the field. The loss of Bourlamaque seems to have shocked Lévis into action and he now realized he could not hope, in the immediate future, to support the advanced French position and ordered his men back to the refuge of the nearby woods. The British pressed on, perhaps perceiving this move to be a general retreat.

However, Lévis was suddenly able to bring into the battle the main French army, which had rapidly come up and, despite severe British fire, he was able to bring the columns into line at the edge of the wood. With little regard for his own safety, Lévis rode along the front of his army exulting them to charge the British. He intended to use his present superiority in numbers to outflank the British. Knox described the French counter:

> While we gained this small advantage over their van, the main body of their army advanced with great expedition, completely formed in columns, in spite of the utmost efforts exerted on our part to prevent them; one of these columns came without loss of time to sustain their flying grenadiers, now pursued by our light infantry, who, being overpowered with great loss, retired to the rear and were of little service afterwards; the enemy, profiting thereby, instantly wheeled round some rising grounds, and charged our right wing vigorously in flank, while M. de Lévis, with another division, made the like movement on our left, and then the action became obstinate on both sides.

This was, no doubt, an understatement, for much of the fighting became hand-to-hand in which the numerical advantage of the French began to tell.

It was at this vital time that the British artillery fire began to slacken, for, as the British had advanced, they found themselves crossing low, marshy ground. A number of cannon soon became stuck and the weakened, exhausted British troops battled to extract them. Furthermore, the ammunition wagons also struggled over the muddy, marshy terrain and the gun crews were forced to manhandle ammunition to their field piece. Inevitably, the British guns began to fall silent, just as Lévis was able to bring his three guns into action.

Murray soon grasped that Lévis intended to outflank the faltering British. He immediately ordered the 35th from the second line to support the right wing and the third battalion of the 6th the left; yet even these fresh troops were unable to stall the numerically superior French for long. Murray was then forced to order Colonel James from the centre to support the third battalion of Americans on the left, and both these corps made a vigorous effort to recover two redoubts lost to the French. Although the attack was successful, the fighting was intense and soon the British were reduced to a handful of combatants, and they were compelled to yield to superior numbers. Elsewhere on the battlefield the story was the same; despite intense bravery, on both sides, the British were being pushed further and further back. The position at Dumont's Mill epitomized the murderous nature of the battle. Here, having first driven the French from the position, the British had yielded, only for the Highlanders to retake the mill once more. Now the French grenadiers returned, determined to regain what had been lost, while, similarly, the Highlanders were not prepared to move. The resultant clash was a hand-to-hand struggle in which the Highlanders, short of ammunition, fought with their dirks. A French officer, Chevalier Johnstone, later wrote of the bitter battle over the mill:

These two antagonists, worthy the one of the other, were no sooner out by the windows, than they returned to the charge, and broke open the doors ... The grenadiers were reduced to forty men per company, and there would not have remained either Highlander or grenadier of the two armies, if they had not, as by tacit and reciprocal agreement, abandoned the desire of occupying the fort.

Now outflanked on both the right and left, Murray had to act quickly, for his remaining force was now in imminent danger of being cut off from the city. Murray ordered the guns to be spiked and the defenders to fall back; a command which Knox stated was one the troops 'were hitherto unacquainted with'. Retreat rapidly became a rout as the French poured forward 'like a hasty torrent from a lofty precipice', as described by Quartermaster Sergeant Johnson. One anonymous British officer wrote, 'we did not retire in very good order'. In their haste, the British not only abandoned their cannon, but also entrenching tools, in fact any item that might slow down their flight, including the dead and wounded. Despite the pleas of the wounded, not all were dragged back to the city walls; many where left to be butchered and scalped by the Indians allied to the French, a fate shared by some of even the French wounded. Although French officers did manage to intervene to rescue some British, the number of wounded prisoners, at twenty-eight, was pitifully small. Captain Fraser was to write after the siege that 'the French allowed the savages to scalp all the killed and most of the wounded, as we found a great many scalps on the bushes'.

The British were saved from total annihilation by a combination of factors. Blockhouses and a strong redoubt outside the city, as well as cannon fire from the parapets, slowed the two flanks of the French army sufficiently to allow the passage of the British back to the city. However, it was perhaps the sheer exhaustion experienced by the French troops, who had marched through appalling conditions and fought in a bloody battle for a full two hours, that allowed so many British troops to escape. This fatigue was to benefit the defenders in the immediate days that followed.

The battle had indeed been bloody. The French suffered 193 killed and 640 wounded, or 22 per cent of those engaged, while the British lost 259 killed and 829 wounded, or 28 per cent. Murray had not only sustained higher casualties, but had been forced to abandon his guns and had lost a much higher percentage of his effective men than Lévis; 28 per cent compared to less than 12 per cent. The Second Battle of Quebec was the most severe of the French–Indian Wars as well as the last that the two empires of France and Britain would fight in Canada and it was one battle that should never have been fought. Murray had taken an impulsive gamble and had endured a spectacular defeat; but for all his concerns about the defensibility of Quebec he must surely have been aware that the city's fate would be determined not by French success on the battlefield, but by which country's fleet first arrived in the basin below Quebec. This is especially true when the lack of French cannon, sufficient to demolish the city walls, is considered. Simple, basic intelligence would have been enough to show to Murray that Lévis' army lacked the artillery necessary to take the city quickly and, therefore, he could have kept his men behind the city walls and used his superior guns to keep the French siege works at bay. Yet Murray chose to attack, an action which appears to have been predetermined in his mind long before Lévis arrived with his troops. This decision cost the lives of hundreds of men and almost lost the city that Wolfe had given his life for.

Just two days after the defeat, Murray attempted to justify his action in a letter to the Commander-in-Chief, Major-General Jeffrey Amherst. It is also clear from this letter that Murray tried to exaggerate French losses, so as to reduce the impact of his own, and he left an intriguing record of his own plans for the British troops if he was forced to abandon the city.

As we have been Unfortunate, I am Sensible I may be universally blamed at home, but I Appeal to Every Officer in the Field, if any thing was wanting in the Disposition, or my Endeavors to Animate the Men, during the Whole Affair. The Superiority these Troops had Acquired over the Enemy ever since the last Campaign, together with the fine Field Train we were firnished with, might have tempted me to an Action, Supposing I had not been thoroughly Convinced of the Necessity of it. We Lost in the Battle about one third of our Army, and I have certain Intelligence the Enemy had not less than Ten Thousand men in the Field – They have already Compleated their first Parallel, but I am in hopes We shall not be Reduced to Extremities, 'till the Arrival of the Fleet, which We Expect daily: IN that Event, I shall Retreat with what I can to the Island of Orleans, and wait the Arrival of Reinforcements, unless I can do better, had We been Masters of the River, in which it is Evident Ships may safely Winter, they never would have made the Attempt.

For Murray to write of his consideration of abandoning the city illustrates how critical the situation now was, but this moment soon passed and he stubbornly resolved to hold Quebec. If Murray can be criticized for the British defeat on the Plains of Abraham, his actions immediately after the retreat can be widely praised. Murray now had a defeated and demoralized force with which to defend the city. That night there was disorder in Quebec; but when some drunken soldiers were caught in robbery and riot, Murray showed his earlier firmness by trying and hanging one of their number. In adversity, Murray's stubbornness strengthened the army's resolve. He and Burton quickly realized that the men must not be able to dwell on their defeat, nor allowed to rest, if discipline and morale was to be restored.

Thus every fit man was put to work making embrasures and platforms for the guns, with the aim of maintaining a vigorous fire upon the advancing French. Writing in his diary, on 29 April, Murray described the tactics required to hold back the French: 'The best we could do was to endeavour to knock their works to pieces before they could mount their cannon.' To this end, Murray ordered artillery to be placed not only upon every bastion, but also upon the far from strong walls. He aimed to use 140 cannon, and the Lower Town was stripped of guns, platforms and planks, with all the defenders involved in this gruelling task. Quartermaster

Sergeant Johnson wrote that: 'None but those who were present on the Spot can imagine the grief of heart the Soldiers felt, to see their Officers doing the common labour of the Soldier, equal with themselves; to see them yoked in the Harness, dragging up Cannon from the Lower Town, at work on the Batteries with Barrow, Pick-axe and Spade, with the same Ardour as themselves.'

At every hour of the day, Murray and Burton were seen inspecting the defences to ensure nothing was neglected. Women were also put to hard labour to strengthen the defences. The parapet walls were re-dressed with fascines, and a quantity of earth rammed down between the lining and masonry work. Convalescents filled sandbags, the hospitalized rolled bandages and made wadding for the guns. The provost was given orders to hang all stragglers and marauders; the insubordinate were sentenced to 1,000 lashes or shot out of hand. To reduce drunkenness, Murray promptly ordered all spirits in the Lower Town to be poured away and even the daily rum allowance was watered down.

Captain Knox was able to record the improvements in discipline and morale introduced by Murray and clearly believed that the French had now lost their opportunity to take the city:

> If the enemy have, or do still entertain, thoughts of storming the place, it seems now too late, and they have let slip a golden opportunity: had they followed their blow on the 28th, 29th or 30th, before the soldiers recollected themselves, I am strongly inclined to think, not withstanding the active zeal and spirit of the governors and officers in general, Quebec would have reverted to its old masters. Batteries are erecting to enfilade the road leading to the lower town; the general and lieutenant-governor visit the guards and working parties frequently, to encourage the men and influence them to diligence and alertness.

Murray, and the rest of the garrison, were, no doubt, surprised that Lévis had not followed up his victory with an immediate assault. Although Murray was glad of the respite, in which he was able to improve his defences, he was also desperate to know of French intentions. To this end, on the night of 29 April, Murray ordered Ensign Maw, of the 43rd Regiment, with two non-commissioned officers and 20 volunteers, to sally out in the hope of capturing a prisoner from whom intelligence could be sought. Unfortunately, luck was not with Maw and his party, for they ran straight into a large party of French troops and, in the resultant tussle, six of the British soldiers were killed or wounded; the remainder fled empty-handed back to Quebec.

As the retreating British shut the gates of the city, Lévis' first concern was not to rally his troops to attempt to storm the walls, but to secure the General Hospital, which lay on the banks of the St Charles, outside the walls. It was here that the nuns were caring for the many hundreds of wounded troops, but Lévis' initial haste was in part from fear that he needed to place French troops in the hospital so as to deter his Indian allies from attacking both the wounded and the nuns. One of the unnamed sisters was to write of her experiences in the hospital in the aftermath of the battle: 'Another pen than mine would be necessary to paint the horrors of sight and sound during the twenty-four hours in which the wounded were brought in ... We saw nothing but torn arms and legs, and to add to the woe of the occasion the supply of linen gave out, so that we were obliged to use our sheets and our chemises.' Five hundred beds were prepared, but these proved totally insufficient; nearby stables and barns were filled with the wounded. Of 72 officers who were brought in, 33 soon died.

With his immediate concern for the hospital and the wounded, and with troops at the point of exhaustion, it appears that Lévis never considered a prompt assault on Quebec, which the British both feared and expected. Lévis hesitated, and it was this hesitation that cost him his best chance of taking the city. A night assault on the city was given but brief consideration, for Lévis felt that his lightly trained Canadian allies, and his reluctant Indians, would perform poorly in a night attack. Although the French now held the Buttes à Neveu, just 900 yards from the city walls, they were unable to commence a bombardment immediately. Not only did they lack cannon – the only guns immediately available were the three field pieces which the French had dragged laboriously through the snow and mud from Saint-Augustin – but British fire from the city walls, the blockhouses and the redoubt seriously slowed the French preparations. Lévis wrote on 30 April that this enemy fire was already having an impact: 'The enemy is unmasking many embrasures, this shows that they can keep up a considerable fire. All this would be nothing if we had the artillery and ammunition to answer them. We can only hope that some aid will come for us from France.'

Although the French artillerymen would eventually drill the touch-holes of the spiked cannons which Murray had obligingly left on the battlefield, this work would take time before the guns could be turned against their former masters, and time was one thing Lévis knew he did not have, for the St Lawrence was now rapidly clearing of ice and would soon be navigable along its length. The only question would be whose fleet would arrive first; the French or the British? To add to Lévis' woes, ammunition was far from plentiful and indeed the British could respond with twenty rounds for every one the French could fire at the city walls. Furthermore the quality of both the French cannon balls and powder was not high. The quality of the powder was such that, on first testing, the French cannon fire could hardly reach the walls. The first cannon ball which the French fired into Quebec was brought to Murray for inspection. Apparently, he was relieved to discover that the missile was of such poor quality.

As French casualties mounted, Lévis began to realize that he would be forced to withdraw from his advanced position on the Buttes à Neveu, for the British cannon could rake and pound the area with impunity, with little threat from the meagre French artillery. Soon the surrounding ground resembled a moonscape. Crucial time was lost in moving the main French camp about one mile back and taking the necessary steps for safety. Every time the French were visible, they were met by fire from the defender's cannon. Consequently they could only approach the exposed positions by trenches and to make these in the frozen ground was extremely arduous. Furthermore, the top soil was found to be only six inches deep in some places, before the French hit hard rocks, and thus many trenches had to be either abandoned or re-routed, again costing time.

The tools and materials for entrenchments had to be carried in sacks over long distances, often exposed to British fire. As fresh artillery arrived, or the captured British field pieces were repaired, they were ferried by boat to the Anse au Foulon and then dragged up the steep slopes and on to the muddy Plains of Abraham. The men were exposed to biting cold, especially at night, as well as the murderous fire of the British. Sleep for the already exhausted French was something of a luxury. When required, the British could bring 60 guns to bear on a single point, and the disparity in artillery between the two adversaries was reflected in the casualties during the siege. The British suffered only 30 casualties, whereas there were 206 on the French side, including 73 fatalities. Every day three or four men were killed and half a dozen wounded; on one occasion a single shot from Quebec killed six French soldiers at work. These experiences truly tested the resolve of the French troops and, in such conditions, with such a resolute defence from the British, it is not surprising that the work went on only slowly. It was later recorded, in the diary of an anonymous British officer, that 'Each night they [the French] were obliged to pay their canadians half a dollar a man before they would go to work in the trenches, our artillery did them so much mischief.'

Despite the determination of the defenders and the commitment of the French, both sides knew that, unless Lévis could rapidly bring a substantial bombardment to play upon the flimsy walls of Quebec, it would be the arrival of the first fleet that would determine the outcome of the siege. The British had gained significant naval victories over the French, at the battle of Lagos (18–19 August 1759) and at Quiberon Bay (20 November 1759), and this meant that, in 1760, the French were simply unable either to challenge the British for supremacy on the St Lawrence River or impede the transatlantic transfer of British ships and supplies.

On 1 May, Murray despatched the frigate *Racehorse* on a fair wind towards Louisbourg and Halifax with orders to hasten the fleet for the relief of the City. For the next week, the French and the British nervously scanned the river awaiting the first sails. At 11 a.m. on 9 May, the anxious wait was brought to an end with the sighting of a vessel round Point Lévis. At first, it appears that both sides thought she was a French ship and welcoming shouts of *Vive le Roi!* could be heard from the French camp. On top of the walls of Quebec, the anxiety and suspense among the British troops reached fever pitch; after months of deprivation and the loss of so many comrades would the garrison now be forced to surrender at the arrival of a French relief force?

The single vessel dropped anchor just off Point Lévis and flag signals were raised from the walls of Quebec, asking the ship's crew to identify themselves. In response, the British colours were hoisted from the mainsail and the British frigate, *Lowestoffe*, removed all doubt as to her allegiance by firing a 21-gun salute towards the City. On the walls and in the streets of Quebec, the besieged went mad with joy and relief; tears flowed, mixed with laughter. Both officers and men rushed to the parapets, which looked towards the French camp, jeered at their adversaries and threw their hats in the air for nearly an hour. To show their glee, the artillery men fired off their cannon repeatedly.

111

In the French camp, despair was heavy in the air. Men who, a few moments before, were shouting the praises of their king, were now sullen and silent. However, the arrival of the *Lowestoffe* brought immediate danger to Quebec for a single ship did not necessarily mean deliverance. Lévis realized that he had, perhaps, only a few hours or days in which to take the City. In the meantime the vessel did indeed bring good news, for the *Lowestoffe* was one of a considerable fleet under Commodore Swanton, which had sailed from England in March. She had been separated from the fleet at sea, and her commander, Captain Deane, confident in his ship, had decided to go on alone to Quebec. Off Newfoundland he met the British fleet from Halifax, under Lord Colville, on the way to the rendezvous point at the island of Bic, in the St Lawrence, about 160 miles below Quebec, where Colville was to meet Swanton.

Despite this good news, Deane also confirmed to Murray that it would be some time before the combined squadrons could reach Quebec. In the meantime, there was a real danger that the imminence of relief might induce Lévis to make a desperate assault. Knox was to write that after the arrival of the *Lowestoffe*, 'The situation of affairs and the circumstances of the enemy, now grown desperate, render it necessary to take every precaution that human prudence and foresight can dictate to prevent a surprise.' Murray, whether by instinct or via intelligence, became convinced the Lévis would attempt an assault on the evening of 9 May. All through the night Murray paced along the ramparts and kept half of the garrison on alert. Even the convalescents were under orders to be ready to turn out at their alarm-posts on the shortest notice, with their firelocks and accoutrements. Murray ordered that a sloop be despatched down the river to encourage the approaching ships to hasten to Quebec.

However, Murray's fear of an assault on the 9th proved unfounded. It appears that, before attempting an assault, Lévis felt that his cannon had to batter the walls of Quebec and, despite his urging, these were not ready until the 11th. On that day the long labours of the French met with some success; at noon the French unmasked four batteries and began firing with great energy. One was opposed to Cape Diamond, a second against the citadel, and the third against the Ursuline bastion. The French were able to bring into play their 24-, 18- and 12-pounders, as well as three nine-inch mortars. Early in the attack, the French dismounted or destroyed five of Murray's guns; however, Knox recorded that the bombardment produced few British casualties. Fate was apparently on the side of at

Quebec before the siege

The Plains of Abraham behind Quebec, as Wolfe would have seen them during his last reconnaissance from the Etchemin bluff on the south bank of the St Lawrence

Wolfe by Brigadier Townshend, 1759

Louis Joseph, Marquis de Montcalm

Grenadiers of the 47th and 48th Regiments of Foot

Soldier of Le Régiment de la Reine, 1759

A view of the Church of Notre Dame de la Victoire, built in commemoration of the raising of the Siege in 1698 and destroyed in 1759.

Chevalier Levis

Brigadier Murray

Brigadier General Richard Montgomery (courtesy New York Public Library Print Collection)

Benedict Arnold

Governor Guy Carleton

least four officers of the 43rd regiment who had a fortunate escape while sitting on the ground in a soldier's tent, eating a dish of pease-porridge. Knox wrote, 'A shell pitched within a yard of the door of the tent, and they had barely time to stretch themselves at their length, when the shell burst; but by being extended flat on the ground, they happily received no other damage than losing their mess, which was overset in the bustle.'

If the French cannon fire inflicted few casualties, it soon began to take a toll of the city's walls and Murray's earlier fears that under sustained artillery fire the defences of Quebec would crumble, and be easily breached, appeared to be justified. For a period of nearly 36 hours, the French were able to sustain a fierce cannonade. This fire had a considerable effect, both in the havoc wreaked upon the structures of the city, but also upon the morale of the garrison. Murray was dismayed at the damage caused by the French bombardment, as well as concerned that his troops would soon be worn out by the stress and tension of remaining under arms both day and night. By the evening of the 12th, four had been killed and nine wounded by the French fire. One French missile that was particularly effective was the carcases, iron shells filled with flammable material, and these soon set fire to the remaining houses in Quebec. Murray was forced to scatter his supplies and magazines to various parts of the town, in case the French were to score direct hits on his ammunition stores.

While it appeared that an assault under the cover of such a vigorous fire seemed imminent, this was not the case. Lévis must have realized that the appearance of the *Lowestoffe* was simply the vanguard for a large fleet and that, even if he could take Quebec, British reinforcements would then see the French besieged. Thus, with this in mind, an assault would have entailed a loss of life for little or no purpose. Lévis' tactics, after the arrival of the British vessel, seem to have been based on destroying as much of Quebec as possible, so as to make the city an unsuitable base from which to launch a British assault upon Montreal later in the year. If, in the meantime, and as a result of the bombardment, the British surrendered, this would have been an unlikely bonus.

Not even this limited objective could be achieved, for the French were unable to sustain their initial rate of fire and for only a little over a day could Lévis make his fire exceed that of the British. Cannon, weak in calibre, proved also poor in quality. Some, including the hastily repaired British ones, burst. French ammunition, too, was also of poor quality and in short supply; much had been ruined by exposure to the torrential rain

113

experienced on the line of march. In consequence, the French fire soon slackened and Lévis was forced to give the order that each gun should fire but 20 times in 24 hours; this was hardly a rate sufficient to destroy a city. The relentless British fire also seems to have had an effect on the outcome of the French bombardment, for the chief French engineer, Pontleroy, decided to site the French batteries some distance from the walls, no doubt to reduce the exposure of his men to the deadly fire of the defenders. This, of course, reduced still further the effectiveness of the French guns.

In the meantime, the squadrons under Colville and Swanton made their way along the St Lawrence. It was Swanton's ships that were first met by Murray's sloop, sent to urge on the British vessels. Rather than await the arrival of Colville's fleet, Swanton decided to hasten to Murray's relief and, when Colville reached the rendezvous point at the island of Bic on 16 May, he discovered Swanton had gone on, two days ahead. Likewise, Colville pushed his sailors on in the race for Quebec. This ascent of the river by a squadron in the spring was the earliest on record, but, thanks, in part, to the observations made by James Cook, and other seamen the year before, the two fleets made rapid, and safe, passage.

On the late evening of 15 May, a strong north-east wind was blowing and it brought into view three ships round the head of the Island of Orleans. Lévis watched, with little hope, and tried to convince himself that they were French; but they were not and his heart must have surely sunk. Swanton, in his ship *Vanguard*, with two other vessels from his squadron, arrived off Quebec that evening. The following day, the remainder arrived. Murray, and the men and women of the garrison, were ecstatic. Gone were the fears of defeat, death and starvation. Lévis, and his troops, were now certain that all hope of inflicting a further defeat upon the British at Quebec was lost. There remained only one decision for the French commander to take, and that was when, and how, his surviving force should retreat.

Murray greeted Swanton with gratitude, yet immediately urged him to attack the French vessels, under the command of Vauquelain, which had been a constant threat. The following day, upon the next tide, Swanton took his three vessels past Quebec and set upon the French ships. The French frigate, *Pomone*, ran aground while trying to evade the British, leaving just Vauquelin, in his vessel *Atalante*, to stand off against the British. Captain Vauquelin, who had been the only master to escape the siege of Louisbourg in 1758 with his ship intact, was fearless. He sailed his warship upriver to Pointe aux Trembles and here ordered his crew to drop anchor. He nailed his colours to the mast and fought with his ship to the last. Only when the British had transformed *Atalante* into a burning hulk did Vauquelin order his men to abandon ship. The apparently pointless defence had allowed Lévis to formulate his plan of escape. Vauquelin, severely wounded, was captured and sent to France, where his gallantry was not recognized, and he met an early death in prison.

Without naval support, and his means of retreat by river denied to him, Lévis' retirement was now inevitable. Furthermore, the British warships were getting the range of his position on the Plains, causing some casualties. His only course was to abandon his lines, under cover of darkness, and get away by land as best he could. Lévis planned that, at ten o'clock on the night of 16 May, his battalions were to march away in silence, no weapons were to be discharged, no fires lit. He was forced to abandon most of his artillery. An attempt was made to evacuate some field pieces by light transports, but most were intercepted and sunk by *Vanguard*. Baggage, stores, wounded and dead were all left behind. Lévis seems to have lost some of his personal control. Contrary orders were given, and for some moments confusion reigned. The Indians went on the rampage, drunk on raided French spirits, as did some French troops. However, despite the noise and confusion, the British failed to appreciate that Lévis was slipping away. A pretence of occupation was continued, for Lévis ordered some Canadian militia to remain in the trenches. On the morning of the 17th these men fired one last volley and then retired. It was not until the evening that a scouting party from Quebec discovered the silent empty trenches.

The British scouts discovered a scene of carnage and devastation. The officers and men killed at the battle of 28 April had not been buried, and their bodies had been treated to great barbarity. The corpses had been scalped and mangled, and had been left away from the camp to be picked at and eaten by ravenous birds and beasts. Hanging on the bushes, around the camp, the British found a great many scalps of their countrymen, a sight that filled them with intense anger. Captain Knox was able to observe the effect of British cannon fire upon the French position; 'It is amazing to see the effect of our artillery in the environs of the late French camp and circumjacent country, for the extent of almost two miles, the ground being ploughed up by our *ricochet* firing.' An anonymous diary entry for 17 May 1760 recorded that 'The french went off so precipitantly that they left all their tents standing and forgot even their church plate which fell a prey to some of our light infantry who did not think it sacrilege to secure it and apply it to their own use.' Captain Fraser wrote, with some relief, that 'We found ourselves entirely freed of very disagreeable neighbours.'

By dawn on the 17th, the French had reached the comparative safety of the Cap Rouge crossing. By the 18th, the army had reached as far as Pointe aux Trembles, and on the 19th they travelled as far as the Jacques Cartier river, the crossing of which proved difficult and dangerous. It was not until the evening that the remains of the army had crossed over. Lévis, having conducted a most arduous six-week campaign with both skill and valour, and his weary army, withdrew to Montreal.

Murray reacted slowly to the news that the French had fled. On 19 May he sent light infantry and grenadiers in pursuit of the French, but an anonymous diarist wrote of the futility of the chase: 'We push'd after the enemy some miles, took some wagons loaded with wounded men, but could not come up with the body.' The time advantage which Lévis had gained proved too much for the British. Murray now wrote to Major-General Jeffery Amherst to inform him of the French retreat, but he also candidly revealed his state of mind after such long months of stress and disease: 'We are very low, the Scurvy makes terrible havock. For Gods sake send us up molassas, and seeds which may produce vegetables. Whoever winters here again must be better provided with bedding, & warm cloaths than we were; our medicines are entirely expended, at present we get a very Scanty supply from Lord Colvills Squadron which arrived this day'.

The supply situation began to be rectified in the days and weeks after the French retreat, and Lévis' fears that Quebec would be used as a staging post for the advance on Montreal proved to be well founded. On 19 May Lord Colville's fleet from Halifax, composed of six ships of the line and seven frigates and sloops of war, arrived at Quebec; after which, ships came up on every tide laden with stores and provisions. In contrast, the French had despatched only a single frigate, with a convoy of transports, to Quebec on 12 April, more than a month after the British fleet had left, and this rather puny effort was completely swamped by the size of the British armada. Furthermore, even this small French squadron was intercepted by the Royal Navy and never reached its destination. The Secretary of State, William Pitt realized that it would take overwhelming forces to win victory in North America and he had been toiling for many months to make victory certain. The pathetic efforts of the French stand in vivid contrast to that of the British and it was her logistical advantage, combined with the determination to win, that enabled Britain to wrest an empire away from the French.

After the retreat of Lévis and his troops, Murray could spare a few moments to reflect upon the achievement of not only Wolfe's success of 1759, but his own in holding the battered city. It seems certain that, if Wolfe had failed, it would have been unlikely that Pitt could have mounted such a major expedition the following year. The political will for such a logistical and financial commitment would have been hard to maintain. Yet, it is likely that a lesser effort would have been made and, given the inability, and lack of determination, of the French to supply their beleaguered colony, the British, given the will, would have eventually taken Canada from the French, despite the crippling financial burden this would have imposed. Murray wrote frequent letters to his brother, George, in Scotland. One in particular, written on 25 May 1760, embodied the hope that the British, after surviving the horrors of the winter and many desperate moments during the French counter-offensive, in the taking, and holding, of Quebec had, at last, achieved something concrete and real. Thanks to the intervention of the Royal Navy, the siege had been lifted, and Murray declared: 'the happy consequence we hope will please our countrymen, as we have given at least uncommon proofs of fortitude of mind, and patience in the most laborious and critical situations that British forces have seen in our time.' These words speak volumes as to the determination of the British to succeed militarily at Quebec in 1759 and 1760, success which assured the fall of New France.

General Amherst sent despatches to Murray which outlined the British plan of attack upon Montreal, now the last citadel of French power. It was to be a multi-pronged attack; after Murray had been re-supplied and reformed his regiments in Quebec, he was to advance along the St. Lawrence, thus approaching Montreal from the northeast. Amherst informed Murray that he could also expect reinforcements from Louisbourg. The second prong, composed of over 3,400 troops, under the command of Brigadier William de Haviland, was to march from Lake Champlain in August, travelling up the St John's river and then north-west to Montreal. The third and strongest prong, of 10,000 regulars and provincial troops, led by Amherst, was to advance from Fort Oswego in early August, move to Fort Frontenac, then journey up the St Lawrence so as to attack from the west, thus completing the encirclement of Montreal.

Throughout the rest of May and June, the British unloaded a mountain of stores at Quebec and Murray used the time to try to restore the health and fitness of his troops. By 13 July, Murray was ready to order the advance towards Montreal and he had somehow managed to cobble together 2,200 men fit for service from the remnants of the garrison. Additionally, Britain's vast resources meant that he had at his disposal 32 armed vessels, nine floating batteries and scores of barges and bateaux. The French defenders of Montreal could make no preparations which could cope with the might of Britain in North America.

Murray soon regrouped his troops and the three forces slowly converged on Montreal. Although his force was not large, it was far superior to the 2,000 men that Lévis had placed to guard the river below the rapids of Richelieu. This tricky stretch of water, with its narrow navigable channel defended by shore batteries, offered the best opportunity of stopping British forces before Montreal, but by 26 July Murray's force had passed the rapids without significant loss and had managed to avoid the French force at Trois-Rivières.

Thereafter, French shore cannon occasionally lobbed rounds at the passing British flotilla, but only the current, contrary winds and the weakening force of the tides slowed its progress. Murray demonstrated his usual ruthlessness by issuing a threat to the Canadians along his route that every farm would be burnt from which the men of the family were absent. His threat had the desired result and the Canadians surrendered in their hundreds and took an oath of neutrality. By the end of August, any forces opposing Murray had simply melted away. He was able to land his troops just north of Montreal at Sorel.

De Haviland imposed a rapid advance upon his troops and, in doing so, successfully cut off Bougainville's force of 1,000 men from their lines of communication with Saint-Jean and Chambly, which left them isolated on the Île aux Noix. Bougainville was forced back first to Saint-Jean and then Montreal, and his force was constantly depleted by desertions. Scouting units from Murray's and de Haviland's advances made contact in early September. Amherst's advance was met with some resistance from small units of French troops, which tried to slow his progress. More of a hindrance were the rapids on the St Lawrence, outside Montreal. Not only did the rapids delay Amherst's advance, but they also claimed the lives of a number of his troops. His battered force finally arrived at La Chine, just nine miles from Montreal, on 6 September.

Lévis now commanded a force of just 3,000 men with which to oppose the combined British army of nearly 17,000 troops. Murray had cut off the city from the east, while Amherst camped his troops to the west. De Haviland approached from the south. When Amherst began to bring up heavy artillery, Vaudreuil held a council of war with Lévis and his other senior officers, at which the hopelessness of the French position was discussed. Seeing no alternative, Vaudreuil began negotiations with Amherst and on 8 September the city, and effectively the whole of New France, capitulated. Following the city's surrender, Amherst despatched Roger's Rangers, and the 60th Regiment, to occupy the French forts in the west, around Detroit and along the Great Lakes. These troops were also tasked to inform the American Indians that the British were now in control of the area. The French regular officers, the majority of their troops, all the senior members of the administration and many of the Canadian nobility and merchants sailed to France in British ships. The farmers and poorest colonists remained, as did Murray, who became military governor and Governor-General until 1766.

The final surrender at Montreal brought a swell of patriotic pride throughout North America, the likes of which would not be seen again. The King, George II, and Amherst were toasted up and down the Atlantic seaboard. In Massachusetts, a day of thanksgiving was proclaimed by Governor Bernard. There were military parades, grand public dinners, fireworks, bonfires, the firing of salutes, carillons from all church bells and a tide of praise, and boasting, from every pulpit in the country. The majority of the colonists in North America had never felt so proud to be associated with the victorious British. In Britain military success was also greeted with rapture, but some of the more perceptive, such as the Duke of Bedford, were aware that the elimination of French power in Canada would alter, in perhaps a very dangerous way, the balance of power between Westminster and the provincial governments in North America.

Although the surrender of Montreal brought the French–Indian War to an end, the larger conflict of the Seven Years' War was to drag on for a further two destructive years. It was finally concluded by the Treaty of Paris, signed by France, Spain and Britain on 10 February 1763. A second treaty ended the conflict between Austria and Prussia five days later. The worldwide conflict was over. The Treaty redrew the map of North

America. France was forced to cede Canada, Nova Scotia and Cape Breton Island to Britain, indeed, all her North American possessions east of the Mississippi, except the city of New Orleans. Sixty thousand Catholic subjects of Louis XV became British nationals, under the British governor, Murray, and his administration. The French Canadians who remained were allowed to keep their laws, language and religion. For America, the Treaty of Paris removed any threat of a French incursion from the north or from the Spanish from Florida. The thirteen English colonies, now freed of their dangerous neighbours, became immediately less dependent on the mother country.

Britain's military success in the Seven Years' War had left her with an apparently lucrative global community but no suitable political structure that was capable of securing an agreed order. Furthermore, she perhaps lacked the willingness or ability to adapt to this challenge. Nowhere was this more apparent than in America. Confusion, misunderstanding, lack of awareness and simple greed were to turn sour the British military success against the French and revolutionary war in North America was barely a dozen years away. This war was again to place the city of Quebec at the very centre of conflict.

3

The Last Bastion

On Thursday, 9 November 1775, Benedict Arnold, American revolutionary commander, peered from the bluffs of Point Lévis, across the St Lawrence River, at the citadel of Quebec. The city had been the target of Arnold and his men for many weeks, as they had toiled across miles of Canadian wilderness to surprise the British and Canadian defenders. The march had been particularly severe and many of the revolutionaries had either died from disease or starvation or had been forced to abandon their efforts. As the snow swirled around Arnold and his advance party, the view of the City must, at times, have been obscured by the weather conditions, but the men would have caught sufficient glimpses for them to know of the magnitude of the task they faced in attempting to storm Quebec. For Arnold, who had helped supply Wolfe and his men in 1759, this was not his first sight of the City. However, for him and his weary, hungry comrades the great stone bulk of the walled fortifications, strengthened since 1760, resting atop what appeared to be an insurmountable cliff, rising to more than 300 feet above the river, must have been daunting. These men, who had endured such hardship, and loss, on their line of march, now had to face an even greater challenge. Quebec, the last bastion of British military and political authority in Canada, was again to take centre stage as the City faced, for the third time in a mere 16 years, another prolonged siege.

What brought Arnold and his men across the Canadian wilderness to attack this stone edifice of British authority? The cause can be traced back to the French surrender at Montreal to Amherst's combined forces in September 1760. That capitulation had witnessed the collapse of New France and the nullification of any threat to America of an incursion from Canada. The victory of 1760 resulted in Britain becoming the dominant power on the North American continent. For the vast majority of her colonial subjects, who were resident in the Thirteen Colonies of America, British military success was met with jubilation, yet it would not take long for pride to turn to resentment among a significant number of Americans.

The year 1760 was indeed the high point of American patriotism towards its imperial master. The thought of secession, and independence, seemed far from every mind. John Mellen, pastor of the Second Church in Lancaster, Massachusetts, spoke for many when he preached: 'Let us fear God and honour the King and be peaceable subjects of an easy and happy government.' Thomas Foxcroft, preaching at the Old Church in Boston, gave thanks for the British victory and the colonists' deliverance: 'Canada must be conquered or we could hope for no lasting quiet in these parts.'

Pastor Ezra Stiles went even further to proclaim his feelings of loyalty: 'All the New England sects are loyal, but the principles of loyalty to the illustrious House of Hanover [the ruling British monarchy] are inculcated on the people of Congregational Clergy with peculiar sincerity, faithfulness and constancy.' When the news arrived at the end of 1760 of the death of George II and the accession of the young king, George III, the new sovereign, and likewise his Secretary of State, William Pitt, was toasted with unqualified loyalty and sincere enthusiasm throughout the Thirteen Colonies of America. Such feelings were soon to be tested and were found to be wanting.

Britain, as an imperial power in North America, had to face a number of obstacles, with the issues of security and of its crushing debts the most prominent and immediate. The nation had amassed a huge deficit as a result of her commitment and participation in the Seven Years' War. By 1763, the war debt amounted to £137 million and on this the annual interest alone was £5 million. This was a huge figure, especially when compared to Britain's ordinary peacetime budget of only £8 million per annum. The French–Indian Wars had cost a vast £60 million, which included £1 million paid in compensation to those of the New England colonies who had made a real effort to contribute their own men and resources to the successful conclusion of the War. However, one of the main issues was that the Thirteen Colonies had been reluctant to become too heavily involved in the conflict and, apart from a few notable exceptions such as the Rangers, the supply of both men and materials from the colonists had not been equal to their own wealth or manpower. Amherst had been very reliant on British regulars to defeat the French, and the events of 1763 made it appear very likely that British troops would have to remain to provide security for the colonial inhabitants of North America.

The British had inherited a growing American Indian problem because colonists were ever tempted to push westwards to open up the interior for settlement, and this placed them in direct conflict with the indigenous peoples. As early as 1761, representatives of numerous tribes, including the Six Nations, demanded an audience with the governor of Pennsylvania to air their grievances as to the encroachment onto their lands. Amherst was determined to maintain peace and did much in his power to support the native Americans. The Ohio valley was a particular area of contention and Lieutenant Colonel Bouquet became very unpopular among the colonists for arresting whites who had entered the area illegally. Despite these efforts, the areas involved were vast and the number of British troops small, so many settlers were able to avoid the British troops, only to find that they then clashed with the Indians. In such violent disputes, the British frequently found themselves caught between the two parties in the conflict. Indian resentment turned on the British, for they were fearful of the number of frontier forts that the British had erected and garrisoned; tribal leaders began to feel that they were being encircled by the white man.

By late 1762, a number of tribes, including the Seneca, Ottawas, Hurons, Delawares and the Miamis, were in rebellion, although the conflict did not incorporate all tribes. A number of the British forts were attacked and the conflict was named after one Ottawa chief, Pontiac, who besieged Fort Detroit in May 1763. By the end of June, all the British forts along the frontier, and in the newly won territories, with the exceptions of Pitt, Detroit and Niagara, had been seized and their garrisons butchered. Two attempts to relieve Fort Detroit were bloodily repulsed in July. British troops were in short supply, as many had been sent to fight Spanish forces in the Caribbean, and Bouquet could only muster 500 troops to march for the relief of Fort Pitt in August.

News of Bouquet's advance was conveyed to the besieging Indians, who deployed east so as to ambush the approaching British. The two forces clashed at Bushy Run on 5 August, where Bouquet, warned of the likelihood of a surprise attack, placed his troops in a circular defence position to await the onslaught from the Indians. This came in the afternoon and fighting lasted until well into the evening and, although the British suffered numerous casualties, they beat off their attackers. The following day, the British were again attacked and further troops were either killed or wounded. With such losses, Bouquet realized that he could not maintain his position and after a council of war among his surviving officers he decided to feign a retreat in order to draw the enemy away from their forest cover. His plan worked magnificently; he was even able to conceal a company of Highlanders from view and as the Indians pursued the supposedly retreating British they were hit by a volley and then a bayonet charge to their flank, and the rest of Bouquet's force was able to pour a coordinated fire into them. This was also followed by a spirited bayonet charge which left the British masters of the field. Fort Pitt was relieved on 10 August. The siege of Fort Detroit continued until October, when Pontiac and his warriors, tired of their work, simply lost interest and melted away and after the battle of Bushy Run the British frontier forts were never challenged by the rebellious Indians again.

Pontiac's War forced the British government to reassess its policy to its newly conquered territories. A Royal Proclamation of 1763 set out that the French settlements north of New York and New England were to be known as the new colony of Quebec, and that all other lands not encompassed within this area was to belong to the American Indians. Colonial governments that had claimed land in these regions, such as Virginia and Pennsylvania, were no longer allowed to grant land to settlers in the area; only the representatives of the Crown could negotiate with the Indians for the sale of land. No whites were allowed to settle in the region and those already present were ordered to withdraw east of the Appalachian Mountains, along a badly defined and hastily drawn line, which placed many of the original settlers within Indian reservations. The authority to ensure compliance with these orders was invested in the Commander-in-Chief of the Army, based in New York, assisted by the governor of each colony, who was also appointed by the home government. Although the Proclamation failed to settle the Indian uprising, it did managed to alienate many of the colonists from the Thirteen Colonies, who felt that they had a right to settle on this disputed Indian land. In addition, at the outbreak of the American Revolution many of those who answered the initial call to arms came from the frontier settler communities who felt betrayed by the British in their dealings with the Indians. They had found the British unresponsive and disdainful of their grievances and it was this, rather than concerns over British economic policies and parliamentary representation, that led such men as

Matthew Smith to journey from the then wilds of the Ohio valley to join the Continental Army outside Boston in 1775.

The difficulties which the home government faced from the Indian uprising resulted in the recall to Britain of Amherst, who was replaced by Bradstreet in late 1763. By the summer of 1764, several of the offending tribes had settled their disputes and received more concessions. Three tribes held out and these were militarily subdued by Bradstreet and Bouquet and, by the end of the year, peace had been restored to the frontier. However, one message from the tribal rebellions which the British well understood was the need for a substantial standing army of regulars in America, not only to maintain the peace and police the disputed areas, but also to provide security and protection to the colonists. The peacetime army eventually became twice the size of the British force in America before the outbreak of the Seven Years' War and the cost of maintaining its presence exceeded over £300,000 per annum. The British government felt that, with the pressing need to reduce its massive wartime debt combined with the reluctance of the colonists to meet their own defence, the cost of maintaining an army in America should be met by those who would benefit from the security it provided. This of course implied direct taxation of the colonists.

It is doubtful whether more than a handful of British politicians considered the implications of imposing direct taxation on the Thirteen Colonies. Few would have doubted Parliament's right, and competence, to take such action for, by the 1760s, British parliamentarians viewed Westminster as an imperial legislature, with the right to exert its authority across the empire. Of course, the raising of revenue, via taxation, would have been seen as central to Parliament's power and it would not have been felt unreasonable that the colonies should contribute to the cost of their own protection.

In 1763, the first minister, George Grenville, began a drive to raise revenue to support the standing army in America by trying to reduce the weaknesses in the Navigation system. Absentee customs officials were ordered to their posts and instructed to be vigilant in the collection of custom duties, and the Royal Navy was given the brief to be more active in its control of smuggling. In 1764, Grenville introduced the Sugar Act, which was designed further to curb the colonies' smuggling and corruption and added a list of colonial products that had to be exported directly to Britain, such as sugar and tobacco, as well as hides, iron and timber. Import duties on such items as cloth, wine, coffee and sugar were also imposed by the Act. Grenville's Sugar Act was not just unpopular for the duties it imposed, but also for the bureaucratic load it placed on American traders. In the following year, Grenville introduced the even more disliked Stamp Act, which sought to extend to America a requirement that was already in existence in England: that of purchasing a revenue stamp to validate official documents, such as marriage certificates, customs forms and even newspapers. In Britain, the stamp was considered not so much a tax but a fee. The colonists did not view it this way.

Although the Stamp Act was undoubtedly hugely unpopular, American resistance to parliamentary taxation was apparent long before this act was passed. At first, colonial opposition was moderate, even conservative; pamphlets were printed and circulated and colonial legislatures despatched petitions and memorials to Parliament and even the King. However, the Stamp Act managed to achieve what even the French–Indian Wars had failed to do, for opposition to it began to bring together the separate colonies so as to unite them against what they perceived to be a British threat. Despite mounting colonial opposition, the royal authorities decided to ignore the various petitions against the Stamp Act and went ahead with its implementation. This unleashed a torrent of anger that swept across the Thirteen Colonies at a rapid and unifying pace. Merchants in the Eastern coast ports pledged to stop importing British goods, in order to bring to bear economic pressure on the British government, pamphlets and newspapers appeared everywhere which condemned Westminster and, at rapidly convened meetings in towns and legislative assemblies throughout America, fierce declarations of opposition were proclaimed. Of even more concern was the fact that even moderates were now openly declaring their opposition to parliamentary rule. For example, Richard Bland of Virginia had been one of the most active and loyal members of the House of Burgesses in supporting Britain throughout the French–Indian War, but even he did not hesitate to freely state his new position:

> I do not deny but that the Parliament, as the stronger power, can force any laws it shall think fit upon us; but the inquiry is not what it can do, but what constitutional right it has to do so: and if it has not any constitutional right, then any tax respecting our internal policy, which

may hereafter be imposed on us by Act of Parliament, is arbitrary, as depriving us of our right, and may be opposed.

Britain was losing the battle of hearts and minds.

It is not surprising that, in such an atmosphere of anger and perceived unfairness, questions began to be raised as to the constitutional relationship between the colonies and Britain. As worrying for the British was the fact that an element of thuggery began to appear. The distributors of the stamps were burnt in effigy and their houses were frequently vandalized. Some were intimidated into resigning. Colonial governors began to report a breakdown of law and order in many of the major towns. A shadowy group, known as the Sons of Liberty, surfaced throughout the colonies and began to coordinate opposition to the Stamp Act. Some of the more extreme members of the group expressed a willingness to adopt armed resistance to British rule if necessary. The constitutional issue was formally raised in the spring of 1765, at a meeting of the Virginia House of Burgesses, which had been called so as to adopt a series of resolutions to denounce parliamentary taxation and to assert the colonists' right to be taxed only by their elected representatives. The resolutions were introduced by Patrick Henry, who used the opportunity to suggest that parliamentary rule was tantamount to tyranny. Although most of Henry's more extreme views were not adopted by the legislature, they were widely reported, and to many colonists it appeared that Virginians had virtually claimed their legislative independence from the home government. Such boldness became contagious and the Rhode Island assembly was next in declaring the Stamp Act unconstitutional and authorized its officials to ignore it. Matters were taken further in October 1765, when delegates from nine colonies met in New York, in the Stamp Act Congress, which issued a series of formal declarations that denied Parliament's right to tax them.

Ultimately, however, it was the power of the mob that saw the demise of the Stamp Act. In August 1765, an angry crowd wrecked the offices, and attacked the home, of Andrew Oliver, the stamp distributor for Massachusetts. The following day, Oliver abandoned all attempts to enforce the act. Violence spread throughout the colonies and local groups of the Sons of Liberty were frequently at the heart of the conflict. It was not long before a network of correspondence was in place to control opposition. In Britain, a new administration, under Rockingham, was prepared to retreat in the face of such coordinated attacks, as well as happy to distance itself from the policies of Grenville. In February 1766, Parliament repealed the Stamp Act.

Although the immediate crisis was averted, the relationship between Britain and her American colonies had been irreversibly damaged and respect for British authority had been lost. However, there remained a continued need for more revenue and British officials concluded that, if the colonies would not accept direct taxation, then Parliament would have to gather taxes via the more traditional methods of custom duties. Thus, in 1767, the then Chancellor of the Exchequer, Charles Townshend, imposed new duties on glass, paper, paint and tea imported into the colonies. In terms of revenue received, this action saw an increase in revenues to £7,000 per annum, as opposed to only £2,000 per annum that had been collected before 1764. However, this still meant that the British government was footing the vast majority of the annual bill for maintaining the army in America.

After the Stamp Act, Americans had become sensitive to all forms of British taxation and Townshend's duties soon met resistance. Pamphleteers, such as John Dickinson, in his *Letters from a Farmer in Pennsylvania*, again defended American liberties and rejected parliamentary taxation. In March 1768, the port of Boston formed an association to boycott British goods and this idea soon spread to other ports. By 1769–70, such non-importation agreements had cut British sales to the colonies by two-thirds. In February 1768, the Massachusetts House of Representatives issued a circular letter to the other twelve colonial legislatures which denounced the Townshend duties as an unconstitutional violation of the principles of no taxation without representation. When Lord Hillsborough, the newly appointed secretary of state of the American Department, ordered the Massachusetts House to revoke and withdraw its letter, the House refused. The Governor, Francis Bernard, therefore dissolved the assembly. This was seen by many Americans as provocative and mob violence broke out across Massachusetts. British officials, particularly in Boston, were targeted by angry crowds and they pleaded for military assistance to quell the violence. Hillsborough authorized the despatch of two regiments of troops from Ireland, which began to arrive in October. This act marked a serious escalation of events; for the first time British troops were being used to enforce authority in the colonies. By 1769, there were nearly 4,000 troops in Boston, a city then of just 15,000 inhabitants. Relations between the Bostonians and the British regulars were far from cordial and the troops were frequently verbally abused and harassed by mobs of agitators. The tensions aroused spilled over on 5 March 1770, when a party of eight British troops fired on a threatening crowd, killing five of them. The 'Boston Massacre' aroused passions still further and it became not only a symbol of revolutionary vigour but also of the ineffectiveness of the British government's authority, which now had to resort to troops to control its colonial subjects.

By 1770 it was apparent that, like Grenville before him, Townshend's attempts to raise revenue from the American colonies were a dismal failure. Since their introduction, the Crown had gathered less than £21,000 in taxation from them, while the loss to British business and commerce, due to the success of the non-importation movement, was estimated at £700,000. A newly reorganized administration, under Lord North, wasted no time in repealing the Townshend duties, for they were clearly, in the words of Lord Hillsborough, 'contrary to the true principles of commerce'. Britain appeared to be increasingly powerless in her dealings with the American colonies and, although many politicians, on both sides of the Atlantic, called for a return to cordial relations, the damage had been done; the prominent feeling among thousands of American colonists was one of suspicion towards Britain. Furthermore, many were now ready to believe that their rights, future and liberties lay away from Westminster. Although the Townshend duties were repealed by Lord North's administration, he considered that the duty on tea should be retained, almost as a symbol of the 'supremacy of Parliament, and an efficient declaration of their right to govern the colonies'.

For the next three years something of an uneasy calm rested over the Thirteen Colonies. Although there were no direct confrontations between the British and the colonists, this did not mean that discontent had been nullified. Boston continued to lead the way in revolutionary fervour. Samuel Adams was at the heart of committees of correspondence, and he, and others, ensured that the proceedings and meetings of the Bostonian committees were widely circulated. At the end of 1772, these views were published in an inflammatory document entitled *The Votes and Proceedings*, which listed all those British acts which the committees considered had violated American rights. These included direct taxation without consent and the use of a standing British army to control agitation and protest. The document was widely debated throughout Massachusetts and, before long, across the Thirteen Colonies. By the end of 1773, independence was being widely debated, even on the pages of the colonial newspapers, and, with the North government still maintaining the belief in the sovereignty of Parliament, further confrontation, and possible conflict, seemed likely.

The crisis was further deepened when Lord North imposed the Tea Act, an additional tax on tea. This was an attempt to increase revenues for the British East India Company, with the ultimate aim of undercutting the Dutch tea supply and passing the surplus tea onto the Thirteen Colonies. Of course, this act of commerce was interpreted very differently by the colonists, who viewed it as yet another attempt to undermine their liberty. In December 1773, a number of Company ships arrived in Boston harbour, loaded with tea. The ships were boarded at night by a group of men disguised as Native Indians, led by Samuel Adams. In an act that became notorious as the 'Boston Tea Party', the mob discharged much of the cargo, to the value of £9,000, into the harbour. The response of the British government to this act, and a number of smaller episodes which clearly demonstrated increasing contempt for royal authority, was to pass the Coercive Acts in 1774. These were a series of measures to try to restore order across the colonies, but particularly in the rebel heartland of Massachusetts. North, and many British politicians, failed to appreciate the depth of suspicion and mistrust that now existed in the colonies and believed that by arresting a few prominent and active individuals, such as Adams and John Hancock, and by keeping control of the mob, order and control would be restored.

The Boston Port Act of 1774 closed the port of Boston to overseas trade, and this was enforced by a Royal Navy blockade. North hoped that this would persuade the people of Boston to compensate the British East Indian Company for its losses. For the Americans, the drinking of tea now became a symbol of disloyalty. Lieutenant General Thomas Gage was appointed the new Governor of Massachusetts and he marched into Boston at the head of an army of 3,500 regulars to restore order. The British Government had completely misread the situation and, rather than restoring and maintaining control, the Coercive Acts inflamed the colonies and provoked open rebellion. Any remaining semblance of respect for royal authority now evaporated. By the end of 1774, many of the colonies' local committees were running and regulating various aspects of American life and commerce. Royal governors could only stand helplessly by as a new informal government literally emerged around them. These new institutions varied from simple town or county committees to provincial congresses and a general congress of the colonies. The First Continental Congress was convened in Philadelphia in September 1774 and it was quickly hijacked by those radicals who were keen to break the imperial bond with Britain. Again, Samuel Adams was prominent, as was his cousin John Adams, and also Patrick Henry, from Virginia, one of many from that colony who pushed for outright resistance to the Coercive Acts. The Congress drew back from endorsing outright independence, but did recognize the new local authorities that were springing up all over the country by establishing the national Continental Association to coordinate activities. This new body instructed all Committees in each of the counties to recognize the 'enemies of American liberty' and to 'break off all dealings' with them.

British parliamentary rule was fast becoming extinct in North America. However, there was one area in which such authority was still recognized, even respected, and that was Quebec. To the indignation of the American radicals, it was here that Britain now introduced the Quebec Act, which was to further alienate the colonists and would become just one more nail in the coffin of British rule in the Thirteen Colonies. It would also place Quebec directly in the sights of those revolutionaries who viewed the city as a bastion of British rule and authority, and which would thus have to be targeted in any future armed conflict.

Sir Guy Carleton had entered the army in 1742 and, in 1758, he served at the siege of Louisbourg, where he acted as quartermaster-general to his friend, James Wolfe. On the Plains of Abraham he commanded the grenadiers and received a wound. He later distinguished himself at the siege of Havana, where he was again wounded. In 1766, he was appointed Lieutenant Governor of Quebec, and succeeded James Murray as Governor of Quebec in 1768. Carleton continued the policies of his predecessor by which the Crown had tried to assimilate the French Canadian population by the introduction of a constitution which recognized their customs, language and Roman Catholic religion. With the recall of Murray, the small minority of British merchants, located primarily in Montreal and Quebec, had hoped that they would be able to obtain substantial political influence within the legislature of the colony and they had high hopes that Carleton would be sympathetic to their desire for greater prominence in the running of Canada. Carleton, however, believed that the best way to reduce the risk of further French military involvement in Canada was to provide the king's French Canadian subjects with employment in both the armed service and administration of Canada and to conciliate the leaders of their community, the noblesse and the clergy. Carleton believed that this could be best achieved constitutionally. In 1770 he returned to England on leave, and this gave him the opportunity to better direct his efforts to gain parliamentary approval for the Quebec Act.

It is hard to believe that Carleton was not driven by reasonableness and fairness in his desire to see the ratification of the Quebec Act, an Act which can also be viewed as far-sighted, even enlightened. However, in 1774 it was viewed by many in the Thirteen Colonies as yet another British attempt to intimidate and surround the American population. Initially Carleton had to overcome much opposition to the Act in Britain for in granting emancipation to Catholics in Canada the Act was well in advance of its time, and it was not until 1774 that Carleton was able to convince both Parliament and the King to pass it. The French population were not only given the right, in law, to exercise their Roman Catholic religion, but the system of tithe collection for the church was maintained. Also retained was French civil law, which operated without juries, and the legislature was to be conducted through the governor and a nominated council of around twenty French Canadians, without an elected assembly. Some taxes were still to be raised by the British Parliament.

For the British minority of around 2,000, living among a Canadian population of 90,000, it seemed that the Act denied them the rights available to every Englishman, notably the right to trial by jury and the right to be taxed only by their own representatives. Additionally, and perhaps most importantly for some of the individuals concerned, it excluded the vocal minority of British merchants from power within the legislature. Men such as John McCord, of Quebec, became one of the leaders of the opposition to the Act and a committed enemy to Carleton, while Thomas Walker, of Montreal, led unrest against the Act in that city. Walker was later to become the principal agent of Congress in Montreal and was to collaborate with the Americans in 1775.

However, it was in the Thirteen Colonies that the Quebec Act aroused the greatest suspicion and, for many, this centred on the British recognition of the Roman Catholic Church in Canada. For those intent on severing the ties between America and Britain, the fears of Catholicism gave them a further opportunity to vilify the British parliament. The colonial press was particularly hysterical and its sectarian utterances simply played upon the fears of the colonists. The *Newport Mercury*, in November 1774, stated that Lord North was soon to visit Rome, with a view to claiming a cardinal's hat from a grateful Pontiff. Alexander Hamilton, a future father of the American Republic, claimed that the Quebec Act would lead to the Protestant colonies being surrounded by 'a nation of Papists and Slaves', while others, such as Josiah Quincy, proclaimed that Britain, via the Quebec Act, had entered into a secret pact with France to restore Canada to her old masters.

For all the perceived fear, and hysteria, the greatest impact that the Quebec Act had upon America was geographical. The Act sought to redraw the western boundaries of the colony of Quebec as far west as the Mississippi. Carleton's justification for incorporating this into the Act was that the new boundary would encompass land treaties made between the British government and Indian tribes following the end of the Seven Years' War. The laws and rights described in the Act would apply in this new area, which recognized that many of the Indian tribes west of the Appalachian mountains had been allied to France, and had been influenced by French customs and many had converted to the Catholic church. This element of the Act can also be viewed as a ploy, on the part of the British, to maintain harmonious relations with the tribes. The inclusion into the Act of the new boundary effectively put an end to any westward expansion by American colonies, particularly Virginia, Pennsylvania and New York. It also put to an end to lucrative land speculation, especially in the Ohio valley and in the proposed Vandalia colony. Speculators, such as Patrick Henry, Israel Putnam and George Washington, saw their stock become worthless. For influential men such as these, the Act had firmly hit their own pockets and this provided an additional justification for them to contest parliamentary rule.

For all the suspicion and fear, as well as economic loss, inflicted by the Quebec Act upon the American colonies, the Act's greatest contribution to the now impending military conflict was to make many members of Congress, and many British merchants in Canada, realize that they had a common cause: opposition to parliamentary rule. Furthermore, this realization convinced some in Congress to see Canada as a potential ally in its expected conflict with Britain, and overtures began to be sent to the British minority community in both Montreal and Quebec. In October 1774, the members of the Continental Congress addressed a long-winded homily to the people of Canada in which they were invited to join the American people so as to win freedom and gain representative government. The address concluded with a warning, perhaps even a threat, to Canadians that it might be dangerous to reject the liberal invitation of Congress: 'You are a small people, compared to those who with open arms invite you into a fellowship. A moment's reflection should convince you which will be most for your interest and happiness, to have all the rest of North America your unalterable friends, or your inveterate enemies.'

Copies of Congress's address were sent, in both French and English, to Thomas Walker in Montreal, with instructions for him to circulate it as widely as possible. This Walker did and committees of opposition, composed mainly of disgruntled British merchants, formed in Montreal and Quebec. The address was prominently displayed in public places throughout the colony. It was not just Congress that had decided to reach out to Canada, for the Committee of Correspondence in Boston, acting independently, decided to send an agent, John Brown, into Canada. Brown was tasked with ascertaining the level of opposition to British rule and then to report back to both Boston and Congress. Although Brown was able to meet Walker, and to speak to many merchants in Montreal, he was unable to convince them to openly declare their opposition to British rule, for fear of losing trade, nor could he convince them to send delegates to the Congress. Brown concluded that the time was not ripe for these dissenters to take positive action. From a military point of view, Brown's journey was not wasted, for as he travelled past the British garrisons at Ticonderoga, Crown Point and Saint-Jean he was able to note how weak, both in numbers of troops and supplies, the British were. Brown advised Samuel Adams that Ticonderoga, in particular, 'must be seissed as soon as possible should hostilities be committed by the King's troops'. In September 1774, Carleton had been forced to concede to General Gage's immediate request for the despatch of two regiments of regulars, the 10th and 52nd, to Boston to deal with the increasing level of unrest there. Carleton was left with only two under-strength regiments, the 7th and 26th, to maintain order in the whole colony of Quebec. Canada was dangerously short of troops and apparently very vulnerable.

By the end of 1774, the British government had concluded that, with its loss of authority, war between Britain and the Thirteen Colonies was becoming a real possibility. In November, the King informed Lord North that 'The New England governments are in a state of rebellion and blows must decide whether they are to be subject to the Country or Independent', and North too began to see no alternative but to use force to bring the colonists to their senses. The start of 1775 saw British military preparations gather apace. The British government, still believing that it was only dealing with mobs stirred up by seditious troublemakers, in December 1774 ordered the British Commander-in-Chief, General Gage, to arrest rebel leaders and to break up known stores of military ordnance. The Earl of Sandwich, speaking in the House of Lords, claimed that the colonists were 'raw, undisciplined, cowardly', and that, furthermore 'The very sound of a cannon would carry them off as fast as their feet could carry them'. However, Gage considered his local forces to be insufficient to deal with even a weak threat and he therefore ordered a concentration of British troops at Boston, consequently depleting the Canadian garrison. By the spring of 1775, nearly thirteen battalions of British infantry were based in and around Boston.

The town of Concord, Massachusetts, just 16 miles north-west of Boston, had been on a war footing for several months. A British spy, John Howe, alerted Gage to the fact that a large cache of weapons and ammunition were being stored there. On 18 April 1775, Gage ordered approximately 650 troops, under the command of Lieutenant Colonel Francis Smith, of the 10th Foot, and Major John Pitcairn, of the Marines, to proceed overnight to Concord, hoping to achieve an element of surprise, to destroy the cache and arrest any rebels. This was despite Howe's warning to Gage that only a fast-moving cavalry force, at least 500 strong, had any hope of conducting the operation successfully. Gage, however, possessed no cavalry. At 6 a.m. on the morning of 19 April, the British force came face-to-face with around 70 American militiamen, under the command of Captain John Parker, a veteran of British service in the Seven Years' War, who had positioned themselves on Lexington Green to oppose the British advance on Concord. After a stand-off, the British moved forward and a shot was fired, it is not known by whom. Thus began the American War of Independence, which would soon draw Quebec into its orbit of operations.

Following this initial skirmish, Pitcairn and the light infantry moved on to Concord to destroy the cache. This they achieved, despite the appearance of further militia along the route. Finally, sufficient American militiamen were mobilized and concentrated at Concord so as to offer a real opposition to the British and the weight of fire from the Americans forced the withdrawal of the British back to the main body, where the order was given to return to Boston. The retreating British, despite support from troops sent from Boston, suffered constant sniping, and casualties mounted. Properly trained troops, fully aware of light infantry tactics, could have, almost certainly, kept the Americans out of effective range, but the British suffered about 70 killed and 170 wounded, before they were able to extract themselves.

During the rest of April and into May, the surrounding colonies sent militia reinforcements to Boston and, by the end of May, some 17,000 Americans had effectively bottled Gage's force up in the city. With reinforcements from Britain, Gage felt sufficiently strong to take the two dominant heights overlooking Boston: Dorchester Heights and Charles-town or Breed's Hill, otherwise known as Bunker Hill. On 17 June 1775, 2,500 British troops stormed the well-entrenched American force on top of Bunker Hill. Although the British were ultimately successful, the butcher's bill was too high a price, for 228 troops were killed and a further 800 wounded. All thoughts of storming Dorchester Heights were abandoned and the British remained holed-up in Boston, effectively under siege, for the remainder of the year. Gage was replaced as Commander-in-Chief by General Sir William Howe in October 1775. However, Howe was in no position to offer any support to Carleton, despite the latter's desperate pleas, as the Americans now turned their military attention towards Canada.

One of the many militiamen who journeyed to Boston in April 1775 was Benedict Arnold, a wealthy merchant from Connecticut, who, in a previous incarnation, had supplied the British troops in Canada with both supplies and horses. At the end of 1774, Arnold had been appointed as captain of the 65-strong second company of the Connecticut Governor's Foot Guard. Within 24 hours of hearing the news from Lexington, Arnold and his militiamen seized the contents of the New Haven powder magazine and marched to Boston. On his way, Arnold had a chance meeting with Colonel Samuel Holden Parsons, who was returning from Cambridge to Hartford, Connecticut, to raise some recruits there. Parsons mentioned to Arnold that there was an acute shortage of cannon among the rebel force and that many could be found in the poorly defended British outpost at Ticonderoga. This news fermented an idea in Arnold's mind and, when he reached Cambridge, he was able to convince the Massachusetts Provincial Congress to commission him as a colonel and appoint him to lead an attack upon Ticonderoga. Leaving his militia behind, with instructions to raise the required 500 troops for the mission, he rushed north.

Similarly, Ethan Allen, commander of the Green Mountain Boys, a group of rough, undisciplined thugs who had been terrorizing both the administration and the locals for several years, heard of the weakness of the British position at Ticonderoga, and he too decided to lead his men against the position. When Arnold arrived at Castleton, he discovered Allen, and 200 men, ready to embark on boats across Lake Champlain and attack the fort. Allen and his men refused to acknowledge Arnold's commission, but did, reluctantly, allow the colonel to join their night-time advance of 10 May. The attack was a resounding success and surprise was complete. The garrison of 44 men, under the command of Captain Delaplace, was overwhelmed, without loss and all were taken prisoner. The Green Mountain Boys took full advantage of the fort's rum supply, much to the disgust of Arnold. The captured British cannon would later in the year be hauled overland to Boston by a small army of men led by Henry Knox. After a herculean effort, the ordnance was dragged onto the top of Dorchester Heights, from where its fire played a major role in the British decision to abandon the city in March 1776.

As more of Allen's men were ferried across Lake Champlain, they were sent, under the command of Seth Warner, down the lake to seize the British position at Crown Point. Like Ticonderoga, the British had allowed Crown Point to fall into disrepair and the small garrison, of one sergeant and a handful of men, was in no position to offer any resistance, and this small band of 'caretakers' meekly surrendered. As well as the importance of the captured cannon, and numerous stores, which now fell into American hands, the capture of the two forts gave a huge boost to rebel morale; at the same time their loss was a huge embarrassment to the British. Furthermore, their possession allowed the Americans to consider further operations along the Lake Champlain–Richelieu river route, which had been, for generations, the traditional invasion route into Canada.

In addition to Warner's success at Crown Point, Captain Samuel Herrick marched 30 men on to Skenesboro, to the home of a prominent Loyalist named Philip Skene. Herrick's sudden arrival allowed him to capture Skene's schooner, *Katherine*. Rechristened *Liberty*, Herrick was able to sail his prize into Ticonderoga on 14 May. Whether or not Allen appreciated the strategic significance of his, and his men's acquisitions,

Arnold most certainly did. As his recruits finally began to arrive from Massachusetts, Arnold began to turn his attention to another important British outpost, that of Saint-Jean which guarded the entrance into Canada, across the New York–Canadian border. An attack on the British here would be seen as a serious border incursion and an attack on Canadian soil. There is little doubt that, for a man of Arnold's intelligence, the consequences of such a move against Saint-Jean, or St John's as the British called it, would have been well appreciated, but this did not deter him. Arnold learnt that Saint-Jean was not only poorly guarded, but also was home to a 16-gun British sloop, *George III*, which was reportedly packed with stores. Acting on his own initiative, Arnold commandeered *Liberty* and, on 17 May, he was able to capture the fort, its 14-man garrison and the sloop, which he named *Enterprise*. Warned by local Canadian sympathizers, such as Joseph Binden, that British regulars were on their way from Montreal, Arnold sensibly decided to avoid a confrontation and sailed south with his spoils.

At first, it appears that Congress was not sure whether it should celebrate or condemn Allen's and Arnold's successes. There were even some members of the Congress who considered that both Ticonderoga and Crown Point should be returned to the British, to appease Canadian fears, and that both commanders should be disavowed, for the seizure of the forts went firmly against the pronouncements of many that arms would only be taken up for defensive purposes. Those in Congress who still hoped for reconciliation with Britain realized that Arnold's action at Saint-Jean, in particular, would stand as a major obstacle in the way of any hopes for peace talks. On 1 June, in an attempt to reassure the Canadian population, Congress went even so far as to declare openly that an invasion of Canada was contrary to its aims. Arnold was appalled to hear that his actions were being condemned by some in Congress, and even more shocked that the return of the forts was being seriously considered. He wrote an assessment to Congress at the end of May, in which he highlighted the strategic importance of Ticonderoga for the British, as a supply base from which they could launch an invasion into New York from Canada, and he went even further by informing Congress that the fort could be used as a forward base for any future incursions by the Americans into Canada. Arnold was not alone in his thinking, for the Massachusetts Provincial Congress held the same opinion. It seems that the New Englanders, in particular, feared that Quebec, and the St

Lawrence, could be used by a large, well-trained army of regulars, sent from England, from which to launch an advance into the Richelieu river valley. The army could then journey south across Lake Champlain and down through the Hudson River Valley to New York City. Such a move would cut New England off from the rest of the provinces and expose the rebels there to the risk of being defeated piecemeal by the British.

By the middle of June 1775, Congress had been completely won over by the strategic argument not only to retain the captured forts, but to use them as a springboard for an invasion of Canada. Congress had finally appreciated the danger of allowing the British to regain the forts, and had also been convinced of the argument that an incursion into Canada, and the seizure of Montreal, would effectively bring to an end any threat of British military action upon New York on the Lake Champlain front. If the reports emitting from Montreal, from the likes of Walker and Binden, were to be believed, then it was likely that the gates of Montreal would be swung open to welcome the American troops, and the chance that Quebec would become the fourteenth rebel colony would be high. If this were to happen, then the likelihood of British reinforcements being able to attack America from the north would be nullified. An invasion seemed to be worth the dangers and risks involved.

Arnold set to work to devise an invasion plan, using no more than 2,000 troops. On 13 June, he was in a position to submit a draft to Congress. Saint-Jean, and nearby Chambly, would be invested by 700 men, while a further 300 would defend the lines of communication. The major force, of 1,000 soldiers, would bypass the Richelieu forts and advance with all speed to Montreal, where they would be welcomed with open arms by the Canadians. With Montreal in American hands, it would only be a matter of time before Quebec would be forced to surrender. Carleton, with so few troops and with little hope of reinforcements from Britain until the spring of 1776, would be unable to oppose the proposed invasion.

Arnold's plan appealed both to Congress and to the new Commander-in-chief of the American army, George Washington. However, neither he, nor Congress, would entrust the plan to its originator. On 27 June, Arnold was crestfallen to hear that, although his plan was to be adopted, command of the invasion force, to be known as the Separate Army, was to be given to Major-General Philip Schuyler, a blue-blooded, landed New York gentleman, who had served as deputy quartermaster-general in the French–Indian War. Arnold was bitterly disappointed and became more

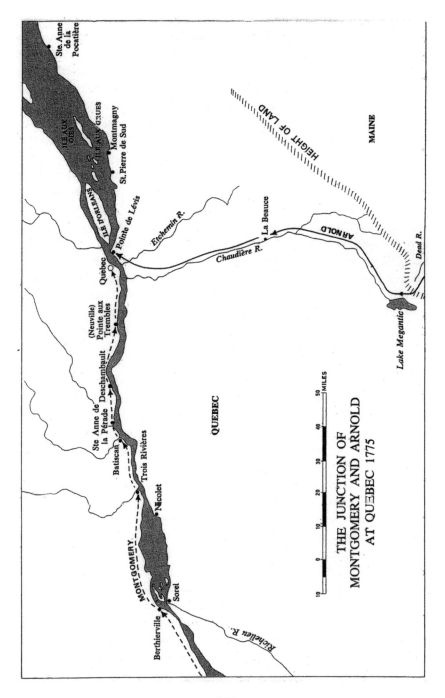

THE JUNCTION OF
MONTGOMERY AND ARNOLD
AT QUEBEC 1775

so when he learnt that Schuyler's second in command was to be Brigadier General Richard Montgomery. Like many participants of the American War of Independence, Montgomery was a veteran of the French–Indian War, and had seen service at Louisbourg and Montreal. He ended the Seven Years' War with the rank of Captain and had served alongside Carleton during the siege of Havana. He disliked the peacetime life of an officer in England and, in 1772, he emigrated to New York. In 1773 Montgomery married the daughter of a prominent local landowner and quickly established himself in local society. Despite being in the colony for less than three years, he was appointed to represent Dutchess County at the New York Provincial Congress and, in 1775, he was nominated by this body to the post of Brigadier General. He appears to have been a rather reluctant rebel for, on both occasions, his nominations were made without his prior knowledge. Even so, he did accept them and he would soon face his old comrades in battle.

Congress authorized General Schuyler 'to Take or Destroy all Vessels Boats or Floating Batteries prepared by Governor Carleton on or near the waters of the Lakes, and to Take possession of St John's and Montreal if he finds it practicable, and not Disagreeable to the Canadians'. This directive signed by John Hancock and despatched to Schuyler by express, encouraged the general to make necessary preparations without delay. That the projected invasion would add a new dimension to the existing situation apparently did not occur to members of Congress; indeed, most thought the Americans would be welcomed. 'The Canadians absolutely refuse to join Carleton, and the Indians assure us that they will observe strict neutrality.' Hancock did, however, caution Schuyler to proceed to Montreal and Quebec only if circumstances seemed to favour success. In Britain the invasion would be viewed as a wanton act of aggression, and it aroused much hostility. The King wrote to North that 'to invade a province to which they can lay no claim, nor pretend no right, seemed such an outrage, as it not only overthrew every plea of justifiable resistance, but would militate with the established opinions, principles and feelings of mankind in general.'

Schuyler arrived at Ticonderoga on 18 July, only to discover everyone, including the sentries, asleep and the fort a scene of utter confusion. The logistical systems, vital for a successful invasion, were non-existent, as was the discipline and training of the troops there. Schuyler would need all his experience, acquired from his service in the French–Indian War, to transform his command into a well-supplied, disciplined, cohesive force. This, of course, took time, and it was not until 2 September that the Separate Army was able to venture out of Ticonderoga on its invasion of Canada. Even then, after weeks of training, Schuyler could only describe his force as 'rough and ready'. He did, however, use the delay to gain useful information as to the disposition of Carleton's meagre forces and the spy John Brown was able to confirm that Montreal would be likely to welcome, rather than oppose, the Americans.

News of Allen's and Arnold's attacks upon the British border forts did not reach Governor Carleton at Quebec until 20 May. He at once hurried south to Montreal, with fusiliers of the 7th Regiment and a detachment of the Royal Artillery, to assess the situation. Carleton decided to make Montreal his new headquarters and he wasted no time in strengthening the city's defences. He quickly realized that the regular forces at his disposal were completely inadequate to the threat he now faced and that he would be reliant on a militia to boost his numbers. Writing from London, the Earl of Dartmouth, Secretary of State for the Colonies, had already urged Carleton to raise a force of 3,000 militiamen, but all attempts to raise such a force met with reluctance and inertia. Despite the urgent situation in Montreal, Carleton's pleas for recruits, even with the active support of Bishop Briand of Quebec, had little response. Certainly, in the British merchant community, there was outright hostility towards Carleton, with some, such as Walker and Price, actively engaged in treasonable correspondence with Congress, and among the Canadian population few seemed willing to come forward. While some young men expressed a willingness to help the British garrison at Saint-Jean, and Carleton had no difficulty in attracting carpenters and boat builders to rebuild fortifications, the lack of militiamen meant that Carleton would certainly have insufficient troops with which to defend Montreal from an American invasion.

Although Dartmouth's demands for a militia force 3,000 strong would have brought forth a certain amount of derision from Carleton, at least he could rely on a newly raised regiment of provincial regulars. Commanded by Lieutenant Colonel Allan Maclean, a veteran of Wolfe's successful attack on Quebec, the Royal Highland Emigrants were a collection of former soldiers from Fraser's Highlanders and the Black Watch, who had served in the French–Indian War and had then settled in North America. Maclean had scoured the Mohawk Valley, the Oswego and Canada for recruits, and each man was to receive 200 acres of land, free of rent for twenty years as an inducement of service. This force was to be the cornerstone of Carleton's defence of Quebec.

Just as worrying for Carleton as his shortage of troops was the perilous condition of his fixed fortifications along the expected invasion route. Montreal possessed only an inadequate citadel, surrounded by a crumbling stone wall, which could not be expected to offer much resistance, while Fort Saint-Jean also needed much attention. Carleton, however, decided to place his faith in the border post of Saint-Jean for he knew that he could ill afford to allow an invading force to gain too much territory before it was opposed. Despite its poor condition, a stand at Saint-Jean did offer some advantages to Carleton. It was connected by a good road to Montreal, which would allow for the easy passage of both men and materials. An invading force, intent on capturing Montreal, could not easily bypass Saint-Jean and the fort's riverfront location meant that vessels could be launched from there to intercept and attack an American force while it was still on Lake Champlain. Finally, the nearby fortification at Chambly, although not strong, was ideally suited as a base from which to keep the garrison of Saint-Jean well supplied. Carleton thus resolved to repair the fort and to provide it with as strong a contingent of regulars as he could afford to spare, and as many militia as he could entice. If the expected American invasion did not materialize, then Carleton could later use Saint-Jean to launch an attack to recover Crown Point and Ticonderoga.

Carleton entrusted the improvements in the fortifications of Saint-Jean to Captain John Marr, of the Royal Engineers, and, in the short space of time available to him, Marr was able to transform the defensibility of the fort. Into this makeshift, but reasonably strong, post, Carleton placed a force composed of 474 regulars from the 7th and 26th Regiments of Foot, 90 Canadian militiamen, 38 gunners of the Royal Artillery and 20 of Maclean's precious Highlanders. These 662 men were commanded by Major Charles Preston, while Lieutenant William Hunter, of the Royal Navy, was tasked with constructing a river force to oppose the American advance. By the time the enemy appeared, Hunter had prepared a schooner, *Royal Savage*, and two galleys. In his weak position, and with the time available, there seems little more Carleton could have done to prepare his defences. He was paying the price for the British neglect of their frontier forts and for Gage's call to supply the main British force with two regiments from Canada.

Carleton could blame himself for being too tolerant of earlier sedition within Canada and for placing too much reliance on the assumption that the Canadians would answer his call to arms. Furthermore, by placing the vast majority of his regular force behind the walls of Saint-Jean, Carleton was placing all his eggs in one basket. If Saint-Jean fell, he would have few regular reserves with which to oppose the American advance and he would be dependent on an unreliable militia. To make matters worse, Carleton's urgent request for two regiments to be transported from Boston, via the St Lawrence, was rejected by Vice Admiral Samuel Graves as 'impracticable', due to the advanced stage of the season, although the St Lawrence would be free of ice for at least another six weeks. Thus, with so few troops, if Saint-Jean fell, Montreal would also fall and that would leave only a weakly defended Quebec as the last bastion of British rule in Canada and an obvious target of American ambitions.

The American invasion plan of Canada, as approved by Congress, had been expanded in both size and scope under the encouragement of George Washington. It was now to be a two-pronged attack, with the ultimate aim of capturing not just Montreal, but also Quebec and thus expelling the British from Canada. The main invasion force was still to be commanded by Schuyler, but it was now to be required to rendezvous with a separate force of troops that would march overland across the Canadian wilderness to launch a surprise attack on Quebec. If the element of surprise was lost, the second expeditionary force would at least divert a part of Carleton's already thinly spread army and thus relieve some of the pressure upon Schuyler's command. After all his exertions to transform his ill-disciplined men into a cohesive force, Schuyler was now a sick man. He was suffering from a fever and his old bones creaked with rheumatism, but he was determined to lead his troops in the invasion and this he did on 5 September. As the invasion boats approached Saint-Jean, the British, on the parapets of the fort, hurled shots at them. The Americans were able to land in a swampy area a mile from the fort.

This was the first of two unsuccessful attempts to establish the siege of Saint-Jean. On this occasion, an advance party was ambushed by around 100 Indians, friendly to the British, and, although American casualties were light, there is no doubt that this incident tested the resolve of Schuyler's men. By the evening of 5 September, the Americans had built a breastwork beside the river, but the British artillerymen had already found the range. Schuyler was confronted by one Moses Hazen, an enigma of a man, who apparently tried to keep one foot in each of the British and American camps, who informed him of the strength of the British position and the imminent arrival of the heavily armed *Royal Savage*. Furthermore, Hazen led Schuyler to believe that the promised support from the local population would not be forthcoming, which was of particular concern. Spooked by this news, and the events of 5 September, Schuyler pulled his forces back to Île-aux-Noix the following day. Here, Schuyler received a contrary report from James Livingston, an American living near Chambly, who told him of the weakness of Carleton's forces, and crucially, that the invaders would receive support from the locals. Livingston inspired Schuyler to attack Saint-Jean once again and, on 10 September, a force of 1,000 troops, led this time by Montgomery, landed in the woods west of the fort. Again, the Americans were nervous in their advance, and comrades even fired on each other, disorientated in the woods. When a rumour circulated that *Royal Savage* had been sighted, Montgomery was unable to restrain his men and the Americans retired, once more, to the Île-aux-Noix.

After these rather farcical attempts, which had gained the British precious time, Montgomery was now determined to force the siege. Continued illness forced Schuyler to hand over all control to Montgomery and the new commander led his force of 2,000 men, including 40 Canadians, back to Saint-Jean on 16 September. Within two days, despite a clash with British regulars on the road to Montreal, Montgomery had completely surrounded the fort. Preston sent news of his predicament to Carleton in Montreal. Over the following days, Montgomery sent small parties of troops, under the command of Livingston and Ethan Allen, across the nearby Canadian countryside in the hope of raising recruits from the locals. While the Canadians did not oppose the invaders, they were lukewarm to the American presence and it seemed clear that many were waiting to see what Carleton would say or do. The Governor took the decision to do very little, for although, militarily, it was probably correct to maintain his small force in Montreal, for an advance towards Saint-Jean would have been reported to Montgomery and an ambush would have been likely, this sent the wrong message to the Canadians who were hoping for decisive British action.

Preston and his command at Saint-Jean now settled down into the monotony of a siege, and certainly, with their initial superiority in artillery, the British suffered little in the first weeks. Small separate bands of Americans, led by Allen, John Brown and Seth Warner, roamed freely around the countryside between Saint-Jean and Montreal and the apparent lack of opposition led Allen and Brown to consider an independent surprise attack on Montreal, in which Allen clearly hoped for a success similar to that he had achieved at Ticonderoga. The plan that Brown and Allen concocted called for Brown to lead a force of 200 men to attack the city from the south-west, while Allen, advancing from the north with just over 100 troops, including 80 Canadians, would penetrate the city from the north. Allen's men were to inform Thomas Walker of the plan so that he might inspire American sympathizers in Montreal to rise up in their support and open the gates of the city. The advance was planned for the night of 25 September, but it was badly coordinated; Brown's force did not reach the agreed rendezvous and Allen found his force completely isolated. Furthermore, Walker's attempts to rally support were reported to Carleton and British forces were alert. Allen tried to extricate his men, before their presence was noted, but they were discovered lurking outside the city gates and Carleton called on the citizens to rush to the defence of the city. The earlier indifference of the population disappeared at the first signs of a real threat to the city and Carleton was amazed to see 120 French Canadians and 80 British volunteers arm themselves and report for duty. This force, combined with a small number of regulars, sallied out from the city to attack Allen's force. At the sight of troops advancing upon them, many of Allen's troops deserted him and he, and 36 of his men, were captured in the resultant fracas, which saw the death of five Americans and three of Carleton's men. The capture of Allen was a propaganda coup for Carleton, who wasted no time in parading him through the streets in chains, before he was despatched to England to face trial for treason.

The threat to Montreal inspired not just the inhabitants of the city, for over the next weeks French Canadians crowded into the city from the outlying districts to join the militia which they had spurned only days before. Carleton was overwhelmed with the numbers: over 1,200 men arrived from the rural areas, and these troops, combined with the 600 men he could muster in Montreal, plus support from Indians, meant that he could now place 2,000 men in the field. Many thought that this would be sufficient to expel Montgomery from Saint-Jean, but Carleton hesitated to use his new force. Again, he feared ambush, and the American presence in the countryside meant that he had no clear intelligence as to the numbers and location of the enemy. After weeks of inactivity, and subsistence on the King's rations, the militia simply melted back to their farms; there were crops to be harvested and farmsteads to be protected from marauding bands of Americans and disloyal Canadians with the result that Carleton lost his newly won army. He did not remain completely inactive during this period, for many of the American sympathizers in Montreal were rounded up, and the capture and imprisonment of Thomas Walker was a very necessary act. However, it must be considered that Carleton had missed an opportunity to harness Canadian outrage and expel the invaders from Saint-Jean.

For Preston and his command, the situation in Saint-Jean began to deteriorate. Montgomery had, at last, been able to transport the heavier guns from Ticonderoga, and he was now in a position to outgun the British. By 15 October, the American fire had levelled the buildings within the fort, although casualties had been mercifully light, and the defenders were forced to seek sanctuary in the cellars of the ruins. In addition, the invaders had constructed a second battery on the east river bank, opposite the fort, and this threatened the British ships and closed a vital route for supplies. Despite British attempts to attack and destroy this battery, the Americans continued to inflict damage and claimed the notable scalp of *Royal Savage*, which was holed by heated shot and sank with the loss of all its ordnance.

The Americans struck an even greater blow on 18 October, when the British commanding officer at the supply depot of Chambly, Major Joseph Stopford, surrendered the fort, with all its supplies and cannons intact, to a mixed force of 400 Americans and Canadians led by Brown and Livingston. Both Preston and Carleton must have now known that Saint-Jean could not be expected to hold out much longer. The Governor now acted decisively and resolved to make an attempt to relieve the beleaguered Saint-Jean. He instructed Maclean to bring 180 of his Highlanders down from Quebec, to Sorel, and recruit as many militia as he could en route. Carleton proposed to lead a mixed force of regulars, militia and Indians, totalling around 1,000 men, from Montreal so as to rendezvous with Maclean south of Chambly. However, with their almost total control of the Canadian countryside, the Americans were able to oppose the movement of the two British forces. On 30 October, Carleton was confronted by a force of Seth Warner's Green Mountain Boys, armed with cannon captured from Stopford, and was forced to withdraw. Maclean, now commanding a force of 400, learnt of this setback when he reached Sorel. He too met opposition, this time from a unit led by Brown and Livingston, and was also forced to pull back.

Montgomery sent two prisoners, captured from Carleton's force, to Saint-Jean, to try to convince Preston of the hopelessness of his position. So as to heap further pressure on the British, an additional battery, to the north-east, began to unleash fire on the fort on 1 November. Reduced to ever-dwindling salt-rations, with officers who advised their commander that the time had come to surrender, Preston began to negotiate terms with Montgomery. Ever mindful of the need to hold on, Preston dragged the negotiations out for a couple of days, so it was not until 3 November that Preston finally marched his force out of the ruins of Saint-Jean and into captivity. Since Schuyler's first attack, the British garrison had held out for a crucial 60 days and thus left Montgomery with little time to capture both Montreal and Quebec, before the arrival of a Canadian winter put paid to all campaigning. The British had suffered 20 dead, while the Americans had endured 100 combat casualties and Montgomery had been forced to discharge 1,000 men, lost to illness. These men would be greatly missed as the Americans pushed further north.

Governor Carleton learnt of the fall of Saint-Jean on 4 November, by when he also knew that a strong party of Americans were heading for Quebec, across the Canadian wilderness. Aware that Montgomery would be hurrying his men towards Quebec, Carleton placed the garrison, and what supplies he could save, aboard a small flotilla, but delayed its departure for Quebec until the American army was facing him across the St Lawrence at Longueuil. This delay proved an error of judgement, for, although Carleton sailed on 11 November, when the Americans arrived at the gates of Montreal, Montgomery had already despatched a sizeable force, under Easton, Brown and Livingston, on to Sorel, so as to intercept the retreating British force. Meanwhile, Montgomery was prepared to show magnanimity to the demoralized citizens of Montreal and promised everyone that they would enjoy 'the peaceable enjoyment of their property'. After two days of talks, Montgomery and his army marched through the Recollet gate and into Montreal without a shot being fired. Those inhabitants who had supported the American cause were not so inclined to be as gracious as the American commander towards the Canadians, and Montgomery's decision to leave the obnoxious Brigadier-General David Wooster, and his Connecticut troops, in charge of the city, while he continued to Quebec, would severely damage relations. This would later benefit the British.

As the retreating British flotilla approached Sorel, on 12 November, one of the vessels ran aground. By the time the boats could resume their journey the wind had died, the British force were compelled to heave to and here they remained until 15 November. On that day, Carleton was amazed to see the approach of a flag of truce, for he, apparently, had never considered that Montgomery might split his force so as to intercept him. A letter was delivered, from the American commanding officer, Colonel Easton, which called for Carleton to surrender: 'If you will Resign your Fleet to me Immediately without destroying the Effects on Board, You and Your men shall be used with due civility together with women and Children on Board – to this I expect Your direct and Immediate answer. Should you Neglect You will Cheerfully take the Consequences that follow.' In the narrow waters in which he found himself, Carleton could not dismiss the threat out of hand. To add further pressure, Major Brown visited the British ships to invite any British officer to visit the 'grand battery of 32-pounder guns', which were in place to blow the flotilla out of the water. Apparently this invitation was not accepted, which was just as well for it was a ruse on the part of the Americans and no such guns were available. Carleton was left to consider the fate of his force.

Faced with such a crucial decision, whether to surrender or risk running the supposed American batteries, Carleton resorted to indecision and called a council of war of all his officers. While one of the ship captains, Belette, bravely offered to take on the batteries, so that the other ships might escape, others expressed more caution. All agreed, however, that the Governor must return to Quebec, where his presence was vital to rally the defence of the last bastion of British rule in Canada, for all knew that if Quebec fell, the British would be unlikely to be able to launch an invasion from the St Lawrence into America. One of Carleton's ship captains, Jean-Baptiste Bouchette, offered to row the Governor, in a small boat, past the Americans in the dead of night, and then on to Quebec. This offer Carleton accepted, so, on the night of 16 November, the Governor, disguised as a peasant, slipped silently past the Americans.

Carleton's second in command, Brigadier-General Richard Prescott, was left with instructions to destroy all stores and throw the ships' cannons overboard, before either surrounding or attempting to run past the American position. Prescott began negotiations with Easton, who successfully convinced the faint-hearted Prescott that his position was hopeless. On 19 November, Prescott duly surrendered, along with 320 men and the cannons and stores which he had been expressly ordered to destroy. On the same day, Carleton arrived at Quebec only to discover that an American force, under the command of Benedict Arnold, were already in the vicinity. The third siege of Quebec was about to begin.

It is not clear who first formulated the plan for an advance upon Quebec, via a journey across the Canadian wilderness, in an attempt to inflict a surprise attack on the city. One commonly held view is that, soon after the capture of Ticonderoga in May 1775, Colonel Jonathan Brewer, of Massachusetts, in a document entitled 'a Diversion of the Provincial Troops into that part of Canada', proposed leading 500 troops through the Maine wilderness and down the Chaudière river to Quebec. Certainly, Washington was considering such a move in the early summer, but Brewer was seriously wounded at the Battle of Bunker Hill and the idea seems to have faded for a number of weeks. Another theory is that Benedict Arnold first approached Washington with the idea, but what is certainly true is that Arnold quickly made the expedition his. Arnold had made his first journey to Quebec in 1759, when he took a shipload of medical supplies to Wolfe's army besieging the city for his then employer, Dr Lathrop, who had the surgical-supplies' contract with the British. He made many subsequent visits to Quebec, trading anything from barrels to horses, and it was probably on one of these early business trips that he learnt of the expedition, led by the young British officer, John Montrescor, from Quebec to the coast of Maine, in 1761, and of the map that Montrescor made of his route. Montrescor had been tasked by the new Governor, James Murray, to produce a military map of the route. Arnold may even have meet Montrescor in 1759, for the officer of engineers served throughout Wolfe's siege of Quebec. At some point, Arnold obtained a copy of Montrescor's handwritten journal of two trips through the wilderness from Quebec to the Maine coast and back. However, what Arnold did not realize was that it was a common eighteenth-century practice for military map-makers, or explorers, to deliberately alter directions and distances, thus deceiving the enemy and preventing them from using the maps effectively, and the copy he possessed had been so altered. The reliance Arnold would place upon the Montrescor map was to cost lives during the expedition.

There is no doubt that Arnold had been disappointed not to receive a command in Schuyler's Separate Army, but he was not the sort of man to disappear from public life as a result of such a setback and, on 15 August, he was able to obtain a private interview with the Commander-in-Chief, George Washington. While Arnold was happy to provide Washington with his views as to the likelihood of Canadian support for Schuyler's invasion, as well as his estimates of the capacity for Carleton to resist the American advance, Arnold was keen to use the meeting to promote his ideas for an attack upon Quebec. The plan was to launch an attack along an overland route between Quebec and New England, by following the course of two rivers that nearly meet, the Kennebec and the Chaudière, hiking over the high land that separates them along the Quebec boundary, to arrive by these cunning means at the enemy's door. Indians of the Abenaki tribe frequented these waterways and forests, but the military potential was not seriously considered until Montrescor's study. Whether or not Arnold made Washington aware of Montrescor's conclusion, that the route was not suitable for the passage of a large body of troops, is not known.

For several days, Arnold briefed Washington on his plan and, as the two men became better acquainted, both the plan and Arnold's determination appealed more and more to the Commander-in-Chief. Arnold stressed that a second invading force, heading straight for Quebec, would surprise the British, scatter their already thin forces, and might even force the surrender of a poorly defended Quebec without a shot being fired. The need for a speedy decision, and rapid preparations, was also emphasized by Arnold and, although he admitted to Washington that it was late in the season to launch such an assault, Arnold felt that this could work in America's favour, for it would discourage the British from attempting to send reinforcements on ships that might become ice-bound in the St Lawrence. By 20 August, Washington was convinced of the merits of Arnold's proposal and he wrote to Schuyler, then still encamped at Ticonderoga, to seek his approval for a second invasion. Washington explained that the purpose of this expedition 'which has engaged my Thoughts for several days' was to make a diversion that 'would distract Carleton, and facilitate your Views. He must either break up and follow this party to Quebeck, by which he will leave you a free Passage, or he must suffer that important Place to fall into our Hands, an Event, which would have a decisive Effect and Influence on the publick Interests.' Schuyler's enthusiastic response was not received until 2 September, by when plans were well advanced.

Washington knew that the American army was desperately lacking good officers, and in particular men who could lead by example and in Arnold Washington saw a natural leader. On 20 August, Washington appointed Arnold a colonel in the Continental Army, with orders to report directly to him. This removed Arnold from the vagaries of provincial politics, much to his relief. Arnold was the only available candidate to lead the expedition who had previously seen Quebec, yet by 25 August he had still not been formally appointed. However, both Washington and Arnold were working together towards that decision, which seems primarily to have required a positive reply from Schuyler. Furthermore, the whole viability of the operation depended upon whether sufficient boats, to carry both the troops and their supplies, could be constructed in time and this seems to have rested on one Major Reuben Colburn, a landowner on the Kennebec river, and the owner of a shipyard. Colburn and his shipyard were vital to the success of the developing scheme. On 21 August, Arnold had addressed Colburn on behalf of Washington, asking how soon he could have ready 200 light bateaux, each built to carry six or seven men with baggage and provisions. Colburn was also asked to inquire into the quantity of fresh beef that could be had on the Kennebec, and was requested to furnish intelligence about the proposed route, 'get particular Information from those people who have been at Quebec, of the Difficulty attending an Expedition that way, in particular the Number, & length, of the Carrying Places, whether Low, Dry land, Hills, or Swamp'. Such basic questions, asked less than a month before the proposed departure of the expedition, illustrates the haste with which the decision had been made.

While waiting for Schuyler's response, Arnold busied himself making detailed preparations for the advance, from Washington's headquarters at Cambridge, Massachusetts. However, for all his planning, Arnold made a fundamental error in that he estimated the distance to Quebec at just 180 miles. In reality the journey would be over 300 miles. Neither did Washington help matters, for he claimed that the expedition would take just 20 days, at most, to cover the distance and, accordingly, he gave his approval to Colburn to gather food supplies with this timescale in mind. The journey itself eventually took 40 days, and would see soldiers facing starvation by its end. Washington also ordered Colburn's boatyard to start construction on the required quota of bateaux. Logistically the operation was beginning to take shape, but the necessary troops who would be brave enough, if not mad enough, to accept this challenging task had yet to be found.

Once Schuyler's agreement had been received, both Washington and Arnold reacted quickly. On 5 September, Washington called for volunteers from among the troops stationed around Boston 'to go upon command with Colonel Arnold' and those that came forward were to be 'active woodsmen, and well acquainted with bateaux'. As later events would demonstrate, it is clear that some of the volunteers were not totally truthful when asked to meet these criteria. All those interested were to assemble the next morning 'upon the common in Cambridge'. Arnold found himself overwhelmed with volunteers, as many, no doubt, saw the command as a means by which they could escape the boredom and disease of camp life. One such man was Jeremiah Greenman, who was to leave a revealing diary of the hardships that these men faced over the next weeks. Over the next two days, Arnold and Horatio Gates, Washington's adjutant general, selected 786 officers and privates, and these were divided into two regiments of five musket companies each. A veteran of the Seven Years' War, Roger Enos, assumed command of the first battalion and the second went to Christopher Greene, who was from a prominent Rhode Island dynasty. Another 300 troops, mostly frontiersmen from Virginia and Pennsylvania, joined Arnold's command. These men, who had been ordered by Washington to join Arnold because their undisciplined behaviour in camp had caused such disruption, were renowned for their marksmanship and their physical resilience. For example, Captain Daniel Morgan, a veteran of the French–Indian War and Pontiac's Rebellion, had raised a rifle company in Virginia and had marched the 600 miles to Cambridge in just three weeks, and Arnold would come to depend on such men.

Once supplies of coats, blankets, tents and firearms had been issued, Arnold's force, 1,050 strong, including two soldier's wives, marched the 40 miles north-east to Newburyport in two days, assembling there by 13 September. All were eager to make sail to Gardinerston, where they would collect the bateaux from Major Colburn, and eleven sloops were waiting at Newburyport to take the troops on this first part of the journey. Unfortunately, strong Atlantic headwinds meant that the planned departure from the harbour had to be delayed; the first of many frustrations for the expedition. Finally, on 19 September, conditions were such that the small flotilla could depart and, despite choppy seas and

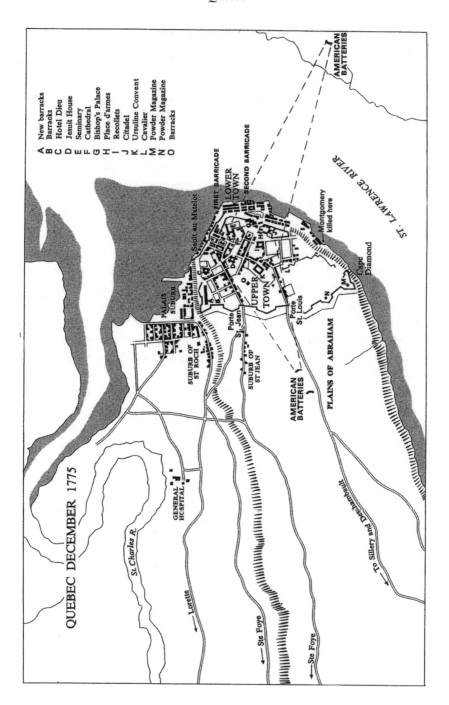

QUEBEC DECEMBER 1775

A New barracks
B Barracks
C Hotel Dieu
D Jesuit House
E Seminary
F Cathedral
G Bishop's Palace
H Place d'armes
I Recollets
J Citadel
K Ursuline Convent
L Cavalier
M Powder Magazine
N Powder Magazine
O Barracks

ST. LAWRENCE RIVER

AMERICAN BATTERIES

FIRST BARRICADE
SECOND BARRICADE
LOWER TOWN
UPPER TOWN
Sault au Matelot
Montgomery killed here
Cape Diamond
Porte St. Louis
Porte St. Jean
PLAINS OF ABRAHAM
AMERICAN BATTERIES
SUBURB OF ST ROCH
SUBURB OF ST JEAN
PALAIS SUBURB
GENERAL HOSPITAL
St. Charles R.
Lorette
Ste Foye
Ste Foye
To Sillery and Desчatiment

much seasickness, all the troops had disembarked at Gardinerston by the evening of 22 September. For many, not used to the perils of the Atlantic at that time of the year, it had been a ghastly start to the expedition.

Before Arnold's departure, Washington issued him with explicit instructions as to the behaviour of his men: the Canadians were to be treated as friends and Arnold was told to try and recruit as many as he could en route. He was to shoot any of his troops found plundering. The Commander-in-Chief also entrusted Arnold with a proclamation. This exhorted the Canadians to overthrow the tyrannical government that Britain had inflicted upon them and assured them that, under American rule, they would enjoy all liberties, including that of religious freedom. Finally, Washington warned Arnold that if he found the Canadians to be hostile, he was 'by no Means to prosecute the Attempt'.

Arnold was presented with the first of many logistical nightmares when he first laid eyes upon the two hundred bateaux which Colburn and his men had constructed. With such a tight deadline, the shipwrights had quickly flung these flat-bottomed craft together and they had been forced to use hastily cut green pine, rather than seasoned wood, and Arnold doubted whether they would be both strong enough and watertight. Apart from being 'very badly built', Arnold noted that the bateaux had been constructed shorter than specified, and to compensate, he insisted that an additional twenty be produced in a mere three days. An embarrassed Colburn complied.

Having gained what limited intelligence he could, Arnold officially launched the expedition on the morning of 23 September, with the despatch of two scouting parties. He then arranged the various companies into four groups, with the idea of placing intervals between each so that they did not become entangled at the many portages, and other likely obstacles, ahead. Morgan's riflemen were the first to embark and these troops were ordered to move as rapidly as possible and 'clear the roads over the carrying places'. Initially, progress was good. By 30 September, Arnold's lead men had reached the crumbling walls of Fort Halifax and, from here to the southern end of the Chaudière River had taken Montrescor only 12 days. Assuming a further eight days to reach Quebec from there, Arnold felt confident his men would seize the lightly defended city by the end of October. However, there were to be many arduous portages en route. The first real test was at Taconic Falls, where every one of the 200 400-pound bateaux had to be unloaded, and both the bateaux and the supplies manhandled over a forest trail of over half a mile. Such work was backbreaking enough for fit men, but as the days progressed, illness, poor diet and physical exhaustion began to take a toll. By the morning of 2 October, Arnold had reached yet another great physical test, that of the Norridgewock Falls, where the Kennebec rose over 90 feet in a series of cascading rapids. It was here that Arnold recognized that the expedition was in trouble.

At the heart of the problem was the rapid disintegration of the poorly constructed bateaux, all of which had begun to leak within six days of departure. One officer expressed the view held by the majority of the men, that 'Could we then have come in reach of the villains who constructed these crazy things, they would fully have experienced the effects of our Vengeance.' Captain Simeon Thayer declared that they were 'villainously constructed' and that the men were always soaked as they had 'to wade half the time'. Furthermore, the leaking vessels had ruined a sizeable portion of their already inadequate food supplies, and much of the salted meat had become rancid. Night-time temperatures had now begun to dip below freezing, causing much hardship for the troops who seemed unable to keep themselves dry. Thayer recorded that his company awoke the morning after the portage of Skowhegan Falls to find their 'clothes frozen a pane of glass thick, which proved very disagreeable'. Fevers and dysentery began to take effect and, by the time Arnold had reached Norridgewock Falls, he could report only 950 effectives.

Arnold called for carpenters to be sent from Gardinerston to make the much-needed repairs to the boats, but this took time, and it was not until 9 October that the expedition could continue. For the next week, Arnold and his men experienced more of the same physical hardship and it was not long before the bateaux were once again leaking. In his journal entry of 16 October, Jeremiah Greenman described the typical terrain the men were having to transverse: 'This morn carri'd all acrost wich was very bad going in sum places half leg deep with mud and mire ware it was not mud and mire it was roks and hils as steep as a hous Side ...' The weather now turned against the expedition; not only were the men suffering from the fall in temperatures, but, from 17 October onwards, it rained almost continuously. On that night, the river rose over 8 feet, flooding the campsite. The men were constantly wet and even more food was ruined. The troops had been able to catch the occasional trout to supplement their meagre rations, but the flooded waterways saw an end to this source of food.

Also, the noise the men made dragging bateaux over portages, and slipping and sliding along muddy forest trails, made game scarce and, although Morgan's men did managed to shoot one moose, this was a rare treat. On 24 October, with his men on half rations, and more and more falling ill, Arnold was forced to hold a council of war of all his officers, to decide whether to carry on or return to Kennebec. All present agreed to continue.

The decision was made that Arnold would proceed onwards with a party of 70 men, so as to obtain supplies, which would then be ferried back to the main body. Greene and Enos would retain only as many men as could be fed for 15 days and all the others, the majority being unfit, would return to Cambridge. Arnold calculated that his force could reach Sartigan, a French settlement on the Chaudière River, within 15 days. Soon after Arnold's departure, Enos announced to Greene that his officers felt that there was insufficient food for them to continue, and Enos led his battalion back to Cambridge. The expedition was now down to little more than 650 troops.

On the morning of 25 October, Arnold and his advance party awoke to find snow had fallen, which would add further to the men's woes. On 26 October, Jeremiah Greenman, who was with Greene's command, wrote that 'the ground covered with Snow and very Cold and our provision very [low] so that we expetckit to kill sum of our dogs to eat'. The following day, he recorded that the decision was at last made to abandon most of the bateaux: 'hear the people [were] cuting up the tents for to make bags to put what small provison they had in here it was agreed to leave our battoes and to fut[foot] it after being gratly fateg'd by carring over such hild mountain & Swamps such as men never pased before'. By 31 October, Greenman stated that sickness and hunger was prevalent among Greene's men and that they now had to resort to extreme measures:

> Set out this morn very early left 5 sick men in the woods that was not abel to march left two well men with them but what litel provision thay had did not last them we gave out of our little every man gave sum but the men that was left was obliged to leave them to the mercy of wild beast this day as we were pasing along the river we saw 3 Cannows that went forward with the advance party stove against ye rok[s] we had very bad traviling th[ro] ye woods and Swamps our provison being very Short hear we killed a dog I got a small peace of it and sum broth that it was boyled with a great de[al] of trubel then, lay down took our blancots and slep[t] very harty for the times.

157

Near starvation was now upon Greenman and he and his comrades were forced to obtain their sustenance from unusual sources, as this quote from 1 November illustrates: 'In a very misrabel Sittiuation nothing to eat but dogs hear will a nother and cooked I got Sum of that by good [luck] with the head of a Squirll with a parsol of Candill wicks boyled up to gether wich made very fine Supe without Salt hear on this we made a nobel feast without bread or Salt thinking it was the best that ever I eat & so went to Sleep contented.'

Arnold, with his advance party, was no better placed for provisions, but, out of sheer desperation, he continued to drive on. Some miles behind, Morgan and his men were crossing the Height of Land, the watershed dividing waters flowing north into the St Lawrence from those flowing south and east to the Atlantic, which drops away to the Canadian plain. Morgan insisted that his Virginians carry their heavy boats. For half a mile, the snow-covered trail crossed ravines and underbrush. Joseph Henry, a Pennsylvania rifleman, declared that Morgan's men had the flesh 'worn from their shoulders, even to the bone'. For men who were now surviving by making soup from shoe and belt leather this proved too much and the remaining bateaux were discarded or swamped trying to descend rapids. For Greene's men, Morgan's route could be traced by the bloodstains in the snow, left by bloody bare feet. Men who fell behind were abandoned; their bones were discovered in the following spring.

The survivors were now becoming delirious with hunger. By 1 November, all parties were approaching the Chaudière river. The men stumbled and fell, but fought themselves to their feet, the survival instinct forcing them on. On the morning of 2 November, Greenman wrote:

this morn when we arose many of us so weak that we could hardly stand we stagerred about like drunken men how sumever we made shift to git our pack on, them that did not thoro them away we marcht off hoping to see Sum Inhabitance by night I hap to git a pint of water that a partrig was boyled in sum of them so weak that a Small Stick as big as mans thumb would bring them to the ground.

Arnold and his party, diverted by the mistakes of a local guide and the inherent errors in Montrescor's map, had finally reached Sartigan on 31 October and had arranged for a herd of cattle to be sent back to the main body. This much-needed food arrived just in time for the starving troops, and Greenman recorded, in his entry of 3 November, the joyous effect upon the men at such a sight: 'In the after noon we came in Sight of the Cattle wich the advance party had sent out it was the Joifulest Sight that I ever saw & Sum could not refrain from crying for joy hear we killed a creatur and Sum of ye men [were] so hungrey before this Creater was dressed thay had the Skin and all entrels guts and every thing that could be eat on ye fires a boyling'.

After nearly a week, during which the troops ate and slept, Arnold finally arrived at the St Lawrence river, on 9 November, with 675 exhausted men, and viewed what appeared to be a formidable fortress. Captain Henry Dearborn wrote of how 'a considerable number' had been 'left on the road Sick or woren out with fatigue and hunger'. Those still with Arnold were 'so fatigued, that they were very unfit for action'. Arnold's force was clearly too weak to mount an immediate attack on Quebec and, furthermore, Arnold had gleaned from the friendly locals that the British were aware of his expedition. The element of surprise had been lost.

When Carleton left Quebec for Montreal, in the summer of 1775, he had left control of the city, and its defences, to the Lieutenant Governor, Hector Cramahé, a somewhat nervous administrator, and secretary to former Governor Murray. Cramahé tried to rise to the challenge that now rested upon his shoulders. He gave orders for essential repairs to the city's walls and requisitioned ships, with their stores, ordnance and crews in the harbour, for use in the defence of Quebec. Such positive measures reassured the inhabitants, and even the English-speaking residents apparently agreed to do their utmost to defend the city, although Cramahé's attempts to raise a militia were not altogether successful. He was not a natural leader, but Allan Maclean most certainly was and, on his return to the city on 12 November, with his Royal Highland Emigrants, he immediately assumed command. Maclean used a firm hand to stop talk of negotiation, or surrender, and he cleverly painted Arnold's men as vagabonds, who had come out of the woods to plunder and to ravage. Such words worked upon the self-interest of even the most doubting defenders and the city's resistance was no longer in any doubt. It can be argued that, if Arnold had arrived at the St Lawrence just a few days earlier, or if his force had been in a condition to mount an offensive at once, then pressure upon Cramahé might have yielded the gates of the city to the Americans. Now, with Maclean in command, there was going to be no easy capitulation.

159

With Maclean's troops, and 100 volunteers that had arrived earlier from Newfoundland on board *Lizard*, the garrison now comprised 1,126 men, almost twice as many as Arnold could muster. Furthermore, Arnold possessed no cannon, while the city was well supplied. Arnold's priority was now somehow to ferry his troops from Point Lévis across the St Lawrence, onto the Plain of Abraham. This was achieved on the night of 13 November when, using 40 captured or borrowed canoes, Arnold eluded patrolling guard boats and landed his force a mile from Wolfe's Cove. Morgan called for an attempt upon the city that night, but he was outvoted during a hurriedly assembled council of war. The following day, Arnold decided that a parade of his troops, a show of force, might impress the British enough for them to consider their position, or might even provoke an attack from the garrison. It was recorded, by an anonymous member of the garrison, that Arnold's men directed three huzzas at the walls, which were answered 'with three cheers of defiance. And saluted with a few cannon loaded with grape and canister shot – they did not wait for a second round.' Arnold now tried to deliver a letter to Cramahé offering to spare private property if he surrendered. The first American messenger was dissuaded in his task by cannon fire, despite being under a flag of truce, and a second attempt the following day was similarly treated. Arnold was indignant that his messengers had been so abused, but clearly Maclean had strengthened the British resolve and, at a council of war, it was unanimously agreed to reject Arnold's offer. In addition, the Quebec gunners were encouraged to fire at any body of American troops that came within range and, on 16 November, they claimed the life of Sergeant Robert Dixon.

Two days later, reports from an English-speaking sympathizer within Quebec reached Arnold and informed him that Maclean was considering a surprise sortie against the Americans. Arnold knew that his weakened force would be unable to offer much resistance, and furthermore, his men had only five rounds apiece. Even the firebrand Morgan saw the sense in a controlled withdrawal and, on 19 November, a dispirited Arnold led his men the 20 miles to Pointe aux Trembles where they could rest, re-supply and await the arrival of Montgomery and his army. In fact, the report was a ruse; the informer had been in the pay of Cramahé and Maclean and the British never intended to venture beyond the walls. Just as Arnold withdrew, Governor Carleton made his less than triumphant entry into Quebec.

Thomas Ainslie called Carleton's return 'a happy day for Quebec' and he wrote in his diary of the 'unspeakable joy of the friends of Government & to the utter dismay of the abettors of sedition & rebellion'. Ainslie saw in Carleton 'our salvation'. Carleton himself was less than optimistic about Quebec's future. In a letter to Dartmouth, he wrote: 'Could the People in the Town, and Seamen, be depended upon, I should flatter myself, we might hold out, till the Navigation opens next Spring,' but he concluded: 'I think our Fate extremely doubtful, to say nothing worse.' Carleton was certain, however, of one thing and that was the need to strengthen his available forces. To this end, he placed great emphasis on expanding the militia, as well as ensuring the men from the sloops *Hunter* and *Lizard*, and from trading vessels, were incorporated into the garrison. Furthermore, all available cannons were taken off the ships and placed upon the city walls. As of 30 November 1775, Carleton was able to report the following return from the garrison in Quebec:

70 Royal Fusiliers
230 Royal Emigrants
22 Royal Artillery
330 British Militia
543 Canadian Militia
400 Seamen
50 Masters and Mates of Trading Vessels
35 Marines
120 Artifiers
A total of 1,800 Men bearing Arms.

Carleton also purged the city of malcontents and American sympathizers, for he had seen what damage such persons had done in Montreal. Cramahé had already arrested the leading orchestrator of dissent, John Dyer Mercier, a friend of Arnold, but, to force the hand of other like-minded individuals, Carleton proclaimed that those who had neither committed themselves to the militia, by 1 December, nor left the city, would be 'under pain of being arrested as Rebels or Spies'. This act had the desired result and a significant number, who had earlier been prominent in political agitation, including such men as John McCord and Zachary Macaulay, fled the city over the coming days. Edward Antill even rushed off to gain a commission in Montgomery's advancing army! Now, at least, Carleton could feel secure within the walls of Quebec.

Montgomery spent as little time as possible in Montreal. He waited just long enough to make some winter clothing from captured British uniforms and to procure weapons and ammunition. He was dealt a severe blow just before his departure, when several hundred men, whose enlistment was due to expire on 10 December, considered their work to be done and left for their homes. Montgomery now had only 300 troops in his small army, although he would gain an additional 160 troops en route. On 2 December this force joined Arnold at Pointe aux Trembles and, by virtue of his seniority, Montgomery assumed command of the combined forces. Instructions were issued that operations to take Quebec should immediately be resumed. There is no doubt that Montgomery rejuvenated Arnold and his men. Joseph Henry wrote:

> It was lowering and cold, but the appearance of the general here, gave us warmth and admiration ... He made us a short, but energetic and elegant speech, the burden of which was, an applause of our spirit in passing the wilderness; a hope our perseverance in that spirit would continue; and a promise of warm clothing; the latter was a most comfortable assurance. A few huzzas from our freezing bodies were returned to this address of the gallant hero. Now new life was infused into the whole of the corps.

The next day, the combined force of just 1,325 men marched to Quebec. Montgomery established his headquarters at Holland House, a large stone building located 2 miles south-west of the City's St John's Gate, near Sainte-Foy. Arnold found accommodation in the suburb of St Roch. All roads leading to and from the city were immediately blockaded and companies of troops were positioned at various points across the Plain of Abraham, extending from Wolfe's Cove to the St Charles river. Morgan's riflemen covered the left of the line, while the New Yorkers occupied the right; smaller detachments were stationed at Beauport and elsewhere to tighten the cordon around the city.

Montgomery now attempted to open a dialogue with Carleton, with the aim of soliciting a British surrender. On 6 December, learning from Arnold's earlier failed attempts, Montgomery used an old woman to carry the letter into the city. The letter spoke of the 'absurdity of resistance' against inspired 'troops, accustomed to success, confident of the cause they are engaged in'. When the letter was delivered to Carleton, he refused even to open it and had it contemptuously burnt and the old woman drummed out of the Upper Town. The following day, the old woman returned to the gates with fresh messages. For this brazen act, Carleton had her clamped in irons and thrown into jail for a few days before being drummed out of the city once more. Montgomery even resorted to firing messages affixed to arrows over the walls, all to no effect. In truth, Carleton knew he had adequate supplies and provisions to withstand a siege of eight months. He had neither the intention of surrendering, nor of making Montcalm's 1759 error by sallying out to attack his foe.

On 15 December, Montgomery made one last attempt to negotiate with Carleton. He sent Arnold, and one of his aides-de-camps, to the city walls, under a flag of truce. Arnold carried a letter which promised both Carleton and Cramahé safe conduct to England, if they surrendered the city. Carleton refused any meeting, stating that he would never negotiate with 'rebel scum'. Montgomery now had to consider other options. When he and Arnold had first met at Pointe aux Trembles, Montgomery had made it clear that he considered that 'until Quebec is taken, Canada is unconquered', and he explained the Americans' tactical options, which included 'siege, investment or storm'. Carleton's intransigence meant that one of these three had now to be undertaken. A siege was out of the question; not only did Montgomery have insufficient artillery to batter the walls, but the ground was now frozen solid and thus trenches could not be dug. Investment too promised little success, for Carleton's stand suggested that the city was well supplied, while the Americans lacked both shelter and warm clothing to withstand a Canadian winter. To Montgomery, an attack upon the city seemed the only option. Furthermore, it would have to be undertaken soon, for the enlistments of Arnold's Kennebec troops would be up on 1 January 1776, and many were already speaking of returning home.

Montgomery resolved to keep the British on constant alert, so as to wear them down and have them fearful of an American assault at any time. Morgan's sharpshooters were employed to kill or wound any targets on the city walls and they claimed many victims. Thomas Ainslie was outraged at such acts and wrote that he considered the rebel snipers 'worse than savages' and that to 'lie in wait to shoot a sentry would ever be held in contempt with men of courage'. Although the British were appalled by such American tactics, it seems clear that such sniping did begin to take a psychological toll upon the defenders.

Less successful were American attempts to cannonade the city. A battery was constructed at St Roch which began firing on 10 December, but the lightness of the American fire buoyed the defenders and had little effect upon persons or the walls. In contrast, the British were able to draw upon as many as 200 ordnance pieces and some of these were now directed at St Roch. In one instance, recorded by Arnold's physician, Dr Senter, a French prostitute was killed while 'in her brothel administering a spirituous potion to one of our lads'. Another rebel battery was constructed 700 yards south-west of the St John's Gate and the American's used ice blocks in the breastworks surrounding the guns. On 15 December, this battery opened up with a steady fire, but it was soon outgunned by the more powerful British ordnance. By the evening, the ice battery lay in ruins. The American cannonade had achieved virtually nothing and Thomas Ainslie was able to gloat that 'Their shot had no more effect upon our walls, than peas would have against a plank.'

At a Council of War, held on 16 December, the decision was taken to storm the city. It was impractical to scale the walls, so Montgomery had no choice but to fight his way into the Lower Town and, from this as his base, attack the Upper. The attack would take place on the first dark night of falling snow, for this would have the advantage of obscuring the attackers and deadening the sound of their advance. The plan called for the defenders of the Upper Town to be distracted by two feints, while two storming columns attacked the Lower Town. Livingston's Canadians were to make a feint against St John's Gate, while John Brown's troops were to lead a second diversion, to give the impression of a major assault at the Cape Diamond bastion. Montgomery himself would lead the attack on the Lower Town from the west and force two barricades, separated by about 100 yards, before reaching a fortified two-storey log house. Simultaneously, Arnold would storm the Sault-au-Matelot barricade to the east. The plan called for the two columns to converge and meet in the marketplace, where they would then assault and take the Upper Town. It was hoped that, by striking with four forces, the British would be thrown into confusion, and once the Lower Town was taken, confusion might turn to panic. Private Abner Stocking was to later record that the plan 'was rash and imprudent', and it was indeed a desperate plan, full of risk and uncertainty, which reflected Montgomery's desperate situation.

Over the next two weeks it must have seemed to Montgomery that the planned assault might never happen for the weather, or the moon, did not favour the assault. Unbeknown to Montgomery, the British were now fully aware of the American planned assault, for a sergeant, named Singleton, deserted and disclosed to the British the essence of the plan. The journal of Sergeant Thomas Sullivan, of the 49th Regiment of Foot, recorded on 23 December that 'This day orders were gave for the garrison to sleep in their clothes till further Orders. A deserter from the enemy confirmed the intention of the enemy to storm us.' Christmas passed almost unnoticed by the Americans, but on Wednesday, 27 December the weather seemed favourable for the assault and Montgomery issued orders to his troops to assemble in readiness for the attack. However, the invaders were to be frustrated, as Montgomery, at the last moment, deemed the night to be too light and stood the men down. Montgomery, conscious that the delays were adversely affecting morale, gave one of his inspirational speeches, in which he urged his men not to be dismayed or disheartened and tried to reassure them that the conditions would soon be right for the assault. However, the nights of 28 and 29 December were also considered unfavourable, but the next day brought a strong wind blowing off the river, accompanied by flurries of snow. In the late afternoon, the snow flurries became driving snow, which would render it virtually impossible for the defenders to see the assault troops moving towards the walls. It was now or never for Montgomery and his men.

Carleton had not been idle. Knowing the details of the American assault, and that it was imminent, he had ordered the repair of the embrasures on the walls, laid gun platforms, erected barriers at the extremities of the Lower Town at Sault-au-Matelot and Près de Ville and fortified these positions with cannons. Barriers were erected between the Upper and Lower Town and additional guns were placed in each of the bastions facing the Plain. Loopholes were cut in buildings, from which fire could be poured down onto any attackers who ventured onto the streets of the Lower Town. The Americans would be rushing into a warren of barriers, crossfire and death.

At 4 a.m. on the morning of 31 December, Captain Fraser, of the Royal Highland Emigrants, was making his rounds in the Upper Town, when he was the first of the defenders to see lights flashing from the American positions. Although no movements could be heard, Fraser's suspicions were aroused and he therefore ordered the guards to stand to arms and rushed to give the alarm. Within a few moments, the whole garrison was under arms; suddenly two rockets shot into the dark night sky from the direction of Cape Diamond, after which the American cannon began lobbing shells into the city. Musket fire was heard in the vicinity of Cape Diamond and the St John's Gate. The American assault had begun.

At the sight of the signal rockets, Arnold led his advance party of 25 volunteers towards the first Sault-au-Matelot barricade. Immediately behind this party was Captain Lamb and an artillery company, dragging a small 6-pound cannon on a sledge, followed by Morgan and his riflemen and then the remainder of Arnold's command. As Arnold raced forward, the snow stinging his exposed face, he heard the peel of church bells, cannons firing and men shouting and realized that the British were fully alerted to the American attack; he could only hope that the two feint attacks would divert the defenders away from his goal in the Lower Town. British fire from the Palais Gate now rained down upon Arnold's men and the Americans were frustrated that they were unable to reply. Joseph Henry wrote that the defenders were 'sightless to us, we could see nothing but the blaze from the muzzles of their muskets'. Now, at the first barrier, Arnold told his advance party to await the arrival of Lamb and the cannon before beginning their attack. Suddenly, and unexpectedly, the Americans were hit by a hailstorm of musket balls, fired from the British at the barricade. Arnold slumped down as a ricocheting ball ripped into his lower left leg. The pain was intense and blood was pouring profusely from the wound. Arnold tried to grasp what had happened as he steadied himself against a wall. Through the snow came the huge bulk of Daniel Morgan, who informed Arnold that Lamb had been unable to drag the cannon through the snow; the barricade would have to be stormed without artillery support. Morgan then noticed Arnold's bloody limb and his commander's weakened state. Morgan took control; he ordered Chaplain Spring, and a rifleman, to take the wounded Arnold to the rear while he assumed command. Arnold, too weak to resist, could only wish Morgan Godspeed, as he was dragged to the rear, to play no further part in the attack.

The rest of Arnold's command was met with the sight of dead and wounded Americans lying in the snow and their commander being dragged away. For many the attack was already lost. Morgan, however, had other ideas. Leading by example, he rushed at the barricade and was the first to place a scaling ladder against it and scamper to the top. Morgan, of course, became the main target for the British defenders. First, surrender on mass. Morgan, defiant as ever, begged his men to lead a final assault to break through Laws' troops, but his subordinates refused to answer his call. Now raging with bitterness and anger, Morgan refused to yield his sword, and it is likely he would have been shot by the advancing British if he had not seen a priest in the milling throng to whom he handed his sword. The American prisoners, including Morgan, Dearborn and Greenman, were marched by their British captors to an improvised prison within the French Jesuit College, where they were to spend the next months.

For the British, victory had been overwhelming; the American assault had been comprehensively beaten back and their losses were substantial. Accurate numbers of those killed are difficult to determine, for it appears that some of the fleeing New Yorkers may have crashed through the river ice and been lost and, in addition, at least 20 bodies were found outside the city walls in the spring thaw. The day after the assault, the British counted 30 bodies, including those lost in Montgomery's assault, and another 42 officers and men wounded. All these were taken prisoner, along with a staggering 389 others. Thus, out of an assault force that did not exceed 1,200 troops, the Americans had suffered a staggering 40 per cent casualty rate. The British lost six dead, which included Captain Anderson, of the Royal Navy, shot by Morgan himself, and five militiamen. On 1 January 1776, the victorious Carleton was able to issue the following triumphant address from the Governor's House:

> His Excellency General Carleton returns his thanks to the Officers and Men of the Garrison for their Gallant and spirited behaviour yesterday. The General was particularly pleased to see the alertness and sobriety of the different corps which greatly contributed to the success of the day. He makes no doubt but that they will persevere in a conduct which rebounds so much to their honour and security, and which is so much beneficial to the King's service.

Sergeant Sullivan was one of the party ordered by Carleton to collect the body of Montgomery on 1 January. Sullivan confirmed that 'Upon viewing the Dead General Montgomery ... had received a shot thro' the Left cheek and thro' both legs with Musquetry.' Carleton arranged for the dead general, along with Macpherson and Cheeseman, to be buried on 5 January in a quiet, dignified ceremony. This act was appreciated by the

a musket ball tore through his hat; then a second creased his cheek, leaving a powder burn and flinging him off the ladder onto the snow below. Winded for a second, Morgan rose and bounded, once more, up the ladder and over the wall. Dropping down among the defenders, Morgan was fortunate that he fell beneath a cannon and was able to gain momentary protection from thrusting British bayonets. His riflemen soon joined him and they were able to beat back the defenders and take the first barricade.

Morgan led the force into the Sault-au-Matelot, a narrow street which was to lead him to the rendezvous with Montgomery's men. Here Morgan hesitated; he was aware he was now ahead of the main body, without artillery support, and to compound his problems many of the men's ammunition had become wet as they marched through the driving snow, and was, therefore, useless. Furthermore, he was outranked by some of Arnold's officers, who were unsure whether they should continue. Argument and hesitation abounded and in the resulting delay the Americans lost the initiative. By now, although Morgan did not realize it, the battle had already been lost.

At the sight of the signal flares, Montgomery had also led an advance. He directed his men, of the 1st, 2nd and 3rd New York Regiments, along a narrow trail below the Upper Town which went past the King's Wharf to Près de Ville, near Cape Diamond. The going underfoot was difficult and the men were slowed down by huge snow drifts and cakes of ice, which had been deposited by the movement of the tidal river. By the time Montgomery had reached the first obstacle, a strong picket fence, he was aware that the advance was behind schedule. Fortunately, however, Montgomery had met no opposition and it seemed that the advance had not been detected. Now, reaching a second picket fence, Montgomery seemed to grow impatient, and, with his staff officers, he found an opening in the fence and pushed on forward along the trail. In the night sky, the advancing Americans could see the outline of a house alongside the path. Montgomery immediately realized that, if this dwelling was occupied by defenders, it could seriously hinder the attack and, wasting no time in speculation, Montgomery unsheathed his sword, shouted 'Push on, brave boys; Quebec is ours' and dashed forward. Almost instantly there was a loud explosion from the two-storey blockhouse and canister and grape fire was unleashed from four small cannon manned by nine sailors and nearly 40 militiamen. This was followed by a stream of musket balls. Montgomery, his two aides, Macpherson and Cheeseman, their Canadian guide and eight others were flung to the ground. Sergeant Sullivan described the effect of the cannon fire upon Montgomery's party as that they were 'mowed down like grass'. All, including Montgomery, were either killed instantly, or died of their wounds as they rolled in agony in the snow.

Miraculously, two men, including Colonel Donald Campbell, to whom command of the attack now fell, were untouched. Campbell was completely overwhelmed by the bloody gore that covered him and lay in the snow around him and, gathering his surviving comrade, he fled back along the path to join the main body of New Yorkers. Campbell's panic was contagious and it transformed the army into a fleeing mob, which abandoned its dead and wounded in the snow. Morgan, and his party, were now all alone. Meanwhile, the terrified militia defenders of the blockhouse were all for retreat; but fortunately Captain Barnsfare, a civilian ship's master, and Captain Chabot and Lieutenant Picard, of the militia, were able to restore some order and discipline and the defenders again turned their cannon towards the Americans.

Following Fraser's early morning warning, Maclean had ordered Colonel Caldwell and a number of militiamen to go to Cape Diamond to offer support there. Caldwell soon established that, following Campbell's rout, his force was not required there and, acting on his own initiative, he led his men to St John's Gate. He considered that there was no real threat from the diversionary attack there and that the guards and gunners on the walls could handle the men of the Livingston and Brown forces. He thus led his command into the Lower Town by the Rue de la Montagne, which led them directly to the south end of Sault-au-Matelot, where Morgan and his men were debating whether to go on. To add to Morgan's difficulties, his hesitation had allowed Carleton to reinforce the second barrier with some 200 troops, which included a few Fusiliers of the 7th and French militiamen. Nervous of the sight of Morgan and his men ready to attempt an attack on the second barrier, some of the militia appeared to be unsteady. However, Caldwell's timely arrival steadied nerves and he assumed command. He placed some of his men at strategically important positions along the barricade and sighted a cannon to fire over the barrier and into the mass of Americans. Finally, he arranged the Fusiliers in a line behind the barrier, with bayonets fixed. This was to be the last line of solid defence should the Americans succeeded in surmounting the barricade.

Arnold's officers had finally agreed to continue the advance and asked Morgan if he would lead it. Wasting not a second longer, Morgan, accompanied by Lieutenants Heth, Humphreys and Steade, rushed forward and planted scaling ladders against the barrier. Before any Americans could venture over, a synchronized volley drove them back. Morgan rallied his men and, for a further four attempts, the Americans rushed at the barrier only to be thrown back. By now, the defenders were firing from upper-storey windows onto the Americans in the street below. As dawn was breaking, making the Americans more visible to the defenders, Morgan gave the order for the Americans to seek refuge in the houses that lined the street and, from here, return fire on the British. The advance had stalled and the Americans were now taking significant casualties. Joseph Henry later recalled that in the street, and its adjoining houses,

some valuable lives were lost. Hendricks, when aiming his rifle at some prominent person, died by a ball through his heart. He staggered a few feet backwards and fell upon a bed, where he instantly expired. The amiable Humphreys died of a like kind of wound ... Many other brave men fell at this place, among them were Lieutenant Cooper of Connecticut, and perhaps fifty or sixty non-commissioned officers and privates. The wounded were numerous, and many of them dangerously so. Captain Lamb had nearly one half of his face carried away by a grape or canister shot. My friend Steele lost three of his fingers, as he was presenting his gun to fire.

Now, free of concern that the Americans might attack elsewhere Carleton could take the initiative and capture Morgan's remaining me like rats in a barrel. He ordered Captain Laws to take a force of Roy Emigrants and seamen from *Lizard* and sally forth into the Lower Tov making for the Palais gate. En route he ran into a group of lost disorientated Americans, led by Captain Henry Dearborn. After a sh fire fight, in which a number of Dearborn's men fell, this part Americans surrendered. Laws continued his advance to the Sau Matelot and caught Morgan's men in the rear; the Americans wer hemmed in front and rear. Laws now pushed forward too far and brief moment, he was captured by Morgan's men. However, wh British began to unlimber a field gun and direct its barrel down th the Americans realized the hopelessness of their situation and

many captive Americans who, like Dearborn, seemed resigned to their fate, for they must have realized that, after such a crushing defeat, a relief force could not be expected for many months. Dearborn wrote in his journal: 'I begun this year in very disagreeable Circumstances, it being the first day I ever Spent in Confinement except by sickness, but I hope I shall be enabled to bare it with a becoming fortitude. Considering it to be the fortune of War.'

For Arnold, and his command of 600 men, the fortunes of war looked equally bleak. The Americans, so few in number and demoralized by defeat, feared that Carleton would lead his army, now almost three times larger than his foe's, out of the city gates and sweep the Americans from the Plain; yet no such offensive measure was forthcoming. While Carleton may have been resolute in defence, events of 1776 would demonstrate that he was not determined in an offensive role, and he remained behind the walls of Quebec. From his sick bed, Arnold was able to maintain a blockade, if not a siege, of Quebec. He maintained command, despite the fact that Campbell was more senior, for, after the latter's flight during the assault, other officers refused to serve under him. In an attempt to reduce desertion, Arnold endeavoured to keep his troops busy. However, low morale and high dissatisfaction were pressing problems and he struggled to stem the flow of deserters. In a letter to General Wooster, in Montreal, Arnold requested that he assume command at Quebec and bring with him reinforcements and supplies. He also asked that, as Wooster journeyed north, he should 'stop every rascal who has deserted from us, and bring him back again'.

For four months Arnold maintained an ineffective blockade of Quebec. In late January, reinforcements arrived from Ticonderoga via Montreal, including new units from New York and Pennsylvania, as well as Seth Warner's Green Mountain Boys. However, these men were exhausted by the winter march and they arrived with few supplies, unserviceable weapons and in poor health. Certainly, such troops could hardly be expected to mount an assault on Quebec. In the meantime, the American camp had become riddled with smallpox and Dr Senter recorded 400 cases at the peak of the disease. The men also suffered from the privations of a severe Canadian winter and it must be wondered why Arnold persisted in his blockade, which appeared to be in no way injurious to the British, when he could have retired to Montreal to re-equip and improve his men's health. It would appear that Arnold was simply obeying Washington's orders, for, in a letter written by the Commander-in-Chief to Arnold, dated 27 January, he stated:

> I need not mention to you the great importance of this place [Quebec], and the consequent possession of all Canada, in the scale of American affairs ... The glorious work must be accomplished in the course of this winter, otherwise it will become difficult, most probably impracticable; for the administration [British government], knowing it will be impossible ever to reduce us to a state of slavery and arbitrary rule without it, will certainly send a large reinforcement thither in the spring. I am fully convinced that your exertions will be invariably directed to this grand object.

Arnold was thus tasked with not only taking Quebec, but in preparing for the likelihood of massive British reinforcements in the spring.

Arnold was never again in a position to attempt another assault upon Quebec, for, over the next months, he was inundated with problems, from sickness among his troops, collapsing discipline and even outright confrontation with the local inhabitants. This last issue came to a head in late March, when a group of 300 locals, outraged by American looting and other violations of Canadian property, assembled to attack a detachment of Arnold's men at Point Lévis. Arnold learned of the proposed attack and, on 23 March, he despatched Major Lewis Dubois, with 150 New Yorkers, to the south shore to intercept the Canadians. In the resulting fire fight, Dubois' men killed three and wounded several. Such actions did nothing to endear the American forces to the local inhabitants.

On 31 March, after falling from his horse and injuring his leg, Arnold was relieved from his command by Wooster. Arnold journeyed to Montreal, where he set about trying to improve both the city's defences and the Americans' relations with its inhabitants, which had been severely weakened by Wooster's heavy-handed approach, particularly towards the Catholic Church. After weeks of planning by Arnold, the Americans were finally in a position to begin some offensive action against Quebec. From 2 April, a battery at Point Lévis became operational, and it began to throw red-hot shells into the city. Despite British attempts to blast away the battery, it remained effective throughout the month and, in his journal entry for 23 April, Sergeant Sullivan noted that the Americans fired 60 shots from this battery on that day. Additional batteries were later constructed in front of Porte Saint-Louis and across the St Charles river but, although some casualties were recorded, for example on 1 May Sullivan wrote that two men and a child were wounded by a cannon shot in the Lower Town, the American fire had little impact. Lacking both cannon and experienced artillerymen, the Americans simply could not compete with the weight and number of the 148 British guns.

The last assault against the British position was launched by Major-General John Thomas of Massachusetts, who arrived on 1 May with 1,200 reinforcements, and assumed command from Wooster. The American 'attack' was launched on the night of 3 May, with the river now clear of ice. In the moonlight, the sentinels upon the walls of Quebec spotted a brig in full sail moving slowly down river. When the vessel failed to respond to the agreed identification signals, Carleton gave the order for the guns of the Lower Town to pound away. In a few moments the ship was ablaze and men were seen fleeing the burning wreck. Like the French in 1759, the Americans had sent a fire ship 'well garnish'd in all parts with shells, grenades, petards, pots à feu' in an attempt to destroy the British shipping at Queen's Wharf. The burning hulk, which failed to reach the harbour, drifted and finally sank. This was the final American assault upon Quebec and its dismal failure was rather symbolic of their disastrous siege of the city.

Within Quebec, the vast numbers of American prisoners had been well treated by Carleton. The officers were placed in the seminary and the other ranks found accommodation in the monastery and college. The officers were allowed to recover their personal baggage and those prisoners of British birth were given the opportunity to enlist in Maclean's Royal Highland Emigrants, rather than face the journey back to England to stand trial for treason. Ninety-four men accepted this offer, but when 14 used their enlistment as a chance to literally jump over the wall and return to their American comrades, Carleton disarmed the new recruits and despatched them to the holds of the ships in the harbour. The other prisoners continually plotted their escape, more in an attempt to relieve the boredom of their captivity than in any hope of a successful release. When plots were discovered, on two separate occasions, the prisoners were placed in leg irons and handcuffs and transferred to the hold of an armed sloop. Both Dearborn and Greenman recorded, in their respective diaries, the sight that greeted their eyes as they looked out of their prison windows on 6 May. Dearborn wrote:

173

This day forenoon, three ships arrived from England to the Great Joy of the Garrison, but much to our mortification as we now gave over all hopes of being retaken, and Consequently of seeing our families again until we had first taken a Voyage to England and there Tryed for rebels, as we have often been told by the officers of the Garrison, that, that would be the case.

Greenman also wrote of the joy among the garrison at the sight of the vessels and stated that 'all the bels in ye City rang'.

Thomas Ainslie wrote of the excitement among the British at the arrival of these first three ships 'the news soon reached every pillow in town, people half-dress'd ran down to the Grand battery to feast their eyes'. The British contingent destined for Canada had sailed in April and the first three vessels, under the overall command of Captain Lindsay, the frigate *Surprise* and the sloops-of-war *Isis* and *Martin*, had journeyed ahead of the main fleet. In early May, the fleet bearing the British troops entered the Gulf of St Lawrence. Some leagues below Quebec, a packet boat met them with the news that Montgomery's attempt to storm the city had been beaten back, that he had been killed and Arnold grievously wounded. The three vessels forged on and brought with them 200 men of the 29th Foot and some Marines. These troops were at once disembarked and Carleton, realizing that panic was overtaking Thomas' American encampment, left the safety of the city and sallied out at noon with the Royal Highland Emigrants, the remnants of the 7th, the 29th and some of the militia, to lead a combined attack of 900 men on the American position.

The rebels, ill-clad, short of ammunition and provisions, decimated by desertion and riddled with dysentery and scurvy, fled in confusion, abandoning their few light cannon and all their camp equipment. No attempt was made to make any sort of a stand and only six sentries discharged their rifles before they bolted with their comrades. Some 600, ill with pneumonia and infected by smallpox, were captured. Sergeant Sullivan wrote of the retreat in his journal thus: 'they ran off with the greatest precipitation, leaving all their Cannon and stores behind, many of them throwing away their Arms that they might run Faster.' Unable to control his men, General Thomas also fled, leaving his still warm lunch to be enjoyed by Carleton. From his prison window, Greenman also saw the flight and wrote of it in disgust in his diary: 'they retreat'd as fast as possible left a number of Sick in ye aspital with sum war lik Stores & see our people retreat wich made us all feel very bad wishing our Selvs tha[ir] to ingage them if thay had only known how bad it was to be a prisoner thay never would retreated anought giving battle.' For all the American prisoners, including both Dearborn and Greenman, the rout of their comrades meant that they would have to endure another four long months of captivity, until 18 September, when they were ferried to New York and exchanged for British troops captured earlier in the War.

By 7 May, the retreating Americans had reached Deschambault, where Thomas planned to make a stand. However, Lindsay had journeyed down the St Lawrence with *Surprise* and *Martin*, destroying American vessels en route, and at Deschambault the Royal Navy were able to bombard the Americans. With the Americans now thoroughly demoralized, Thomas had no hope of maintaining this position and he ordered his troops back to Sorel, at the mouth of the Richelieu, where hastily collected reinforcements, commanded by Brigadier-General William Thompson, awaited them. The third siege of Quebec was at an end; the British, once again, had been victorious.

The lifting of the siege was just the beginning of British military activity in Canada in 1776. The British strategy for the year was that a northern army, some 10,000 strong, commanded by Carleton, with the support of the newly arrived Lieutenantt-General Sir John Burgoyne, should clear the Americans from Canada and then proceed down into New York, via Lake Champlain, and on to a junction with Sir William Howe's main army operating in the lower Hudson valley. Carleton was slow to proceed south from Quebec, much to the frustration of men like Maclean who believed that the delay, and Carleton's rather conciliatory approach towards the enemy, would only allow them to grow stronger. Indeed, the Americans were surprised and relieved that Carleton's inactivity gave them some time to reorganize their forces. Despite the retreat from Quebec, the Continental Congress was ever hopeful 'that they would spend the summer of 1776 inside the walls of Quebec'. This hope was supported by an additional 5,000 troops, which arrived at Sorel on 1 June. The following day, General Thomas died from smallpox and Major-General John Sullivan assumed command of the combined American force. On 6 June, Sullivan despatched Brigadier-General William Thompson, with 2,000 troops, to investigate the British position at Trois Rivières, where, it was believed, Maclean was in command with only a few hundred British troops. However, when, on the following day, Thompson attacked the British, his troops received a bloody welcome from the troops of the 9th, 20th and 62nd Foot. These men combined well with the guns of *Martin* to force back Thompson's four advancing columns. The Americans retreated, leaving behind 60 dead and wounded and over 200 prisoners, including Thompson.

Lieutenant William Digby, of the 53rd, was present at Trois Rivières and left an account of the battle:

> About 4 in the morning an alarm was given by an out piquet of the approach of a strong body of the enemy ... soon after the alarm was given a few shots were heard from one of our armed vessels that was stationed a small way above the village who fired on part of the enemy advancing between the skirts of the wood and the river. In the mean time the troops on the shore were ordered to line every avenue from the village to the wood, and take post in the best manner possible ... About 5 o'clock strong advanced parties were sent towards the wood, where they discovered the enemy marching down in three columns, who immediately began a heavy fire with small arms, which was instantly returned. In the mean time a strong reinforcement of our troops with some field pieces arrived, which soon swept the woods, and broke their columns, the remains of which were pursued by us, as far as was prudent. The enemy from that time did nothing regular, but broken and dispersed, fired a few scattered shots, which did little execution.

This battle broke the American will to remain in Canada. Sullivan wished to defend Sorel, but was overruled. On hearing the news from Trois Rivières, Arnold ordered the evacuation of Montreal, and American forces withdrew to Crown Point. On 18 June the British reached Fort St John's, which they found abandoned and on fire, and then moved on to the shores of Lake Champlain. Here, Carleton stopped for nearly four crucial months, to construct a flotilla for operations on the lake. This delay represented a lost chance for the British. The Americans were given the opportunity not only to elude their British pursuers, but also to strengthen their posts at Crown Point and Ticonderoga, as well as to build the country's first Navy to oppose the British. Eventually, on 11 October, Carleton resumed operations. His flotilla met and defeated Arnold's squadron off Valcour Island, but, once again, Carleton was slow in his pursuit of Arnold's men, both on Lake Champlain and its shoreline.

Between them, Carleton's army and the Royal Navy should have been able to pin down and destroy or capture the entire enemy force with a rapid advance. It appears that Carleton did not want to do that. He let the Americans escape, as he reported to the Secretary of State for the American Department, Lord George Germain: 'to convince all His Majesty's unhappy subjects, that the King's mercy and Benevolence were still open to them'. This illustrates what a poor grasp Carleton possessed of the situation, for such a conciliatory approach, at this stage of the war, had little chance of modifying the American Whig mentality. In contrast, a stern dose of military reality, that a comprehensive defeat in Canada would have brought, might have both modified American behaviour and their expectation levels.

In the wider strategy of the war, the Americans probably benefited from being driven out of Canada; the extended lines of communication and the heavy commitment of supplies and manpower which an occupation, by necessity, would have entailed, could have led to a collapse of the Continental Army in late 1776 or early 1777. The taking of Quebec would have only been beneficial if it had stopped the arrival of British reinforcements. Of course, at the time, the failure to take Quebec was not viewed as a blessing. Washington wrote of the inability to take Quebec thus: 'hence I shall know the events of war are exceedingly doubtful, and that capricious fortune often blasts our most flattering hopes.' The British ballad, 'Captain Ephraim or the Yankee Entertainment', was less reflective than Washington, and certainly more cutting:

> Brother Ephraim sold his Cow,
> And bought him a Commission,
> Then he went to Canada,
> To fight for the nation:
> But when Ephraim he came home,
> He prov'd an errant Coward,
> He wouldn't fight the Englishmen,
> For fear of being devoured.

The Americans continued to fall back, abandoning Crown Point. Now, just 12 miles from Ticonderoga, Carleton was expected to take the fort to use as a supply base for a further advance into America itself, probably in 1777. However, American determination to defend the fort, combined with Carleton's timidity, meant that the British backed off from their attack. Carleton reasoned that the fortress was too strongly defended to start siege operations so late in the year and he thus decided, to the incredulity of some of his officers, to withdraw from Lake Champlain and winter his troops in Canada. Certainly, having made this decision, there was no realistic way that the British could winter by the Lake. The harsh season would have claimed the lives of many British soldiers and Carleton's slow advance did at least avoid the possibility of British troops being caught in an ambush. Carleton's caution was not well received in London and, when the British returned to the offensive the next spring, the descent from Canada was entrusted to Burgoyne.

The failed attempt by the Thirteen Colonies to capture Quebec, and thus conquer Canada, was not the last time that the Americans would be considering operations north of their border. Historians have been critical of Carleton's timidity during the 1776 northern campaign and some have gone so far as to make the assertion that Burgoyne's failure at the battle of Saratoga, in October 1777, was as a direct result of the delays he encountered early in the 1777 campaign, when his troops were forced first to take Canadian territory that Carleton should have reclaimed in 1776. This, undoubtedly, is too much of a simplification. Burgoyne's recapture of Canadian forts along Lake Champlain in 1777 hardly slowed him at all and, indeed, if Ticonderoga had been taken in 1776, it would have most certainly been left as a smoking wreck which Burgoyne's troops would have been forced to repair in 1777, before it could be used as a forward supply base by the British. A hypothesis can be made that, if Burgoyne's force could have left Ticonderoga in late April 1777, then Howe might have been obliged to join forces with him and the combined armies would have been too much for the Continental Army to defeat. Burgoyne's failure at Saratoga, which would so inspire the Americans, and did so much to encourage outside intervention by France and Spain on the American side, cannot be attributed to Carleton's reluctance to advance in 1776, but owed far more to Burgoyne's overconfidence, his army's inability to solve its logistical weaknesses and the lack of support he received from General Sir William Howe's army, which had decided, independently, to make Philadelphia, the home of Congress, its main objective. For all his apparent timidity, Carleton was never defeated by an American army, unlike the overconfident Burgoyne.

The defeat at Saratoga again placed Canada in danger. With the British unable to replace their losses, until May 1778 at the earliest, Congress voted in January 1778 to launch another invasion. It was hoped that the new American alliance with France might encourage more Canadians to support an invasion. To further entice the support of the locals, Congress appointed the Marquis de Lafayette as commander of the invasion force. However, an early assessment by Lafayette of both the availability of troops and supplies for an invasion, along with news that Carleton had strengthened British defences along the invasion route, led the new commander to conclude that a fresh invasion would be impracticable and unlikely to succeed. By March 1778, Lafayette had convinced Congress that this was the case and all thought of invasion was abandoned. After 1778, neither the British nor the Americans considered any large-scale operations across the border and, by 1780, Congress had formally abandoned any thought of making Quebec the Fourteenth Colony.

However, a draft peace proposal, presented to the British delegates during the 1782 Paris peace negotiations, did include a demand that Britain should cede Canada to America. This demand was rejected out of hand by the British delegates and, when the preliminary peace treaty was signed, on 30 November 1782, it was omitted. At the conclusion of the American War of Independence, Canada opened its borders to between 50,000–60,000 Americans who remained loyal to Britain. Their descendants became the very heart of the United Empire Loyalists' movement, which played such a major part in repelling the second American invasion during the war of 1812. On three separate occasions Quebec endured the hardship of a siege and, despite the fact that it would remain the home for a British garrison well into the nineteenth century, it would never play such a central role in Canadian military history again. Today, the legacy of French and British rule still lives on in the politics and culture of a modern vibrant city.

Conclusion

Historians are, of course, blessed with a wonderful gift, that of hindsight. Unfortunately, it has led some to adopt a 'What if?'school of history, which allows them to postulate about how historical events would have differed if alternative actions had been taken, or contrary decisions made. This approach also permits a debate, however pointless, as to the likely consequences of an alternative action or approach. The three sieges of Quebec provide bountiful scope for the 'What if?' historian. This is particularly true of the first siege of 1759, and the numerous debates surrounding Wolfe's actions, both before and on 13 September, seems to have drawn the conspiracy theorists and those keen on conjecture to it. For the military historian, there is certainly value in examining decisions which lead directly to success or failure on the battlefield, or in the operation of a siege. This approach differs from 'What if?' for it critically examines the performance of commanders, and their subordinates, and attempts to explain how the decisions taken led to victory or failure. Once again, the sieges of Quebec provide many opportunities to assess how events and decisions influenced their ultimate outcome.

While there is little doubt that it took a moment of brilliance by Wolfe to place his troops upon the Plains of Abraham, this, of course, did not guarantee British victory. Crucially, there were a number of actions and decisions that eventually combined to achieve success for the British. Both Montcalm and Wolfe knew that the British had only until the end of September to take the city, after which the rapid approach of winter would have forced them to abandon the attempt. With this in mind it must be considered that the French should have tried to delay the approach of the British squadron as it sailed up the St Lawrence towards Quebec. Certainly, well-positioned and entrenched shoreline guns, particularly at the Traverse channel, could have damaged and delayed the British flotilla. However, more critically, it is clear that, within a matter of weeks, the British pilots had gained a better understanding of the complexities of the St Lawrence river than the French seamen had in decades and the reliance placed by the French upon the river as the city's first line of defence proved totally unfounded.

The French should also have realized the importance of the position of Point Lévis, as Wolfe was so quick to do, and steps could have been taken either to deny this to British cannon, or at least delay their deployment. However, despite the damage inflicted by the British guns upon the city, it was not this that determined the siege, but the success, and mistakes, upon the Plains of Abraham. When examining the decisions made on and around 13 September, it is easy to agree with the eminent Canadian historian W. J. Eccles, that 'the most overlooked determining factor in history has been stupidity'. Considering all the hard work and effort by the French to defend the Beauport shore and to shadow British forces in the upper river, the lax defences at Anse au Foulon must be viewed as the height of folly. The French were aware that the pathway at Anse au Foulon allowed for an ascent from the shoreline and thus should have ensured that the area was sufficiently defended. Although Wolfe achieved the element of surprise, and demonstrated a brilliant use of the tides to place his troops at the foot of the slope at the required time, the relative ease with which the British then ascended the slope and overwhelmed the small number of defenders was as much a factor of French negligence as British brilliance.

Once upon the Plains, Wolfe deployed his forces so that any French attack would have to be a frontal one, since there was no opportunity to outflank the British position. The fact that Montcalm did indeed decide to sally out from the city and attack an enemy that was superior in training and quality must be considered a mistake. The French commander should have waited for Bougainville and his men to join him, or, at the very least, waited to bring a larger number of field pieces into play before beginning the advance. Montcalm was guilty of beginning an engagement, which he did not immediately have to fight, where he knew he was disadvantaged, and this can only be viewed as a grave error.

The following year, the French and the British were once more in a bitter fight over the control of Quebec and, of course, on this occasion it was the British who were the besieged. Both Murray and Lévis knew that the fate of the city depended on two things: first, whether the French could bring sufficient cannon to fire upon Quebec's weak walls, and second, who would be first to navigate up the St Lawrence and thus reach the city with fresh troops and supplies. Warned, by chance, of the approach of the French army, Murray initially withdrew behind his defences. He should have obtained as much intelligence as possible as to the composition of Lévis' force. If Murray had done so, he would have realized that the enemy did not possess sufficient artillery with which to batter the city into submission and thus the British could have simply waited behind the city walls until reinforcements arrived from Britain. Unaware of the weakness of the French artillery, and convinced in his own mind that Quebec's defences were inadequate, Murray risked all in an unnecessary general engagement. The battle should never have been fought, and, furthermore, Murray compounded his mistake by advancing from his superior position upon the Buttes à Neveu towards the French. His force soon became bogged down in the muddy terrain and were easily outflanked by the French. Only a hasty retreat saved Murray's force from destruction. The arrival of a squadron of Royal Navy ships ensured that Quebec would remain in British hands.

Fifteen years later, the British were at war against their former American allies and Quebec became, once again, central to the armed struggle in North America. It is without question that Arnold's march across the wilderness of Canada was heroic, yet it proved to be ultimately unsuccessful. It has been argued that, if Congress had promptly given its approval, and supplied ready cash to equip the expedition properly and pay for Canadian volunteers, then Arnold would have captured Quebec. Indeed, if Arnold had arrived outside the city walls only a few weeks earlier, before Maclean had arrived to strengthen the city's defensive resolve, then Arnold might have obtained the surrender of Quebec without a shot being fired. This is, of course, conjecture, but a more persuasive military argument can be made that Arnold's march should, on military grounds, never have taken place, for the only addition that it offered to the Americans was that of surprise, which was soon lost, so that the defenders of Quebec knew of Arnold's approach. Instead Washington should have directed Arnold and his men, many of whom were of the highest quality, to Montgomery's command. Here, the added troops would have surely enabled Montgomery to have taken Saint-Jean earlier, so that they would have arrived outside Quebec before the full onset of winter. The extra numbers of quality troops would have allowed the Americans to bring with them additional supplies and even cannon with

183

which to blast the city walls. Despite the gallant resolve of Maclean and Carleton to defend Quebec, the city was there for the taking and it was the Americans, through an ill-conceived plan, that failed to take it.

Three eighteenth-century sieges of Quebec and three British successes. While there are clear moments in the history of each siege that defined success for the British, there remains one element to this success which has been largely overlooked in this work. It was the Royal Navy who, in 1758, had been able to deter the French Navy and allowed for the landing of British troops to capture Louisbourg, thus opening the way for an advance upon Quebec. It was British pilots who discovered the secrets of the St Lawrence and safely delivered Wolfe and his army to Quebec. It was only the cooperation and skill of the men of the Royal Navy which placed Wolfe's troops upon the Plains of Abraham. It was British sailors who delivered British troops to the base of Anse au Foulon and supplied them with cannon. Elsewhere, the British Navy decimated their French counterparts at the naval battles of Lagos and Quiberon Bay, which meant that in the following year the French were unable to effect a re-supply of troops and provisions to New France, and it was the Royal Navy that first arrived in the basin of Quebec, much to Murray's relief. In 1775, it was not just America's wish to make Quebec the Fourteenth State that made the city, once again, a military target, but it was also the realization that Quebec was the key to the St Lawrence river, which, in turn, allowed the British Navy to reinforce its troops in North America. It was British sailors who stood shoulder to shoulder with British troops and Canadian militiamen behind the barricades to defeat the Americans. If Montgomery and Arnold had succeeded in their attempt to capture Quebec then the British would have been deprived of an important avenue with which to continue the fight in North America. Thus, on three separate occasions during the eighteenth century, Quebec was at the heart of a continental, if not world, conflict and it was both British troops and sailors that were crucial to British success in these engagements. Thanks to the exploits of James Wolfe, the city has gained a renown which certainly places it high in British military tradition. However, there is much more to the military history of the great city of Quebec than one brief engagement upon the Plains of Abraham and it is hoped that the importance of Quebec in the history of France, Canada, America and indeed Britain will long be taught and remembered.

Bibliography

Anderson, F. (2000), *Crucible of War – The Seven Years' War and the Fate of the Empire in British North America, 1754–1766*. London: Faber & Faber.

Black, J. (1991), *War for America – The Fight for Independence 1775–83*. Stroud: Alan Sutton.

— (1992), *Pitt the Elder*. Cambridge: Cambridge University Press.

Bonwick, C. (2005), *The American Revolution*. Basingstoke: Palgrave. 2 edn.

Bray, R. and Bushnell, P. (eds) (1978), *Diary of a Common Soldier in the American Revolution, 1775–83*. DeKalb, IL: North Illinois University Press.

Brown, L. and Peckham, H. (eds) (1969), *Revolutionary War Journals of Henry Dearborn 1775–1783*. Freeport, NY: Books for Libraries Press, reprint.

Brumwell, S. (2002), *Redcoats – The British Soldier and War in the Americas 1755–1763*. Cambridge: Cambridge University Press.

— (2005), *White Devil*. New York: Da Capo Press.

— (2006), *Paths of Glory – The Life and Death of General James Wolfe*. London: Continuum.

Connell, B. (1960), *The Plains of Abraham*. London: Hodder & Stoughton.

Conway, S. (1995), *The War of American Independence 1775–83*. London: Edward Arnold.

Corbett, J. (1907), *England in the Seven Years' War*, Vol. I. London: Longman.

Dixon, D. (2005), *Never Come to Peace Again – Pontiac's Uprising and the Fate of the British Empire in North America*. Norman, OK: University of Oklahoma Press.

Garrett, R. (1975), *General Wolfe*. London: Arthur Barker.

Griffith, S. B. II (2002), *The War for American Independence 1760–81*. Urbana: University of Illinois Press.

Hébert, Jean-Claude (1974), *The Siege of Quebec in 1759 – Three Eyewitness Accounts*. Quebec: Ministère des Affaires Culturelles.

Henry, J. (1877), *Account of Arnold's Campaign Against Quebec in the Autumn of 1775*. Joel Munsell; Albany: reprinted New York: Arno Press, 1968.

Hibbert, C. (1999), *Wolfe at Quebec*. New York: Cooper Square Press reprint.

Higginbottom, D. (1988), *War and Society in Revolutionary America: The Wider Dimensions of Conflict*. Columbia, SC: University of South Carolina Press.

Huston, J. (1968), 'The logistics of Arnold's march to Quebec'. *Journal of Military Affairs*, 32 (3) (December), 110–24.

Knox, Captain J. (ed. Connell, B.) (1976), *The Siege of Quebec and the Campaigns in North America, 1757–60*. London: Folio Society.

Lawson, P. (1989), *The Imperial Challenge: Quebec and Britain in the Age of the American Revolution*. Montreal: McGill-Queen's University Press.

Lenman, B. (2001), *Britain's Colonial Wars 1688–1783*. Harlow: Longman.

McCullough, D. (2005), *1776*. New York: Simon & Schuster.

McLynn, F. (2004), *1759: The Year Britain Became Master of the World*. London: Jonathan Cape.

Marston, D. (2001), *The Seven Years' War*. Oxford: Osprey.

— (2002), *The French Indian War 1754–60*. Oxford: Osprey.

— (2002), *The American Revolution 1774–1783*. Oxford: Osprey.

Martin, J. K. (1997), *Benedict Arnold, Revoltionary Hero*. New York: New York University Press.

Middleton R. (ed.) (2002), *Amherst and the Conquest of Canada*. Stroud: Alan Sutton.

Morrissey, B. (2003), *Quebec 1775: The American Invasion of Canada*. Oxford: Osprey.

Parkman, F. (2001), *Montcalm and Wolfe – The French–Indian War*. New York: Da Capo Press reprint.

— (2001), *The Battle for North America*. London: Phoenix, reprint.

Pocock, T. (1998), *Battle for Empire – The Very First World War 1756–63*. London: Michael O'Mara.

Reid, S. (2000), *Wolfe*. Staplehurst: Spellmount.

Reilly, R. (1960), *The Rest to Fortune*. London: Cassell.

— (2001), *Wolfe of Quebec*. London: Cassell, reprint.

Rogers, Col. H. C. B. (1977), *The British Army of the Eighteenth Century*. London: George Allen & Unwin.

Sheppard, R. (ed.) (2006), *Empires Collide – The French–Indian War 1754–63*. Oxford: Osprey.

Stacey, C. P. (ed. with new material by Graves, D.) (2002), *Quebec, 1759 – The Siege and the Battle*. Toronto: Robin Brass.

Stephenson, R. S. (2005), *Clash of Empires – The British, French–Indian War 1754-1763*. Pittsburgh, PA: Regional History Center.

Sterne Randall, W. (1990), *Benedict Arnold, Patriot and Traitor*. New York: William Morrow.

Warner, O. (1972), *With Wolfe to Quebec*. Toronto: Collins.

Williams, N. (1997), *Redcoats along the Hudson – The Struggle for North America 1754–63*. London: Brasseys.

Wrong, G. (1914), *The Fall of Canada 1759–60*. Oxford: Oxford University Press.

— (1928), *The Rise & Fall of New France*, Vols I and II. London: Macmillan.

Primary sources at the National Army Museum, London

NAM 9109-122-1 Extract from the Orderly Book of the Rebel army before Quebec which Book was found in the Baggage (of a Major Fishery) taken on the Point Lévi side, 7 May 1776, after the precipitate retreat on the Arrival of the Ships the day before.

NAM 9109-118 Journal of Sergeant Thomas Sullivan – 49th Regiment of Foot 1775–1778.

NAM 2005-01-47 Diary of the Siege of Quebec 1775 by J. Danford.

NAM 7204-6-2 An anonymous diary covering the period 1758–65, including an account of the sieges of Louisbourg and Quebec.

NAM 7311-85-3 The Expedition against Quebec 1759– The Papers of Colonel George Williamson and Lieutenant Adam Williamson.

NAM 2005-01-45 A Journal of the Siege of Quebec 1759 by Edward Coats.

NAM 7803-18-1 An Account of Abercrombie's failed attempt to capture Ticonderoga in July 1758 by Captain Charles Lee of 44th Foot.

NAM 9203-174 An Account of the Attack of Quebec 1776 by Fitzwilliam Burke.

NAM 8202-17-1 Memoirs of Philip van Cortlandt – an American Loyalist.

NAM 8202-17-2 Philip van Cortlandt, An American Loyalist.

Index

189

191